PATHS THROUGH
THE FOREST

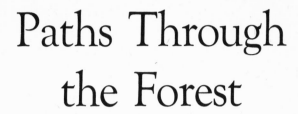

Paths Through the Forest

A BIOGRAPHY OF THE
BROTHERS GRIMM

Murray B. Peppard

HOLT, RINEHART AND WINSTON
· NEW YORK · CHICAGO · SAN FRANCISCO ·

First edition

Designer: Paula Wiener

SBN: 03-085076-2
PRINTED IN THE UNITED STATES OF AMERICA

For Jo

Contents

Acknowledgments

I WISH to express my gratitude to Richard and Clara Winston, whose imagination initiated the project and whose encouragement accompanied its progress; to Miss Alison Bond of Holt, Rinehart and Winston, whose invaluable critical judgment and advice were matched only by her patience; to Roxanne McCabe, under whose patient fingers the manuscript became legible; to my colleagues, E. A. Johnson, Jr. and Benjamin M. Ziegler— *e tanta fede, e si lungo costume;* to the Tikos, the fairy godparents of the tale of the brothers. I cannot begin to thank adequately Dr. Hennig, the director of the Brüder Grimm-Museum in Cassel, whose deeply appreciated generosity has made possible a contribution to this volume; *dass gepfleget werde der feste Buchstab', und Bestehendes gut gedeutet.*

Preface

THE POET Ludwig Uhland once said of his contemporary Jacob Grimm that he had spun a golden thread of poetry everywhere. Jacob and Wilhelm Grimm, the "fairy tale brothers," lifted the musty veil obscuring Germany's past and wove it into a magic web that captured the imagination of all Europe. The poetic qualities inherent in old and quaint customs needed a fresh vision and a new perspective for their discovery; to previous generations they were uncouth matters best forgotten. Yet Jacob and Wilhelm found poetry in everything: in old legal customs, in formulas of law, and in the humblest documents of daily life. The imagination of the brothers imparted an aura of wonder and delight to material that earlier had seemed dry, dull, and sooty with age. The tendency to admire what was sophisticated, French, or classical meant the rejection of the Germanic past as a barbarous time of national adolescence. The Grimms' new perspectives and enthusiasm helped to restore pride in their country's heritage. For them enchantment lay in the romance of words and the lure of language, and so they lavished care on individual words, rejoicing in their history and development. Without such a gift, they could not have started their monumental dictionary with its exacting, detailed work.

Jacob and Wilhelm collaborated so harmoniously that they are generally known as "the Brothers Grimm." Most of their works they wrote together, and even their separate publications were shared undertakings inspired by a common spirit. Born a little more than a year apart, they passed their lives in a harmony of interests and effort: from childhood on they were inseparable, living and growing together throughout their long and industrious lives. As mature scholars they continued to share a common study, with desks and books conveniently arranged for both. When they were buried side by side in Berlin, they had already become a symbol of friendship and creative cooperation.

Their modest yet productive careers spanned an era of great events and changes in Europe: the French Revolution, the Napoleonic Wars, the Romantic movement, Kantian philosophy, the age of Metternich, the July revolution in France and the struggles for constitutional government in the German states, the revolution of 1848 and the rise to power of Bismarck. The brothers were attentive observers of the historic happenings around them and sometimes participants. Twice they were active in political events: in 1837, when their famous protest against Hannoverian autocracy made them symbols of liberty in all the German states; again in 1848, when Jacob served at the Paulskirche in Frankfurt.

The brothers' patriotism and love for the spiritual treasures of their homeland were expressed in their study of the language, traditions, legal customs, mythology, and folklore of their own as well as other Germanic countries. They had the rare gift of being able to see the German cultural heritage as a whole and to relate it to the entire Germanic past. This overview, combined with their substitution of scientific observation and reliable sources for speculation and deductive reasoning, made them the leading philologists, antiquarians, lexicographers, and folklorists of their age. Their enthusiasm for older German cultural monuments was imbued with a piety—in great works they saw something divine—and a reverence for all that the mind of man can create. It has been said of them that they delved for the gold of early literary monuments in serene humility, as if they themselves felt homesick for those ancient times, as if they were seeking a lost poetic paradise.

Diligence in detail and respect for the seemingly insignificant enabled them to pioneer in gathering source material for the study of the German cultural past. Their works mark such important departures that it has become customary to talk about "before" and "after" the Grimms. By systematically applying a comparative-historical approach in their investigations, they put an end to the long period of speculation and fanciful constructions about the Germanic past. With *The Children's and Household Tales* (1812)—better known as the *Fairy Tales*—and *German Heroic Tales* (1829), they established the basis of German folklore. The *German Grammar* (1819, 1822) laid the foundation of Germanic philology. The *German Mythology* (1835) was the first to present the chief sources for the study of the religion and mythology of the continental Germanic tribes. Their last and greatest undertaking, whose vast scope prevented their living to see its completion, was the *German Dictionary,* a new departure in lexicography that has no precise English analogue, but whose properties may be imagined in a combination of Dr. Johnson's dictionary with a complete *Oxford English Dictionary.*

Since their lives were spent in such close cooperation, it is not always easy to discriminate between them. Yet there were nuances in both their characters and their works that distinguish them, if only in emphasis. Jacob was the bolder and more experimental of the two, and it was his "iron diligence" and enormous capacity for work that gave him an advantage over his less robust, less adventurous brother. There was something ascetic and monastic in Jacob's severe and unrelenting devotion to forms of work that demanded the closest attention to detail. To many of his contemporaries he seemed stern and forbidding; within the family circle he kept rigidly to schedule, but he could also unbend and be a lovable uncle.

Wilhelm was the gentler, more poetic brother, with a gift for popular speech and a "silver style," as his older brother expressed it. Jacob was at one and the same time his greatest admirer and severest critic. Wilhelm's qualities were deeply appreciated by Jacob, who realized that Wilhelm, as a devoted husband and father, was more social and needed family life in fuller form. Wilhelm's nature expressed itself in more literary and poetic paths than Jacob's. But he too had reverence for significant detail and could share his brother's interests and exacting forms of research. One of his more charming essays is on the Old German names for the different fingers of the hand—nothing was too insignificant to be a source of the quaint and interesting.

The Grimms were in many respects typical of their time and representative of important aspects of nineteenth-century Germany—they were compilers in an age that was rediscovering the importance of source material, they took part in collective enterprises in the spirit of Romantic group philosophizing, and they came from a middle-class family with a tradition of teaching and preaching, thus representing in their lives as well as their work the best ideals of their class. Their provincial origins and loyalties contrasted sharply with their broad intellectual horizons—again a characteristic of many nineteenth-century German scholars who reached out widely in the realm of ideas while leading restricted lives. They were a pair beloved by all for achieving excellence in those areas in which the common ethos strove for excellence. By embodying the best of their time, region, and class, they became famous far beyond the limits of their origin.

Although not always the discoverers who made the first, inventive steps, the brothers were often the systematizers and refiners who supplied the rationale, so ordering and presenting the material and its principles that it became firmly established. Thus even in the case of the famous "Grimm's Law," much is owed to the work of previous scholars, so that the rules of correspondence cannot be termed an entirely original discovery of Jacob Grimm. Both brothers loved the excitement and adventure of exploring the world of ideas. Generally they improved on what they found, with much of their effort spent in clearing away the wild conjecture and fanciful guessing in their chosen fields.

One of their most endearing traits was their great capacity for friendship. All their lives they made friends, even with people whom they never saw but with whom they only corresponded. They had an extraordinary gift for loyalty and sympathetic understanding and possessed the ability to inspire these feelings in others. The dedications of their books were always planned carefully to honor their friends and helpers, and the words of appreciation and gratitude found in these dedications are among the finest they wrote.

Their happiest role was that of teacher, for the chief purpose of all they planned and published was the education of their nation in the wealth of wonders in its past. At heart both were devoted to instructing and informing their fellow countrymen, and service to the fatherland was both their motivation and goal. The urge to enlighten is strong even in their private correspondence. Yet they were never happy in the classroom; as professors they were not content, so their academic life was mostly a trial for them.

Methodology and erudition alone would not have made the Grimms masters in so many fields if these abilities had not been sustained by contagious enthusiasm and the gift of communicating it. Their ability to enter wholeheartedly into new fields and generate interest was not just a characteristic of their youth. The mature Jacob's lectures on the Finnish epic *Kalevala* in 1845 earned him an appointment as corresponding member of the Finnish Academy. These same lectures led Russian scholars to turn their attention to Finnish folklore for the first time. The Grimms' sense of wonder and delight in the unaffected and folklike led them to provide the source material for many later generations. But it was not the material as much as the glow of excitement in their writings which captured the imagination and held the interest of scholars and laymen alike.

The consonance of their scholarly work with their daily lives has been a source of admiration for succeeding generations. Jacob, who treasured variant spellings of older words, also loved bric-à-brac in his living quarters. Both brothers were very fond of flowers—took them with them when they moved, cherished them in their rooms, and happily observed them on their long walks. The brothers' unaffected simplicity concealed minds of great subtlety, for they wore their learning lightly. Their modesty and reserve conformed to the bourgeois ideals of the time, yet over the years they maintained friendships with many aristocratic families. Their lives and achievements were thus part of a harmonious whole—lives of learning dedicated sincerely and generously to their country.

MURRAY B. PEPPARD

Amherst, Massachusetts
February 1971

PATHS THROUGH
THE FOREST

❧ I ❧

Hesse-Cassel. The Family

OVER A CENTURY has passed since the death of Jacob Grimm in 1863, a year that saw memorial volumes dedicated to him in both parts of the Germany he loved so well. The passage of more than a hundred years has not dimmed the memory of one of the world's greatest philologists and folklorists, nor that of his brother Wilhelm, whom millions remember as the editor of the famous *Fairy Tales*. In the popular mind they will always be the "fairy tale brothers": their modest and exemplary lives are recalled with as much warmth and gratitude as their many contributions to our knowledge and pleasure, for the brothers have become symbols of the best scholarly tradition of old Germany. They lived during an era of great upheavals in Europe, so that the constancy of their quiet scholarly productivity has made them all the more appealing.

The Germany into which the brothers Grimm were born was not the Germany of today clearly divided into East and West, but rather a loose conglomeration of petty principalities, duchies, and kingdoms, some as large and powerful as Prussia, some so tiny that an oft-related satiric tale tells of one ruling prince who accidentally dropped his realm out of his pocket and lost it forever on an afternoon's stroll. Theoretically this patchwork quilt of approximately one sovereign state for every day in the year was

ruled over by the Emperor Joseph II, the son of the famous
Maria Theresa. In fact, each petty prince considered himself an
absolute ruler and reigned with unquestioned authority within
the boundaries of his territory, however small it might be. Some
princelings were enlightened despots who controlled the privileges of the arrogant aristocracy, curbed the military, and har-
bored the best intentions. Others were merely despots who imi-
tated, within or beyond their means, the pomp and luxury of the
French Court or the military display of Prussia.

Hesse-Cassel, a small and politically insignificant principality
in the heartland of the old Germanic territories, has seen the settlement of Hessians since the time of the Great Migrations. The
traditions and history of the region were untouched by Slavic
memories or influences, quite unlike the newer, reconquered territories to the east of the Elbe. Americans are most familiar with
the Hessian mercenary troops who fought in the Revolutionary
War, many of whom settled in this country after the war. In the
late eighteenth century Hesse-Cassel was ruled as well or as
badly as any other principality large or small. The Landgrave
Wilhelm IX represented a dull mixture of stupidity, greed, and
unenlightened notions of absolutistic grandeur, and his hand
often lay heavily on his subjects. During the Napoleonic Wars he
also proved to be cowardly and inept in military matters. But he
nevertheless commanded the loyalty of most of his subjects, who
instinctively respected and obeyed him in spite of all the abuses
of his regime. Patriotism seems to have been a matter of habit and
ingrained loyalty to the region without regard for the person of
the ruler. The aristocracy found its advantage in support of the
ruling house, whereas the middle class remained mostly unpolitical, and the peasants, of course, had no voice at all in how they
were governed. Local patriotism and particularistic pride flourished right through the sweeping changes and drastic redrawings
of the map that resulted from the Napoleonic Wars.

In the small town of Hanau, not far from Frankfurt am Main,
in an old and still medieval section of Hesse-Cassel, Jacob Ludwig
Carl Grimm was born on the fourth of January, 1785, the son of

Philipp Wilhelm Grimm and his wife Dorothea Zimmer Grimm. The year before their first-born son, Friedrich, had died when still only a few months old. On February 24, 1786, another son, Wilhelm Carl, was born. Philipp Grimm, the town clerk of Hanau, was a solid and respected member of the middle class. His ancestors had been clerks, lawyers, or clergymen, all sound citizens of the principality; and for nearly fifty years Philipp's father had been the pastor of the Reformed Church in Steinau. His grandfather in turn had been an important clergyman in Hanau. Dorothea, née Zimmer, was a native of Cassel and therefore as much a true Hessian as the Grimms. Family tradition was strong, with ancestors remembered and kept alive in the thoughts of each new generation. It is characteristic that Wilhelm and Jacob learned their catechism from a form prepared by their great-grandfather.

The Grimms and Zimmers represented the best of the emerging middle class—they had received formal educations and had risen to professional careers. Education, especially for the lower middle class without family fortunes, was the only path to a higher station in life, for the upper echelons of the army and civil service were closed to commoners in the highly stratified, almost feudal society of the late eighteenth century in Germany. But there were possibilities of upward mobility, for society offered honors and advancement to those who achieved in the scholarly field. The universities were becoming more important in the overall life of the nation even before the French Revolution and its egalitarian influence. The middle class, emerging as a force in the social life of Germany, began to achieve power in politics as well as in the field of learning where it had long been dominant.

The sense of belonging to a solid family with roots and achievements was a natural heritage of the brothers Jacob and Wilhelm. Wilhelm, only thirteen months younger than Jacob, was in many respects a quite different personality, but the remarkable features of their relationship were the lack of rivalry and sibling jealousy and the presence of a unique special intimacy. During childhood a deeply felt inner affinity kept them together in all their doings: they worked at one desk, sharing interests and reinforcing their common goals. The feeling of responsibility for other family members served to strengthen these bonds. In 1805, when Jacob left for France (Jacob was then twenty, Wilhelm nineteen), they made a solemn resolution never to separate and to preserve their special bond in all their undertakings. Even Wilhelm's marriage did not change their habit of working together, for they long had two desks in one room and only later, in Berlin, did they work and write in adjacent rooms. In their publications this intimate cooperation is seen in the absence of their Christian names—*Old German Poems,* the *Songs of the Elder Edda,* the *Fairy Tales,* and the *Folk Tales* are by the "Brothers Grimm." The whole family was closely knit and united by ties of affection and loyalty not only for its immediate members but for a large circle of relatives. Reverence for ancestors, respect and care for living relatives, and a strong sense of duty and family obligation were the heritage of the brothers. Jacob and Wilhelm very early helped in the supervision of the younger children, feeling responsible for them even when both parents were alive. Philipp and Dorothea had nine children, three of whom died in infancy. The one daughter, Charlotte Amalie or Lotte, was a family favorite and received special treatment as the only sister.

Grandparents were a vital part of family life in those days. The maternal grandfather, Johann Hermann Zimmer, who lived from 1709 until 1798, took an active interest in his grandchildren, especially the eldest, Jacob. His letters to Jacob were often admonitory and didactic in tone, full of piety and sincerity as well as concern with Jacob's education, but his well-meant advice was appreciated, as we can judge from the few letters surviving which Jacob wrote to him. No letters to Wilhelm have come down to us. Wilhelm as a child was quite delicate and in need of special care: he was often bathed with warm water and wine to restore his vigor. Wilhelm's account of his childhood in Hanau is less detailed than Jacob's, who later recalled his life in the town with tenderness and nostalgia, although he was never sentimental nor did he romanticize the period. But from his autobiography, which he began when he was twenty-nine, and the references in his letters, he and Wilhelm had a very normal childhood, sharing most of the joys and sorrows of their contemporaries. Their time at home was spent in the company of the maids and the younger brothers and sister—only in the evening did the family gather together for reading or prayers. Jacob was rather reticent, even if respectful, about his father, who played a small role in both his and Wilhelm's reminiscences. Yet he made a deep impression on Jacob, who at the age of forty-five claimed that he could still recall his father exactly. For the most part Jacob seems to have remembered his father more as a magisterial than a parental figure. Philipp Grimm, as a German official, wore a uniform in the course of performing his duties. Although he was not very tall, he must have been an impressive figure in his blue frock coat, red collar, leather breeches of eighteenth-century cut, and silver-spurred boots. Even when not in uniform he appeared to the children in a kind of official capacity, escorting them to church on Sunday, reading prayers to the family, and in general presenting a figure of authority and guidance. Jacob often spoke fondly of his father's neatness, orderliness, and his love for work, qualities which he himself inherited and cherished all his life. Work was a positive, almost religious value in itself for the Grimms.

Much more vivid were the brothers' recollections of a kindly and industrious mother who always seemed to be sewing or knitting. Since several children were born to Philipp and Dorothea in rapid succession, Jacob's memories of her may well have been influenced by the series of pregnancies and childbirths. Her grief at the death of her husband—Jacob was eleven years old and Wilhelm only ten—was recalled with pain years later by the older brothers, who helped her to hold together the family in a time of trouble and financial difficulty. On a day-to-day basis, however, it was Gretchen and Marie, the maidservants, who were most directly responsible for the upbringing of the small children. Even more influential was Aunt Schlemmer, Philipp's elder sister, widowed in the year of Jacob's birth, who undertook the care of the older children. When they were quite young and well before school age, she taught Jacob and Wilhelm to read, write, and use the multiplication tables, skills which the brothers were quick to learn. She was the first important educational guide in their lives, and some of her stern method and insistence on careful and correct learning stayed with them throughout their careers.

The family was in several senses a closed circle. The boys did not play with other children or come together with their peers until late in school. Quite naturally for the times, the family was also a strict religious unit. Jacob later recalled that their early religious education was pronouncedly Reformed Lutheran, and that he looked on Lutherans as foreigners, while the few Catholics who occasionally passed through the town he viewed with awe and curiosity. Catholicism and predominately Catholic countries always remained alien to Jacob, who was rather rigid in his Protestantism, if not to the point of real intolerance, then at least to a degree of incomprehension and rejection. In the light of his assumption "that through the Reformation and Protestantism intellectual culture has been furthered," he thought Austria suffered from cultural lag because it had had no Reformation. He preferred Protestant hymns to Catholic ones, and he objected to the Catholicizing tendencies of the later stages of Romanticism. Sometimes his anti-Catholicism was of questionable taste, as when he wrote rather bitter remarks on the conversion of Protestants to the Roman Catholic faith in letters to his teacher Savigny, who had married into a Catholic family and moved in circles where such remarks would hardly be tolerated. Jacob believed very sincerely that the modern German language was a product of Protestant thinking, and in the preface to the second edition of his *German Grammar* asserted: "One may well designate New High German as the Protestant dialect whose liberating nature has long since overwhelmed poets and writers of the Catholic faith, quite without their realizing it." In his defense, however, in his personal and social contacts and in his many friendships, he never allowed his bias to interfere or to become an obstacle.

Except for prayers and the learning of the catechism there was little formal religious training within the family, but the boys naturally received instruction in the Reformed Steinau Church.

Jacob later recalled that he had never felt a greater surge of piety than when he received communion after his confirmation in the same church where his grandfather had been pastor. Religious and familial piety were intimately connected in the lives of the brothers. The picture that we gain from Jacob's autobiographical material is one of quiet, dutiful provincialism. Patriotism, like religion not discussed at home and inculcated more by example and the force of observed attitudes than by talk, was a local loyalty for Hesse-Cassel. Jacob was to recall that "we looked down with condescension on people from Darmstadt," a short distance to the south of Frankfurt.

At an early age the two brothers were instructed in French by a private tutor who lived nearby. These lessons were later recalled by Jacob with mixed emotions, but eventually his knowledge of French was to serve him well. At the age of six Jacob entered the local school, soon followed by Wilhelm, who, although thirteen months younger, always was quick to catch up with his older brother. Jacob was supposed to become a pastor like his grandfather in Steinau. Temperamentally he was well suited for such a career, and had his father lived longer, he might well have entered the ministry. But Jacob was also open to worldly pleasures and forms of entertainment. It comes as a surprise to learn that the serious-minded, to some even dour, philologist of later years had dancing lessons, often danced at ceremonial occasions, and as a student in Marburg was considered a lively dancer. The boys' everyday life was unexciting and ran according to routine; they relished the seasonal changes that people close to an agricultural society enjoy. No great events were later recalled by any of the family from the childhood days in Hanau, but it is interesting to note that Jacob wrote his Grandfather Zimmer about the murder of the King of France, indicating that happenings in the larger world outside Hesse-Cassel did not pass unnoticed. In 1791, when Jacob was six, Philipp Grimm was appointed magistrate for the districts of Steinau and Schlüchtern, not far to the east. The whole family, now increased by more children, had to move together with Aunt Schlemmer to Steinau. Hanau never forgot the

Grimms, just as they never forgot the town. In 1837, when the brothers were expelled from Göttingen, the town collected money and sent the generous sum of four hundred thalers to its illustrious sons. In Steinau Jacob and Wilhelm spent the next seven years, a period which they always looked back on as an idyllic part of their lives.

Steinau, which lies on the road from Fulda to Gelnhausen, was a small town with many monuments dating from medieval times. Castles, towers, and the town walls were both landmarks and historical reminders. The brothers' sense of tradition was due not only to their family life but also to the experience of living in conservative towns like Steinau where the past was very much alive in the present. They made excursions into the country, enjoyed the flowers, trees, rivers, and rolling hills, and began their lifelong interest in botany and in trying to capture some of the beauties of nature in drawings and sketches. For the rest of their lives, the charms of open landscape and unspoiled nature were to be a source of solace and recreation. But like many small towns Steinau offered inadequate schooling for youngsters as awakened as the brothers Grimm. Jacob claimed that he learned nothing from the schoolmaster Zinkhahn but classroom studiousness and strict attention.

Although absorbed in their studies and personal matters, the brothers were also aware of events in neighboring France which were to have such a profound influence on the whole continent of Europe. The immediate political effects of the revolution in France were not felt in rustic Steinau, nor is any mention of the implications made in the documents from Jacob and Wilhelm that have come down to us. Grandfather Zimmer was horrified at the regicide, and his letters were full of reports on events beyond the Rhine. As France began to push across Europe in the burst of energy released by the revolution, Hesse-Cassel inevitably came into the arena of military activity. Troops moved through the area, some of them native Hessians, but more picturesque and terrifying were the foreign troops—Austrians, Dutch, Prussians, and Russians. The wild behavior of the troops, especially the drunken and marauding stragglers, frightened the citizens of the town and the peaceful, unmartial Grimms. The looting and pillaging were dreaded by all, since even the "German" soldiers from other regions of Germany did not spare the country. The most feared were the Austrians, the most disorderly the Dutch, and the best behaved and disciplined the French, who after all entered as conquerors, but were restrained at first in exercising their rights. It was the French troops who seem to have been the most sympathetic and appealing. Even when ragged they made the most cheerful impression, and even when retreating seemed to have the highest morale. Steinau itself did not suffer during the 1790's as much as more important cities like Frankfurt and Cassel, but the Prussian withdrawal through Hesse-Cassel in 1794 made a deep impression. The rapidly changing fortunes of war interfered with the duties of Philipp, who as magistrate was necessarily involved in the resulting disorders. The children seem to have lived relatively undisturbed lives, even though they were later able to recall vividly some of the martial events and the pillaging.

The Steinau years ended abruptly with the sudden death of Philipp Grimm on the tenth of January, 1796, leaving Dorothea with six small children to support and educate. The situation within the family never became desperate, because the older brothers—especially the dutiful and responsible Jacob—helped in every way possible. But financial resources were scarce, and the formal education of two of Germany's most famous scholars might have come to a premature end if Aunt Zimmer (Henriette Philippine Zimmer), a lady-in-waiting at the court of the Landgrave of Hesse, had not come to their rescue. With her help the two brothers went off to the Gymnasium (called the Lyceum) at Cassel in the fall of 1798. There Jacob studied until ready for the university in 1802, and Wilhelm until 1803. Their preparation in Steinau had been inadequate, so that at first both Jacob and Wilhelm had to struggle. Both were quick and eager; Jacob was soon the first in his class and began to rise through the grades rapidly. He was able to skip several classes and advance at a pace that was unusual for the time. Looking back Jacob expressed severe criticism of the school, and his strictures on the faculty were not flattering. Jacob was especially offended when called by the old-fashioned "Er," while his classmates from the city of Cassel were addressed by the formal and correct "Sie." Neither brother was ever aggressively egalitarian, but both had at various times in their lives to contend with the class distinctions that were the hallmark of German society in those days. Minor rebuffs and slights were noted especially by Jacob with some bitterness, although politically he accepted the historical ordering of society without many complaints until much later in life.

Jacob was also very critical of the curriculum at the Gymnasium, which "wasted much time with geography, natural history, anthropology, morals, physics, logic, and philosophy, while the instruction in philology and history, which should be the soul of all education at the Gymnasium level, was neglected." In addition to six hours of school every day, both brothers then had four or five hours of private tutoring, especially in Latin and French. They made rapid progress under this stern regimen, but later Jacob admitted that too much had been demanded of them and that they had no leisure for fun or for playing with their friends. They did find time to practice drawing and sketching, a habit from their Steinau days, at which they developed much skill. Ludwig Emil, a younger brother almost always referred to as Louis, continued in the field of art and became a well-known artist. To him we owe many portraits of the Grimm family as well as illustrations for the books his older brothers published.

The death of Philipp in 1796 had given them many immediate problems to settle, with family affairs and the progress of their education absorbing most of their interest and energy. Aunt Schlemmer, who was still living with them, also died in 1796; by now in real financial difficulties, the family had to give up the official residence and move to a rented house. In September 1798, the brothers moved to Cassel, and the childhood days were over.

❧ II ❧

Marburg

AT SCHOOL in Cassel Jacob and Wilhelm missed their mother and the family life, but they were at least still together and able to give each other moral support. But the move to the University of Marburg in the spring of 1802 marked Jacob's first separation from the brother who was so dear to him. Wilhelm was very ill at the time, and it was no doubt more difficult for Jacob to leave his beloved brother than Cassel and the rest of the family. Jacob chose law as his field of study "because my father had been a lawyer and because mother wanted it that way; what do children or youths understand about the true meaning of such a study at the time when they make such decisions? But there is something natural in clinging to the paternal position in life, in fact something harmless and rather advisable. In later years I would have chosen no other science than botany." Jacob lived very modestly in Marburg, since he was unable to obtain the slightest financial help. Stipends were handed out to members of the aristocracy and rich landowners who did not need the money but received it as a reward for their social position. The widowed Dorothea Grimm had had to submit a most humble request to the Landgrave of Hesse-Cassel for permission for her son to study at the university. Her request was necessitated by Landgrave Wilhelm's curtailment in 1793 of the number of students who could attend the university, limiting the right to study to those servants of the state who stood at least in the first seven ranks of the civil service. Since Jacob's father had only been in the eighth rank, special dispensation was necessary, and was not given to the Grimms until 1802.

Again one can sense Jacob's bitterness and resentment of the privileges which accrued to the aristocracy of birth and not of mind. But typically he also saw the positive side of his enforced poverty: "Lack of money is an inducement to diligence and work, protects one from many forms of distraction, and inculcates the noble pride which the consciousness of one's own merit maintains with regard to that which others are given by their status and wealth." Jacob further expressed the thought that Germany's achievements might be ascribed to the fact that it was not a rich country. Jacob was quite sincere in his praise of the blessings of poverty, for even though he often complained that he had not enough money to buy the books he wanted, he had very modest demands on life. His wants were simple and frugal. When he was able to purchase the volumes he needed for his work, he could be content with very few material possessions. Both he and Wilhelm were more concerned with things of the spirit than with objects, ornamentation, or even with comfort. They did not make a virtue out of necessity in this regard, but were so completely absorbed in their studies or in plants, pictures, and other simple pleasures that they never felt the need for luxurious living.

Marburg changed Jacob's life decisively. He thought very highly of the university, of its spirit, of the student body and the faculty. He also praised the great sense of freedom evident during his student years, and contrasted it with the later attempts of the state to regulate and control the university which had been founded in 1527 as Germany's first Protestant university. Government regulation of education, he believed, only promoted mediocrity.

At first Jacob pursued the usual course of studies leading to the degree in law, mostly without enthusiasm and borne up chiefly by a sense of duty and the habit of succeeding in his studies. Only in one field was he inspired to develop not only interest but a profound concern. A young instructor at the university called Savigny caught and won Jacob's admiration. Soon the relationship between student and professor became one of friendship and mutual respect. Jacob began to visit Savigny's home and to browse in his library. Here he found medieval manuscripts and reprints of medieval literature. Savigny not only fostered Jacob's interest in law but inadvertently gave him the first impulse toward that field of study in which he was later to gain fame. Contact with Savigny's in-laws, the Brentanos of Frankfurt, well-known Romantic writers, the study of law, and especially of older Germanic law, and the awakening to his true calling all proceeded from the Marburg experience. Jacob was clearly aware of this and realized that his life had progressed from youth to manhood during the Marburg years.

Of the influences on Jacob's career, Savigny was the one who stood out above all others. Friedrich Karl von Savigny (1779–1861) was born in Frankfurt am Main and owned hereditary family property between Hanau and Gelnhausen. In 1800 he came to Marburg as a lecturer and was made a professor in 1803. In the same year he became engaged to Kunigunde Brentano, a sister of the famous poet Clemens Brentano, and married her in 1804 before leaving the university for a trip to Paris. It is characteristic of Jacob and his instinct for quality that he immediately felt the greatness of Savigny and was able to appreciate his intellectual powers, although some students saw him as a dull lecturer lacking in temperament. Savigny, unlike most professors of the time, did not dictate, but lectured at a comfortable pace, often interrupting his talk to direct questions to students. He also assigned written exercises to his students and returned them with comments and evaluations. In all this he was an innovator, since most instruction in law at the time consisted of taking down lectures in notes and learning them by rote. Savigny's life is so intertwined with that of the brothers Grimm that we shall often refer to both his personal life and professional career. He had a high regard for both brothers and valued their opinions in law as well as literature. Savigny's empirical method of dealing with texts, in contrast to the customary speculative procedure of the times, had a profound and lasting influence on Jacob and Wilhelm. Jacob frankly confessed that he owed a lifetime debt to Savigny for having taught him scientific method in research. The *German Grammar,* the book that established Jacob's world reputation as a philologist, he dedicated to Professor von Savigny with a noble and generous statement of his debt to him.

Of importance and interest but of quite different nature was the acquaintance with the poet Clemens Brentano, the brother-in-law of Savigny. Brentano was an erratic and unstable person, subject to moods of alternating depression and exaltation, an improviser who was scornful of pedestrian precision, yet at times an inspired poet and narrator. His comings and goings were as unpredictable as his moods and whims. He was a dabbler in many fields, at times a gifted amateur, at others a harborer of bizarre notions. Always full of plans and projects, most of which were dropped before completion, he was able to generate ideas and enthusiasm and his infectious ways contributed much to the work of others. He later boasted that it was he who first interested the Grimms in older German literature, and there may be some truth in the assertion. He had already begun preparations for the book of folk songs which made him famous, *The Boy's Magic Horn (Des Knaben Wunderhorn),* which he collected and published in collaboration with Achim von Arnim. Clemens certainly introduced Arnim to the Grimms, and for this act alone he deserves kindly mention. The brothers were at first attracted to Brentano as well as charmed by his sister Bettina, later wife of Arnim. But over the years they became wary of his idiosyncrasies, his marital problems which he shared with all who would listen, and his unreliability. In the long run Bettina turned out to be the steadier friend and more reliable sponsor. Bettina sang the praises of the brothers to everyone she could, and her loyalty to them was to last as long as she lived, long after her husband had died.

The separation from his beloved brother was just as painful for Wilhelm, who spent a lonely year in Cassel after Jacob went to Marburg. Wilhelm's misery during this period was reflected in his tender and melancholy letters to both his brother and his school friend, Ernst Otto von der Malsburg. In the autumn of 1802 Wilhelm suffered an acute attack of asthma, not his first respiratory trouble, nor unfortunately his last. For nearly six months he was sick and alone in his room at Cassel, unable to read or study, but through it all he remained cheerful and courageous. He was always able to face his physical weaknesses with courage and good humor, even finding a positive side to his handicaps. Later in life, when still plagued with many ailments, he could confidently assert that illness had its advantages, since lying in bed gave one opportunity for quiet thought and reflection. In spite of all obstacles he was able to complete his Gymnasium studies in 1803, leaving school with a brilliant record and finishing his preparatory work in half the required time. In the same year he joined Jacob at the university and also chose law as his field, although he too felt no special call to the subject.

The fourteenth-century town of Marburg is picturesquely situated on a sentinel hill overlooking the beautiful winding Lahn Valley. Guarding a prominent bend in the river and dominating the steep cobbled alleys and steps is the castle of the Hessian landgraves, where Luther and Zwingli once met during the turmoil of the Reformation. From the town many pleasant vistas open up, with views of the rolling wooded Hessian countryside that preserve still a romantic atmosphere suggestive of the setting for a fairy tale or fanciful folk tale. Gray slate roofs lie nestled among fields and darker woods to mark sites of civilization, but the countryside remains unspoiled even today. The brothers, who appreciated the beauties of nature wherever they were, found the region very attractive.

In his first letter to his school friend, Paul Wigand, Jacob wrote: "I like the new place very much. The situation of Marburg and the surrounding region is certainly very beautiful. Especially when one stands near the castle and looks down; the town itself is, however, very ugly. I believe there are more steps on the streets than stairs in the houses. There is one house which one enters by the roof." The life of the town centered around the university.

There is only scattered evidence that the brothers participated in the student social life, which at that time ranged from barbarous drinking bouts and duels to more civilized forms of entertainment such as riding horseback, attending the teas and dances of the local gentry, and playing card games with and without gambling.

Most of the students were wealthy and came from highly placed families on the carefully graduated social scale. Yet the Grimms' social status proved to be no obstacle in forming a firm and intimate friendship with the aristocratic Savigny and his circle of friends and relatives. The brothers were consciously and deliberately middle class in all their values and views, and only occasionally did they express resentment of the privileges of the aristocracy. Wherever they went, their outstanding intellectual and personal qualities won them friends among those of higher social station, including Brentano, von Arnim, von der Malsburg, and others, and they were usually content that it should be so. Both brothers were sociable enough when time and opportunity presented themselves, and both were good conversationalists who could enter into polite chatter as well as weightier discussions. They developed so many interests and were always so well read and informed that they were able to take their place easily and happily among like-minded people. The capacity for forming lasting friendships throughout their lives was one of their most appealing qualities. At the same time they could be brutally frank in forming adverse judgments. In their letters they often spoke with almost cruel candor of persons whom they did not like. From 1803 to 1813 Jacob kept a guest book in which guests and visitors wrote rhymes or sayings beside their names. Some of Jacob's marginal comments were caustically sarcastic, even where friends were concerned. He was quite impartial in calling nonsense nonsense, without regard to the source, and when friends wrote what he considered silly rhymes he could display biting invective. Jacob's sharp tongue did not go unnoticed by his fellow students, who nicknamed him "the old man," probably not out of respect but from fear of his sarcasm. Wilhelm, who obviously earned the affection of the other students much more readily, was called "the little fellow."

The rather terse references in Jacob's autobiography to any other aspect of Marburg than the faculty and curriculum can easily create the impression that study and hard work were the only activities of the brothers in their university days. In fact they managed to see the family in Steinau, where their visits were a great joy for their widowed mother and for the younger brothers, who looked up to Jacob and Wilhelm as guides and mentors. They did not indulge in the beery pastimes of many of their fellow students, but their literary interests, which had already been awakened in Cassel, soon brought them into contact with families in the area besides that of the Savignys. Through a fellow student from Cassel, von der Malsburg, they came to know the Chief Forester von Wildungen, who lived near the Savignys. In his home several young gentlemen and ladies, including the two daughters of the house, formed a "reading circle" which not only discussed the latest literature but also put on amateur theater productions, among them Shakespeare's *A Midsummer Night's Dream*. Various parlor games and *thés dansants* were also part of the attraction. Both brothers seem to have found time outside their study of law to do an enormous amount of reading in both classical and contemporary literature. When asked to go for a walk or pursue some other form of entertainment, Jacob often refused, saying that he intended "to take a walk in literature." The latest works by Goethe and Schiller were read and discussed with great interest, often with surprising judgments. Wilhelm, for example, did not like Schiller's *Wilhelm Tell,* and like many another student before and after him, was unable to finish reading Klopstock's *Messias*. Wilhelm was not content with the literary activity that he found already established when he arrived; after a little over a year in Marburg, he founded his own reading circle with some twenty-eight members. In order to keep up with his reading, he devoted his entire fall vacation in 1804 to filling out what he felt to be gaps in his reading list.

By the end of their period of study in Marburg, both brothers had read widely in the new Romantic literature, which strongly appealed to them. Jacob especially was enthusiastic about Tieck's stories with a medieval background, and was stimulated by Schlegel's collections of poetry from the Middle Ages. In Savigny's library Jacob first came to know medieval literature in the original Middle High German, and many years later he could still recall the thrill and excitement of the discovery. Their law studies had already brought them into contact with the medieval period in a scholarly way, because Savigny's method was historical and genetic. Since childhood they had felt a strong continuity with their national past; now at the university they began to discover sources and to acquire that historical-analytical method which was to make them the greatest scholars of their time in their chosen field. Their letters of this period tell us little about their formal studies, but much more about their growing interest in literature, especially older German literature. The Romanticists had rediscovered the magic and charm of the German national past in their own way, which was highly imaginative and fruitful where it was not methodical and historical. For many Romanticists the Middle Ages represented a timeless, unhistorical period of adventure, nobility, European unity, and German greatness, an "era when knights were bold and ladies fair," virtue was triumphant, evil was punished, and the exotic nature of the past was recaptured in fanciful tales of love and wonders. This approach was enough to satisfy the brothers at first, to win their enthusiasm and devoted interest, and to stimulate further research. Their subsequent strictures on the Romanticists' lack of scholarly method, and their personal dislike of several individuals, must be understood as a later reaction on the part of careful scholars who never really forgot where their first inspiration had come from. Even their harshest judgments were always tempered by gratitude.

❈ III ❈

France and the French

IN THE SUMMER of 1804 Savigny went to a Paris library to do source studies for his history of Roman law in the Middle Ages. In January 1805 he sent a message to Jacob, who had not finished his studies, asking him to come to Paris to help in the research. The offer was very flattering to Jacob, who accepted immediately. Upon his arrival in Paris in February, he lived with the Savigny family and immediately began to work with his professor in the library. Jacob's help was so valuable and so highly appreciated that Savigny officially recognized his assistance in the preface to the first published volume of the history. Jacob enjoyed living and working with the Savignys, but he also found time to investigate some of the medieval German manuscripts in the Bibliothèque Nationale and thus started on what was to become his major field of work for the rest of his life.

Life in Paris was very stimulating for a young man from a deeply provincial background, and his letters to Wilhelm reflect both his excitement and enthusiasm. Jacob was a keen observer of folk customs, national differences and peculiarities, as well as cultural differences of a scholarly nature. The people and the atmosphere of Paris were as interesting to him as the art works he carefully observed in the Louvre. The paintings of the Italian Renaissance seem to have made the deepest impression, but he also appreciated the Flemish school. Architecture in all its forms, even in the manner of building peasants' homes, was carefully observed on his travels and reported in detail in his letters to Wilhelm. Savigny often invited him to go along to the theater, but Jacob found Parisian theater productions not to his liking. He complained of the noise made by the audience, disliked the repertory, found the comedies shallow, and often laughed during the tragedies. The constant applause, even for the mere entrance of an actor, disturbed him. Racine and Corneille he considered the best playwrights, but he objected to their polished and rather boring language. Some of his judgments are remarkably keen, whereas others betray the young man from a rustic background. There are often notes of national pride to be heard in some of his criticism of the French way of life. No real Hessian boy is ever truly at home in Paris.

While Jacob was working and studying in faraway Paris, his mother, who had agreed to the trip only reluctantly and with much anxiety, worried and fretted at having a son who had traveled beyond the bounds of her ability to visualize his condition. But she neither spoke of it nor did she write him, and Jacob only learned later from his sister Lotte how much he had been missed. Jacob returned with Savigny toward the end of September 1805, stopping in Marburg to take Wilhelm along for a home visit to Cassel, where Dorothea had moved in 1805 in order to be with her elder children. Although Jacob had not completed his law studies in Marburg, he immediately set out to obtain a paying position to help support the family. He hoped to become an assessor or secretary in the government in Cassel, but was unable to secure such a position, partly because he had not finished his studies, partly because of the system of privileges and preferments in such appointments. Yet Jacob was fortunate in having the best possible recommendations, especially from Savigny, who sponsored him in all his undertakings with great enthusiasm. Then in January 1806, he finally became secretary to the War College in Cassel with a salary of one hundred thalers a year, a sum which hardly made him affluent. Jacob was glad to receive any salary at all under the circumstances, and he complained less about his remuneration than about the amount of mind-deadening work he had to perform. In addition he had to appear in a stiff and uncomfortable uniform with powdered wig and high collar. When doing his own research, Jacob was capable of very demanding and precise work with careful attention to detail, but he was offended by dull and empty routine of a bureaucratic nature, and his letters over many years were full of complaints about mindless routine and meaningless ritual. The delight he took in reconstructing bygone forms and rituals contrasted sharply with his annoyance at court protocol and ceremony. In his autobiography he noted with satisfaction that he was able to devote his leisure time to the study of medieval literature.

While Wilhelm continued his studies at Marburg and Jacob was looking for a position, political and military events brought about a fundamental change in the status of Hesse-Cassel. The year 1806 saw the final dissolution of the Holy Roman Empire of the German Nation. In his imperialistic sweep through Europe, Napoleon won the great battles of Jena and Auerstedt and destroyed the power of Prussia, and even Russia was helpless against the French in 1807. By the Treaty of Tilsit, Prussia lost approximately one half of its territory and was forced back entirely to the east of the Elbe. To the west of the Elbe, Napoleon founded the new kingdom of Westphalia, which consisted of the former territories of Prussian Brunswick, parts of Hannover, and Hesse. The capital of the principality of Hesse had been occupied as early as November 1, 1806, and the ruling Elector Wilhelm I had had to flee. As king of the new state Napoleon established his youngest brother, Jérôme, a rather frivolous and extravagant person who never won either the respect or the love of the Hessians. Cassel now became the capital of a kingdom, an advance in status from one point of view, but a source of irritation and oppression for most of the populace. As in every occupation there were those who cooperated with the new regime and profited from it, but in general the citizenry resented the conquerors more than they appreciated the pomp that went with the new kingdom. Although a new and much enlarged bureaucracy arose to administer the affairs of the new state, Jacob remained unemployed for most of the year 1807. Wilhelm, who had taken his law examinations in May of 1806, was unable to find a job also. Financial distress finally forced Jacob to apply for a position as librarian with King Jérôme, but nothing immediate resulted. In his autobiography he modestly stated: "I considered myself qualified to seek a position in the public library in Cassel, since I had some practice in the reading of manuscripts, had become quite familiar with the history of literature through private study, and also felt that I would make greater progress in this field, whereas I hated the learning of the French law into which our whole jurisprudence threatened to be transformed." But the position was given to someone else, and Jacob remained without employment. Wilhelm had also been unable to find a source of income, and since the widow's pension which Dorothea received was small and quite inadequate, times of real deprivation came for the whole Grimm family.

The problems of financial support and gainful employment were abruptly overshadowed in the brothers' lives by the sudden death of their beloved mother. In May 1808, at the age of fifty-two, Dorothea died, leaving six children without any means of support and adding profound grief to their precarious situation. Her death was a blow to all the children, for she had been the emotional center of the family and her warm love and care had maintained the sense of unity, intimacy, and belonging that made family life so precious. Perhaps the later aberrations and failures of Ferdinand, the problem child of the family, can be attributed to the death of his parents while he was still young and immature. The older brothers tried to replace the parents, helped, guided, and advised as best they could, but at least in the case of Ferdinand they failed to adequately replace parental leadership. The emotional impact of the mother's death was reflected in many of the letters the older brothers wrote during the difficult weeks following her funeral. Wilhelm reported dreams and nightmares, and both he and Jacob were later moved to sorrow on the anniversaries of her death. Many years later, in 1826, Wilhelm visited the scenes of his youth in Steinau and sadly noted that he still dreamed of his mother sitting with her knitting work and talking to him with mild reproach.

At times of crisis the Grimms were obviously sustained by their religious faith. Deaths in the family always brought to the surface their deep trust in God's laws and His ordering of the world. In the normal routine of life they were not ostentatious about religion, churchgoing, or the formal expressions of faith, but in times of stress they were able to find simple, sincere, and moving words for their belief in God's guidance of the universe. Jacob never expected favors from the Deity, but his wishes for a quiet, domestic life devoted to his hobbies often took the form of asking God for just so much material welfare that he might lead a productive life. He felt that God's will worked for the best, and found comfort in this thought in times of bereavement. When Aunt Zimmer died, he had found his faith reconfirmed and wrote Wilhelm to comfort him with the assurance that God would continue to help. Even in the growth and decay of literature, Jacob believed that he saw the will of Providence, and he considered the cycles of development and decline as a cause for joy. He later came to believe that Christianity had preserved Germany's pagan past and had fulfilled an important historical function in transmitting the pagan heritage to posterity. Later on, Wilhelm's fortitude in sorrow was touchingly expressed at the death of his little son Jacob. The faith that love is the prime principle of the world and that children who have been loved will surely enter heaven sustained him, so that he was able to write his friend Karl Lachmann that in the midst of grief he experienced "moments of intense happiness when the indescribably loving heart of my wife and the heart of Jacob overflowed with love as Jacob sat for twelve hours by the child's bed, bent down over him to the last breath."

While fortune smiled on Napoleon, whose power grew from day to day, and while the political and military events that disturbed Europe had their depressing effects on the brothers, Ludwig, who had now begun his serious career as a painter, found a position as an illustrator for the journal *Trösteinsamkeit,* edited by Arnim and Brentano in Heidelberg. Jacob's efforts at securing a paying appointment were finally rewarded in 1808 with a position as director of the private library of the new King Jérôme. Jacob remarked rather bitterly that there must have been a total lack of other applicants for the position, since he received it without anyone having certified his abilities. In fact Jacob owed the post to a recommendation by Johannes von Müller, the Swiss historian, who used his influence with one of the king's secretaries. The job was a real sinecure which left Jacob much leisure for his own pursuits. Yet his fierce Hessian patriotism made him report his appointment to Savigny in deprecating, almost apologetic terms.

By reason of his appointment, Jacob became a citizen of the kingdom of Westphalia and therefore subject to the military draft. In August 1808, he narrowly escaped being drafted into the Westphalian army. But his luck held, since conscription took place by lot and he was fortunate enough to draw a blank. Thousands of others were not so lucky, and many loyal Hessians were forced to serve in the imperial forces of Napoleon. In this way many acquired military experience which was ironically turned against Napoleon in 1813. Jacob's heartfelt relief at Napoleon's defeat was expressed in all his letters, for the foreign regime had been unable to win the loyalty even of its paid and pampered servants.

At the library, from July 1808 on, he immediately began to receive a quite adequate salary for duties that were far from onerous. The library, left behind when the Elector of Hesse-Cassel fled, contained about fifteen thousand volumes, rather haphazardly collected and not representing a valuable collection in any field. There were a few history books which attracted Jacob, but there was no system and none was expected. Early in 1809 the king unexpectedly informed Jacob that he had been appointed auditor to the Council of State, with a raise in salary that brought his total income to about one thousand thalers (circa seven hundred dollars) per annum. All financial worries disappeared, and for the first time in years the family was able to exist without constant concern for money.

Jacob used his new well-paid leisure to pursue his studies of older German literature. Occasionally he had to enter new books in the catalogue and sometimes to appear at meetings of the council, but as time went on he discovered that not much was expected of him and that the king had less trust in him than the other members of the council, who were all French. Various people near to the king protected Jacob, so that he had only his resentment of the French occupation as a disturbing element in an otherwise advantageous situation.

Wilhelm, who remained unemployed, had several spells of bad health, and the year 1808 marked one of his lowest and most depressed periods. His usual cheerfulness even in adversity seemed to have left him and being unable to work over long periods of time depressed him all the more. The same year saw the beginning of his work in Norse literature, the field which first established his reputation as a scholar.

Both brothers had also started their collection of folklore material, mostly for fun, and in 1808 contributed several folk songs to the first volume of Arnim and Brentano's *Des Knaben Wunderhorn*. Work on the reediting of old manuscripts was becoming a main concern of the brothers. Several of Wilhelm's translations of Old Danish songs of chivalry were later published by Arnim in *The Journal for Hermits* (*Zeitung für Einsiedler*).

The Grimms' turn to older German literature and history was at once an escape from the depressing contemporary political situation and an attempt to find solace in the ancient glories and achievements of their nation. Although Jacob spoke with remarkable tolerance of King Jérôme (Wilhelm hardly ever mentioned him), it is clear that they suffered under the occupation. Inflation and ever mounting taxes added to the strain of French rule. Life in Cassel, now capital of the kingdom of Westphalia, became so expensive that the family often sent to Steinau to buy necessities. King Jérôme was a luxury-loving exhibitionist whose ostentation obviously cost dearly, but in addition all Napoleonic kingdoms were expected to defray the cost of the occupation and help maintain the French troops in the field. Wilhelm, who was often ill and for a long time unemployed, could contribute little but moral aid and comfort to the family. Jacob even had to help with the household chores at times—something quite unusual for a German man—since Lotte, the only sister, was not skillful in housework and was always considered too delicate and precious for any real work. Jacob, so orderly and precise in his own life, had not the heart to discipline the other younger children, and led them by good example, but not without many misgivings and occasionally giving vent to his displeasure. Fundamentally all the brothers and the sister liked each other, were loyal and helpful, but there were moments of irritation and frustration to bear at home as well as in service. In 1809 Wilhelm's health reached such a dangerous point that he was sent to Halle to take a cure under the direction of a physician. The family could ill afford the expense; Wilhelm's letters asking for money are touching in their apologies and deference. The "magnetic" treatments lasted for nearly six months, half a year of suffering for unhappy Wilhelm that cost the family dearly since the physician, a well-known doctor by the name of Reil, also ran a resort and spa and charged accordingly. Wilhelm's one consolation was that he was able to continue his studies in spite of his poor health.

Napoleon's defeat at Aspern raised the hopes of occupied Europe for a short time, but after the battle of Wagram Austria was humbled once more and Napoleon's power seemed more irresistible than ever. In June 1809, Jacob wrote to Wilhelm that he was so depressed by life in Cassel that he would leave if it were not for the fact that his mother's grave was in Cassel. A desire to travel overcame him, and although he explained it as a wish to find new books for his studies, it is clear that he really wanted to escape the French. But even in his blackest moods he was able to find a positive note—he observed in the same letter that he believed that people in Germany had never prayed so nobly and so unanimously. Even Wilhelm, who should have had enough to do with his magnets and studies of Old Norse, noted in his autobiography that the general popular concern for the troublesome events was more profound than ever. Their letters of this period reflect the first stirrings of the great national movement of the Wars of Liberation, a movement which was borne and led chiefly by the intelligentsia. The intellectuals were the leaders and instigators—the popular enthusiasm so often observed by historians frequently stems from the writings of poets and other intellectuals. The prayers of many were for the liberation of the fatherland, and piety and patriotism were united as never before. The specific union of religious faith and the desire to liberate the nation may be seen very early and with elegant clarity in the brothers' letters, for they were proud to be the kind of citizens who could and would contribute to the spiritual wealth of the nation.

During this period they began their correspondence with several Scandinavian scholars, notably Nyerup in Copenhagen. Wilhelm's attempts to obtain old manuscripts of Old Norse poetry were often unsuccessful, but he was able to establish contact with helpful advisers. Although Wilhelm was constantly ill and often unable to work at all, even when not taking the cure in Halle, he did travel to Berlin for the first time. He was not too favorably impressed by the city but for a time his complaints about the lack of contacts in Cassel ceased. In December 1809, he went to Weimar to visit Goethe. The celebrated, admired poet received Wilhelm rather formally, but cordially enough, yet probably did not sense the profound admiration and respect which the young scholar held for him. Wilhelm made many attempts to obtain Goethe's support for his publication of older German literature and requested several forewords which he never received. Goethe's enthusiasm for epics like the *Song of the Nibelungs* suffered from the fact that he always compared them unfavorably to the *Iliad* and *Odyssey*. So in spite of several formal statements of encouragement and approval, the brothers were never able to secure much help from the Olympian of Weimar. Goethe did not share their patriotic enthusiasm, nor did he truly appreciate the Grimms' efforts to present the nation with the documents and evidence of its past achievements.

Jacob's first contribution to the rediscovery of Germany's half-forgotten ancient literary heritage was an essay on the Old German *Meistergesang*. Jacob's theory that the troubadour tradition of the Middle Ages had persisted with unbroken continuity down to the Master Singers of the time of Luther and Hans Sachs was not generally accepted by many scholars of the time. A *Meistergesang* was a song written according to strict rules of specific schools, composed mostly of middle-class artisans, from the fourteenth to the sixteenth century. For the Meistersinger, whom Richard Wagner's opera made famous throughout the world, the art of music was much like any other handiwork or craft; both the poetry and the accompanying music were considered learnable techniques that could be taught by a system of formal rules. The strophic form of the medieval Minnesinger was retained, but the content and essence became very different. Jacob, while noting this similarity in form, chose to play down the great difference in spirit.

Both Jacob and Wilhelm firmly believed that poetry could be used to illuminate the history of the nation. Language, like history, had for them an organic growth that proceeded from the national community and was then sustained by it. They felt very deeply that poetry was an essential part of life. With one of their characteristic metaphors, they expressed this belief as follows: "All genuine poetry is confirmed by the fact that it cannot exist without reference to life, for it has come forth from life and returns to it, just as the clouds return to the place of their birth after they have watered the earth. . . ." In the preface to *Old Danish Heroic Songs,* the book he was working on, Wilhelm wrote: "Because poetry never deceives, it has within it grace and a never failing solace, and it leads us out of the valley of despond and we see above all the clouds the blue firmament eternally arched."

Language, however, also mirrors the history of a nation. All his life Jacob considered the history of language and the related literature as the most convenient key to national history, and wrote in the preface to his *History of the German Language*: "It seemed worthwhile to see if the basis of our national history could not be better uncovered by proceeding from the history of our language." Their motive in discovering the old language and reediting old manuscripts was not primarily academic, in the pejorative sense of the word, but rather patriotic: it was a means of discovering the spirit of the past. More than most of their contemporaries they were aware of Germany's continuity with its past, and they felt that to learn the origins and development of one's country would strengthen one's love for the homeland. Jacob believed that the medieval chroniclers derived their knowledge of oldest history from the heroic songs created and declaimed by the bards. This faith involves a belief in the accuracy of medieval chroniclers and in the historicity of the epics, problems to which we shall return.

Ever since his training under Savigny in Marburg, Jacob had become an historian in everything he undertook. And Savigny's legal training taught him close attention to detail. Sometimes his love for fine points would verge on the crotchety: "In general I feel ever more clearly a decided antipathy to everything that is not detail, for in it alone the truth is truly alive." But it is not fair to a genius to emphasize only his idiosyncrasies. Jacob really felt that language was a living being, and he hypostatized a "spirit of language" which evolved and created as if it were alive. Poets, writers, and even historians he considered only servants and tools of this spirit, which was like a principle of organic nature. Thus he could later formulate his "sound laws" as natural laws. Jacob's exalted view of his mission was combined with a certain rigidity in his views that prevented a ready acceptance by the reading public. Armed with Savigny's historical-critical method, Jacob felt certain that he was right and that his hypotheses had the validity of empirical discoveries.

It is easy for later generations to point out and criticize the force of systematic error in Jacob's views: he wished to emphasize the continuity of Germany's culture and therefore bent the evidence to fit his thesis. Jacob was still in these years very much under the influence of German Romanticism. The Romantic rediscovery of the past had overtones of nationalism and political reaction; it tended to sentimentalize and distort in an imaginative and fanciful way not only the national past but also such artificial contrasts as town versus country, popular culture versus learned culture, and perhaps most damaging of all for scholarship, the contrast between reason and intuitive imagination. Most of these Romantic ways of thought were inherently alien to an ordered, analytic mind like that possessed by Jacob, but for years he was under their spell and his work combined in curious fashion Romantic notions with his own modes of thinking. Those Romantic ideas that were by nature congenial with his method and beliefs persisted throughout his career. The Romanticists had discovered *das Volk,* the common people, and raised them to the level of creators of culture, with the result that peasant culture became both synonymous with national culture and an object of research for the intelligentsia. Both Jacob and Wilhelm tended to idealize *das Volk* and to take a sublime view of things that to soberer realists were not so noble in nature. They must often have seemed naive idealists to more pedestrian contemporaries. Their nobility of character was combined with great simplicity and directness in expression; they shunned stilted and florid language, finding that the most profound thoughts were best conveyed in the most disciplined language. They expected a great deal from literature, which they believed to have an ennobling, ethical power, and were sincerely convinced of the moral as well as pedagogical value of their contributions. Wilhelm once defined poetry as "the raising of reality to the level of higher truth and a spiritual existence." In the most profound sense of the term, the Grimms believed in the humanistic value of poetry. Wilhelm once wrote to Savigny: "I mean that a poem by itself does not exist—it exists only through its relation to man and through his joy in the poem." Jacob shared Wilhelm's noble view of poetry and expressed his belief in its power and beauty in the preface to his article on *Meistergesang*: "Poetry is life itself, captured in its pure form and contained in the music of language."

The Grimms had hardly started publishing the results of their private research when they found themselves involved in constant polemics. These scholarly quarrels, which were as often concerned with trivia as with real issues or questions of principle, were taken seriously by all interested parties. The Grimms, although by nature not contentious, were convinced that they were right and that they had found a method and procedure which enabled them to restore old texts to their proper form. They were genuinely distressed at popularizing editions based on insufficient philological knowledge and full of sloppy scholarship. Most of their disagreements were with minor figures who tried to capitalize on the reawakened interest in older German literature. The feuds were not academic in the strict sense, although they did involve professional jealousy of a kind a modern faculty would immediately recognize, but were disputes, carried on in the journals, with scholars who were usually not professors, but only independent amateurs without academic connections. Most of the polemics have long since been forgotten, but only because the Grimms' principles triumphed so completely that their rivals and competitors have been deservedly consigned to oblivion.

Regrettably there were differences in principle which arose with friends such as Arnim and Lachmann. The Grimms insisted on standards of reproduction that were not easy for all to accept. The bitterest arguments arose over the question of translation. The Grimms had taught themselves to read Old High German, Gothic, Old Norse, Old English, some Sanskrit, and various other ancient and modern languages and some dialects without school texts or tutors. They had done this casually and in their spare time, considering the learning of languages merely something one does when the need arises. Jacob especially, confident that anyone else could do the same, saw no need to translate older German texts; what was required for the study of older German literature was the correct editing of the manuscripts. Wilhelm, more conciliatory, in fact began his career with translations from Old Danish. The necessity of modernizing in order to reach a large public never really became clear to Jacob.

As in so many other respects, the pioneering Grimms stood here at an important crossroads in scholarship. Jacob became the father of modern Indo-European philology, while writers such as Ludwig Uhland and Karl Simrock became the transmitters of older German literature to millions of readers. The spate of translations and adaptations that burst forth in the early years of the nineteenth century came to an end during the 1820's. Scholarly method and painstaking procedure triumphed. Only people with university training in philology and older literature occupied themselves with editing texts. Many new special skills became necessary for the scientific study of older languages and literature. Jacob and Wilhelm hardly speak of it, in their usual casual assumption that everyone learns what he has to, but it is remarkable that they were their own best paleographers. They read manuscripts in their original condition in a dozen languages and in the handwriting styles of several centuries.

The Grimms' dream of recapturing for the nation its ancient heritage was in great part defeated by their successful methods of scholarship, for their loving devotion to detail and historical accuracy made them inaccessible to many readers. And both Jacob and Wilhelm gradually accepted the fact that their more recondite scholarship would never become part of the popular culture.

In the year 1811 Napoleon's power was still the dominant fact of European life. Preparations for the great invasion of Russia in 1812 were being secretly made, and the end of foreign control seemed farther away than ever for the occupied nations of Europe. At this low point in the history of the German nation, Jacob reedited two of the oldest surviving documents in the Old High German language, the *Lay of Hildebrand* and the *Prayer of Wessobrunn* (the *Hildebrandslied* and the *Wessobrunner Gebet*). Both works had been published before, but carelessly and without any understanding of the problems involved. Since the language of the *Lay of Hildebrand* was unusually difficult, Jacob, contrary to his principles, included a translation along with the corrected text and commentary. Both documents go back to the early ninth century, the *Lay of Hildebrand,* a fragmentary Germanic version of the Sohrab and Rustum motif, being the oldest preserved heroic song in a Germanic language. It was written down by monks in Fulda in a curious and baffling mixture of High and Low German in the first decades of the ninth century. The *Wessobrunner Gebet* is a poem written in Bavarian dialect from the Upper Bavarian cloister of Wessobrunn. The editing of these two ancient documents was not in itself such a remarkable feat, but Jacob did more than reprint forgotten texts —he rediscovered the old Germanic meter and the principle of alliteration and restored the texts, which had until then been considered prose, to their proper form. Scholars had long known that Old Norse poetry had used alliteration as a structural element, but Jacob's discovery proved that the continental Germans had used a very similar style. Wilhelm collaborated both in the preparation of the text and in this important discovery. They were suitably modest about their achievement, but they were also proud for their nation. In a letter to Goethe, Wilhelm stressed the historical importance of the poems.

Wilhelm's medieval research had received an important impetus in the year 1807 when he visited his Aunt Zimmer in Gotha, where she was living with the Hessian Court in exile. While searching for manuscripts, something which by this time had become a fixed habit with both brothers, Wilhelm discovered the *Goldene Schmiede* of Konrad of Würzburg, a great deal of material which subsequently went into his edition of *Freidanks Bescheidenheit,* and some significant documents which he later used for his *Heroic Tales*. These were valuable finds, but he was still occupied with his studies of Norse literature. The Scandinavian world with its magnificent medieval literature stands at the beginning of Wilhelm's career. Herder was the first German poet to recognize the grandeur of the world of the Edda. With their penchant for the dark and mysterious, the Romanticists followed him in their admiration. Indeed, appreciation of the Edda and Old Icelandic literature was strongly admixed with Romantic notions of the exotic and heroic. Both brothers were usually very generous in expressing their debt to their predecessors; Wilhelm gladly acknowledged the assistance he had received from Scandinavian scholars, and cheerfully admitted that it was his knowledge of Norse literature which had helped him so much in his early research in older German literature.

In a letter to Savigny in 1808 Wilhelm said: "Almost my whole work recently has been a translation of the Old Danish heroic ballads. You will find some samples in *The Journal for Hermits*. I first hit upon the idea when I translated some of them as annotations for the history of the *Nibelungenlied*. But now I have found that these genuine old poems have a poetic depth, beauty, and grandeur such as those of few other nations; they surpass those of the Englishman Percy in this respect and in their purity. To be sure they lack the colorfulness and grace of the Spanish romances, but their advantages make up for that adequately and there is no lack of poems that are very cheerful and childlike like a children's fairy tale. I am sure that Goethe has the ideas for his best romances, the 'Erlkönig,' the 'King of Thule,' the 'Fisher,' from such Danish songs." By 1809 he had finished work on the *Old Danish Heroic Songs, Ballads and Fairy Tales* in Halle, encouraged by Savigny, to whom he had sent samples, and much helped by the German philosopher Henrik Steffens, in whose house he lived for a time. When he had real difficulties with the translation, he turned for help to Professor Nyerup in Copenhagen. Publication did not come until 1811, however, because Wilhelm had hoped for a time that Goethe would write an introduction. Reimer, the publisher, agreed to accept the book only if Goethe wrote a preface. When no word came from Goethe, Brentano suggested that the poems appear in a fourth volume of the *Wunderhorn*. However, in 1810, with the help of Arnim and Brentano, the publisher Zimmer in Heidelberg agreed to announce the book and finally published it in 1811. Arnim and Brentano again helped collaborate in the announcement, which has a ring of high Romanticism and the characteristically Norse spirit—something that Wilhelm was never as close to in his later writing.

The heroic songs which make up the first part of the collection Wilhelm thought were documents of the Great Migrations and therefore probably Germanic rather than specifically Danish in origin, because of their similarities to older Germanic verse and their preservation of very ancient traditions, apparently pre-Christian. He had come to the study of the material from his research in German literature written during the relatively sophisticated period of the thirteenth century. Thus he was struck by the more archaic tone of many of the poems and supposed them to be more ancient than they really were. His interpretation is readily understandable at a time when there were no guideposts and, instead of accurate relative dating, only the wildest speculation and surmise.

In spite of Jacob's strictures—Jacob was his brother's severest critic—Wilhelm continued his work in translation. In 1813 there appeared, after some delay in finding a publisher, three old Scottish songs in the original and in translation, and then some poems by the Danish poet Oehlenschläger, the only time that Wilhelm ever translated from a living author. Much more significant for his career was the work already started with the Icelandic Eddas. In May 1811, Wilhelm wrote to his old friend Wigand saying that he and Jacob were editing the Elder Edda with an historical introduction and translation. Wilhelm, deeply impressed by the poetic power and grandiose style of the songs of the Edda, was naturally intrigued by the variant versions of themes familiar from the German *Song of the Nibelungs*. Goethe wrote Wilhelm an encouraging letter, promising nothing but expressing his pleasure and congratulating him on his efforts. Unfortunately years were to pass before *Songs of the Elder Edda* could appear in print in 1815. The delays and difficulties in getting their edition published taught the Grimms a lesson. Jacob vowed never again to announce the publication of a text, but rather to keep on working quietly and publish when ready. The practice of making prepublication announcements of forthcoming books might well serve to keep scholars informed of progress, but it also made for many unnecessary disputes and poor reviewing practices, stimulated races against the announced publishing dates, and in general promoted quite unscholarly competition.

The Grimms' interest in mythology was stimulated by their study of the Edda, but the purpose of the edition was quite another one: "These songs of the Edda belong to us Germans in so many respects that they can hardly be called something foreign." They were beginning to work at the problem of recapturing not just the continental German past, but the whole Germanic sphere of older literature and tradition. They were spurred on in their studies by the fumbling efforts of Hagen, a private scholar and amateur publisher, with whom they disagreed in principle and practice, and whom they reviewed caustically when his *Songs of the Elder Edda* appeared in 1812. The Danish scholar Arendt also published an edition at almost the same time as the Grimms. So the book on which the Grimms had labored long and hard had a poor reception. Hagen's adverse review brought in its train more polemics and literary feuding. Not all was nobly humane in the field of older German studies.

The Grimms' book contained a free translation in prose and a more literal one for scholars, together with a commentary. Wilhelm was thoroughly convinced that the songs of the Edda represented *Naturpoesie,* that is, anonymous poetry created collectively by *das Volk,* and not *Kunstpoesie* by individual poets. This Romantic view did not help the reception of the book; in 1817 Reimer, their publisher, reported that not more than one hundred copies had been sold. But in the same year the Scandinavian Literary Society of Copenhagen rewarded the brothers by making them corresponding members. Recognition from abroad came quicker than fame in their own country. As P. E. Müller, the secretary of the society, graciously wrote in the covering letter accompanying their diplomas: "It was natural that the famous pair of brothers in Cassel were the first to be named." This was gratifying, but not an adequate compensation for the failure to reach a larger public.

For Jacob there simply was no such thing as an accurate translation; at most, a rendering in another language could only dimly reflect the original text, and it usually distorted, misinterpreted, or failed to find the original's inner beauty and excellence. Since Jacob's attitude toward his field of study is important for any understanding of his problems and achievements, it is proper to digress for a moment and consider more generally the questions involved in renewing and recapturing the treasures of older German poetry. Romanticism was in its finest flowering during the first years of the nineteenth century. Writers and the reading public had never been so open to literatures of other lands: Voss's translations of Homer, Tieck and Schlegel's translations of Shakespeare, Schlegel's translations from Hindu literature, and various translations from the Spanish golden age were being widely read in the early 1800's. The time was thus ripe for translations and adaptations of older German literature. Tieck introduced the mode with his adaptations of medieval *Minnesange* in 1803—the copy in Savigny's library was the first and decisive impetus for Jacob Grimm's own studies of the Middle Ages. The Romanticists for a time had a real rage for translations—Novalis even stated that in the end all poetry is translation—but accuracy in rendering a text in modern German was not one of the Romantic ideals. Insistence on the primacy of the idea and the spirit over external form led to very free translations that were in effect adaptations. Very often attempts were made to retain as many archaic but still understandable words as possible, thus retaining the magic and charm of the original even at a lexical level.

For Jacob such adaptations were dilettantish aids for lazy readers. Attempts to preserve the flavor of the original by changing the spelling of old words to fit modern orthography he looked upon as treason. The additional retention of older word order in an effort to retain older metrical features combined to produce a macaronic language, neither New nor Old High German but an improbable mishmash. Something comparable could be achieved in English by translating Chaucer into Spenserian English with a dash of Milton. To dignify such efforts by appealing to the need to popularize was, for Jacob, wretched evasion. To Savigny, who was enthusiastic about Wilhelm's translations, he wrote: "If the old poetry is limited to a strict, learned study, that would suit me very well, only I am afraid that even fewer publishers can be found. We'll soon see what the public's amateur urges mean, for the people can at least hang pictures and collect them, but their vanity does not lead them to old poems." Jacob even delighted in the variant readings of the old manuscripts with their quaint and irregular orthography. In another letter to Savigny he mentioned how intrigued he was with these spellings: "One could gain much from mistakes in spelling by peasants for the subtlety and divergence of the dialects, and in this aspect the theory is valid that what is innocent and naive is, in its way, always right and good, and is only wrong if held up to comparison." Wilhelm had an equally sublime concept of language, but he always remained more realistic than his brother with regard to the potential reading public.

❦ IV ❦

The *Fairy Tales* I

CHRISTMAS IN 1812 was not a season to be jolly for most people of central Europe. Of the six hundred thousand soldiers who set out to conquer Russia, only thirty thousand returned. Thousands deserted, were prisoners of war, or died of their wounds. Disaster lay heavily on the occupied countries, which had supplied most of the troops for the invasion. Even the Grimms, who were fond of festivals and always celebrated holidays in traditional fashion, could not escape the general atmosphere of depression and anxiety that lay over Europe while Napoleon's power was rampant. As news of the disaster in Russia and the true extent of the losses reached Hesse, the early stirrings of Prussia's resurgence could be felt. The alliance between Prussia and Russia that would eventually bring Napoleon to his knees was being formed, and the first gleams of hope could be seen on the political horizon.

At this moment of the turning of the tide, the world received one of its finest and most precious gifts: *The Children's and Household Tales* of the Brothers Grimm. Next to the Bible, this collection of fairy tales is the most widely read book in Germany, and has become a household book in many lands and languages. All over the world it is the family book of fairy tales, the first and often the only book to come to mind when one thinks of such tales. The very definition of a fairy tale for many is "a tale like a story from *Grimms' Fairy Tales.*" Even in Russia over eighteen million copies have been sold. Not only have the tales been a source of joy and wonderful entertainment for children, but they have also served as the basis for learned investigations into folklore, thereby providing source material for many scholars.

It is ironic that this gift to the world had its origins in the Grimms' patriotic fervor. What was originally a collection of tales from Hesse, with a few from Westphalia, became an enduring part of international cultural heritage. The brothers presented the book to their nation as an encouraging reminder of its spiritual history at a time when Germany was about to rise with renewed courage from its days of defeat and despair; in fact, so much of what they wrote is suffused with this love of their country and its culture. In his autobiography Wilhelm clearly stated their motives for publishing:

> Those days of the collapse of all previously existing establishments will always be unforgettable for me. . . . The ardor with which our studies in older German were pursued helped overcome our spiritual depression. . . . Undoubtedly the world situation and the necessity of withdrawing in the peacefulness of scholarship contributed to the reawakening of the long-forgotten literature; but we did not only seek consolation in the past, but we hoped naturally that this course of ours would contribute somewhat to the return of a better day.

Jacob and Wilhelm were, however, not just responding to an upsurge of patriotic enthusiasm; they also had serious pedagogical purposes in mind. Their wish to revive and give new value to a genre that had fallen into disrepute is one of their lasting achievements. *Grimms' Fairy Tales* have become international property in part because of the educational value of the tales, a value which the Grimms were among the first to see. Jacob wrote to his childhood friend Paul Wigand that he hoped Wigand's children would learn a great deal from the book: "It is our firm intention that the book be regarded as an educational book. . . ." Since the brothers intended the book to be read aloud by parents to their children, and not read by the children themselves, he added a warning note that Wigand not read too much at once until the children could understand, "but give them little by little another morsel of this sweet food." Wilhelm, in the same vein, wrote to Savigny: "We really wished the *Fairy Tales* to be an educational book, since I know nothing that is more nourishing, more innocent and refreshing for childlike powers and nature." In similar style Jacob explained to Savigny his motive for collecting the fairy tales: "Faith in the sacredness and truth of the children's tales was what caused us to collect them, and because we are only publishing what we have collected, I can praise the book to you, since few others can be so rich in fresh and eternally new facts."

The reading public they had in mind, as Jacob wrote to Arnim, was "adults and serious people," and the reading of the text by children would be secondary. Jacob countered Arnim's objection that not all the tales were truly children's stories by emphasizing that nothing had been done to the traditional tales to make them right for children, and in any case it was wrong to distinguish between the interests of adults and children. Jacob's interests were clearly more sophisticated and complex than those of a child, but the lifelong bachelor and marvelously successful uncle to Wilhelm's children was a child at heart and all his life preserved an intuitive response to what was pure and genuine, whether it was simple or complex.

By an odd coincidence Wilhelm and Jacob were not the first Grimms to publish fairy tales. In 1809 a certain Albert Ludwig Grimm, unrelated to their family, published a collection of tales for children that has long since been forgotten. The attitude toward folk tales and literature had recovered by 1809 from its great decline at the end of the eighteenth century. In spite of efforts by thinkers and writers such as Herder, who bequeathed much to subsequent Romanticists, and occasional ballads by Goethe, the period of the Enlightenment was not favorable to folk literature. Sophisticated writers helped to debase the fairy tale by pointing out that it smacked of superstition and a naive belief in the irrational and supernatural. Even writers of Wieland's stature had exploited the narrative elements in popular tales for satiric purposes in moralizing and edifying stories, or had reduced the plots to farces and trivial tales of magic, or perhaps worst of all had kept many elements of oral tradition but had felt the need to embellish the simple narratives and adapt them to the current style. The notion that the fairy tales as told by old grandmothers needed no prettifying never occurred to writers such as Musäus, the most important predecessor of the Grimms. His *Folktales of the Germans* (*Volksmärchen der Deutschen*) had appeared in five volumes between 1782 and 1787. Some were genuine folk tales from oral tradition, later to be taken over by the Grimms, but there were also popular tales retold to conform to rational form, and free additions and variations in the style of the literary short story. The books were addressed to adults who could enjoy the frequent irony and occasional satire—elements always conspicuous by their absence in a genuine fairy tale. They had a surprising popularity and were frequently reprinted throughout the nineteenth century. Wieland even edited these tales in 1804. The five volumes, containing many stories of robbers and ghosts, somewhat in the English Gothic tradition, had none of the charm and sense of wonder that the Grimms preserved so well.

Ludwig Tieck, one of the leading Romanticists whose influence was felt for many years, published some *Volksmärchen* in 1797, but at this stage of his career Tieck, not yet fully converted to Romanticism by Novalis and the Schlegels, used the folk tales only as plot material into which he could insert jokes, literary satire, and rather trivial discussions of philosophical problems. In his way he was as far from the genuine folk tale as Wieland with his ornamentation, versification, and embroidery. By 1812 several different authors had published what were called popular fairy tales, but no one had hit upon the basic idea of publishing the stories as they were actually told by mothers to their children. The prejudice that only lofty language can convey lofty ideas prevented the discovery of the treasures hidden in the simple folk tale, a legitimate and important part of a nation's culture. Subsequent generations have found profound truth as well as beauty in the fairy tale, but only after the Grimms had shown the way. The popular tale might have passed into oblivion if the Romantic movement had not dominated the literary scene.

The Romanticists inaugurated an age of exciting discoveries and innovations at the end of the eighteenth and the beginning of the nineteenth centuries. Renewed appreciation of the classics, translations from many lands and cultures, exotic literature from India, and adventures in literary ideas and philosophy gave the period its stamp of ever expanding horizons. The Romanticists' love of the unsophisticated and their delight in the simple, natural, and almost corny led them to a totally new appreciation of folk culture. The Romanticists' ability to find charm in the rustic and homespun was sometimes affected and doctrinaire, but their theories inspired and stimulated and succeeded in changing the tastes and values of future generations. Herder had ascribed power and passion to folk poetry, but the Romanticists valued its tenderness, temperament, and profundity in apparent childlike form. The term *Volkslied,* or folk song, had been coined by Herder in 1773 (the English term "folklore" was coined by William Thoms in 1846), but the age of the folk song only came about when the Romanticists made it popular in their literary works. It may be said that they *invented* folk culture; they certainly invented the myth of folk culture and its creation, for their enthusiasm was contagious and their early efforts were rewarded by a receptive public.

In some ways the success of Romantic literature helped to produce a craze for all that could be prefixed with "folk-." The number of books published during the first decade of the nineteenth century concerned with folk literature—and older, medieval literature—was astounding. But the first important publication of lasting value was *The Boy's Magic Horn (Des Knaben Wunderhorn),* edited by Arnim and Brentano, in 1805. It was a pioneering, epoch-making collection of folk songs, ballads, and rhymed sayings derived from both oral and written sources. In the appendix to the first volume, Arnim issued an appeal to scholars everywhere to help preserve folk songs and tales by collecting them before it was too late. His emphasis on their timeless value and appeal must have touched the hearts of the Grimms. Goethe greeted the volume enthusiastically and wrote a review in 1806 in which he recommended it "for every household in which alert and unspoiled people live."

Arnim's appeal, which renewed the call Herder had issued many years before, and Goethe's warm approval might have been enough to start the Grimms on the path that was to lead them to fame. But there were also strong personal ties. In 1803 they had come to know Clemens Brentano, an intriguing personality who was constantly generating ideas and stimulating others, starting projects, inspiring and inciting, but rarely finishing anything himself. But he did offer the unlikely suggestion that Jacob and Wilhelm write a "critical history" of the *Magic Horn*. Wilhelm turned him down, and Arnim approved the refusal. Wilhelm pointed out that Brentano had modernized some songs, while leaving others in dialect or replete with archaic words. The whole procedure was inconsistent, no sources were named, there was no account given for method and theoretical views, and original songs were intermingled with reworked ones. He also regretfully noted that in the category of "old" and "oral tradition" some recently composed songs had been smuggled in, something which he considered "an error if not downright dishonesty." Meanwhile Arnim and his future wife, Bettina Brentano, visited the Grimms in Cassel in November 1807. Arnim remained in Cassel, becoming very intimate with the Grimms, who appreciated his nobility of mind and character and were deeply attracted to him personally even when they did not agree with him in literary matters. Arnim worked on the second volume of the *Wunderhorn* during his stay in Cassel, consulting with Jacob and Wilhelm, who not only followed the progress of this volume, but also contributed their own collection of folk songs to the *Wunderhorn*, most of them appearing in the third volume. Arnim's move to Heidelberg did nothing to interrupt the close cooperation between the friends; on the contrary, *The Journal for Hermits* (*Zeitung für Einsiedler*), founded in Heidelberg by Arnim and Brentano, began to publish the early works of the brothers, who were grateful for a sympathetic and like-minded publisher.

In assigning their folk songs to the *Wunderhorn*, the Grimms ended their own period of collecting and turned to the gathering of folk tales and fairy tales. Jacob had collaborated in the folk song project with some inner reservations, more out of friendship than from conviction. Arnim and Brentano were trying to reach a general reading public and were therefore less concerned with scholarly aspects than with popularizing procedures. Jacob, more than Wilhelm, had doubts about the public's response to unedited texts that preserved archaic language, and as noted earlier, he considered modernized texts of no use to the historian or scholar.

Three events combined to set Jacob on the path that was to lead the brothers to fame. The first was the immediate success of the *Wunderhorn*, which was acclaimed by intellectuals and the general public alike. The second was the publication in Arnim and Brentano's *Zeitung für Einsiedler* of two folk tales in their original Plattdeutsch (or Low German dialect) by the famous Romantic painter Philipp Otto Runge—"The Fisherman and His Wife" and "The Juniper Tree." Both of these, but especially the first, were among the most famous items included in *Grimms' Fairy Tales,* where they were reprinted in their original dialect form. Runge's letter accompanying the two tales was perhaps even more important because he pleaded eloquently for the further collection of such stories and emphasized the rewards from gathering tales that live only in oral tradition. The appeal of the stories, their obvious quality, and the summons to preserve such tales before they were lost forever urged the brothers on. The principle of collecting living folk culture in its original form without seriously altering the texts was now becoming firmly established in their minds. But a third factor also played a role of some importance. Aware that Brentano was also collecting fairy tales and folk tales for another possible publication, they were not disturbed by the thought of competition, but they were skeptical of his methods and erratic ways. So they wanted to collect the folk tales in their own way. By this time they were firmly convinced of the correctness of their principles, had worked out their basic procedures, and had started their own project.

In 1929 in the monastery of Oelenberg in Alsace, a manuscript was discovered that had been in Brentano's possession. On closer examination it turned out to be some fairy tales which Jacob and Wilhelm had sent to Brentano in October 1810. Brentano had requested material from the brothers for his projected collection, and in 1809 had already used some of Wilhelm's translations from the Danish. His first request was in July 1809, when he wrote asking for their assistance in compiling his volume. Wilhelm answered very generously, saying that all that he and Jacob had "is as much yours as ours." A month later Jacob wrote to Wilhelm, who was in the midst of his "magnetic" cure in Halle: "Clemens is heartily welcome to our collection; it would be petty of us not to repay in some small way his kindness, even if his way of working is not ours." Brentano did not accept their offer until 1810, when Jacob, writing to Wilhelm, noted that he was sending off what he had to Brentano: "He wants to treat them freely in his own manner, so we have nothing to lose. We must certainly let him have them. (All the same, I think we should make copies first, otherwise we shall lose them.)" Chance would have it that the working copies of Jacob and Wilhelm were lost, but the tales sent to Brentano have survived, permitting us to obtain a picture of the early stages of the collection. Brentano's fairy tales were never published during his lifetime, although for several years, from 1810 to 1813, he frequently referred to his plans.

The Oelenberg manuscript and the letter of the brothers are our chief sources for an understanding of the six years of search and compilation which began in 1806. The work was one of collaboration between the brothers, but since Wilhelm came to be the chief editor of succeeding editions, the fact that Jacob was at first the initiator and major contributor to the project has been forgotten. Although Jacob in principle had his model and guide in Runge's local tales, he seemed for a time to have given nearly equal weight to translations, notably from the Italian (Basile's *Pentamerone*) and other literary sources. Taken together, the

Oelenberg versions represent about one third of all the tales in Volumes I and II of the *Fairy Tales*. Some of these early versions are garbled, with variants and repetitions, and some already represent rewritten forms gathered from oral sources. Many tales are incomplete, as if the ending had been forgotten. "Snow-White and the Seven Dwarfs" has a beginning quite unlike the final version, and other tales retain the basic narrative elements but with quite different motifs. There are also tales which were never included in the published editions. All in all, the Grimms collected hundreds of stories, some complete, some fragmentary, some merely variant versions. The Oelenberg manuscript allows us now to see their process of selection and editing. During the long period of collecting, the brothers were of course busy with many other things. Jacob was a librarian and Wilhelm had long periods of illness and other times of concentration on Old Norse. The years 1808, 1811, and 1812 mark the times of their most intensive work on the *Fairy Tales*.

The brothers' interest in the oral traditions of the "folk," or common people, was intimately connected with their already profound concern with the national past. Their study of folklore was part and parcel of their work in medieval literature and history. They had the same attitude toward the fairy tales and folk tales that they had toward the written documents from Germany's history. Work on *Reynard the Fox* (*Reinhart Fuchs*), the famous medieval beast epic, had been started by Jacob as early as his trip to Paris with Savigny, and Wilhelm had joined him in his research. Both brothers felt that popular, oral tradition could be used to reinforce the lessons learned from literary documents. Wilhelm had already expressed his high opinion of fairy tales in the preface to his Danish ballads: "In the fairy tales a world of magic is opened up before us, one which still exists among us in secret forests, in underground caves, and in the deepest sea, and it is still visible to children. These fairy tales deserve more attention than they have been given up to now, not only because of their poetry, which has its own special charm and which gives everyone who has heard them in childhood a golden rule and happy memories for life, but also because they belong to our national poetic heritage, since it can be proved that they have existed among the people [*Volk*] for several centuries."

It was not just for their historical importance that the Grimms valued fairy tales. Both, but especially Jacob, believed that many of the tales were very ancient in origin and represented, in imaginative form, the core and kernel of old myths. Only a month before the *Fairy Tales* appeared, Jacob wrote to Savigny, continuing a discussion of the relation of history and myth, that he believed that both must be given their due and that both were interrelated. "This relationship may be something unfathomable, but it is enough that we believe in the existence of this miracle and strive to approach it. . . . I see in mythology and popular beliefs a necessity and a truth which are far beyond the ability of individual people. . . ." His belief in the collective origin of folklore, in its fundamental "truth," led him to treat fairy tales with the same reverence as other evidence from the past. Even history is not the product of one historian's cerebrations, according to Wilhelm, who entered the discussion with Savigny with as much verve as Jacob. In referring to recent historical writing, he said: "I do not believe that it is within the power of one person, but rather that it must grow and develop in a whole people; once it is there, then the mouth which will express it will not be long lacking, just as in no early era the prophets were lacking." In this view of the brothers, the individual author consciously or otherwise expresses the collective "truth" which has been "growing and developing" in the nation. The brothers did not use organic and botanical metaphors by accident, but very deliberately chose them in describing the processes of the creation of folk literature. Jacob believed that the fairy tale "has preserved most purely the nature of early epic poetry and has transmitted a whole element of it down to our present times. It is a poetry which belongs to the childhood of the race—and therefore children take to it so readily." But by being closer to the origins of mankind, the tales were also closer to their Creator; for the religious core of the fairy tales was as important to the Grimms as any other aspect. Their piety extended to the pagan past—they were not narrow in their Christianity—and wherever they thought they had found a faith men once lived by, they adopted an attitude of reverence.

On the eve of publishing they wrote to Savigny: "It is our intention to present the origin of poetry as a common possession of the common people which was not separate from daily life and whose origin mortal eyes cannot see and which therefore is full of mystery like all living things." Their sense of the sanctity of what had been inherited made them annoyed with those who, like Brentano, tampered with the texts of songs or tales. "The wonderful last echoes of ancient myths" which they believed they heard in the fairy tales they did not wish to see deflected in any way. Years later, in the introduction to Vuk Karadzic's collection of Serbian tales, Jacob believed he could trace fragments of ancient common myths in the Slavic fairy tales, and thus explained the relationship of these tales to those of other countries.

The view that the fairy tales stem from an old, probably Indo-European common origin in the mythopoeic age owes much to the older German dialects which the Grimms were studying at the time they searched for folk tales. The parallels with the system they were evolving to explain the relationships among the Indo-European languages were too obvious for them to ignore. Once again their widespread interests turned out to be one cohesive whole: they brought to bear all their knowledge in whatever special aspect of their research they were working on at any time. Their efforts were always harmonious parts of one grand, total attempt to rediscover the nation's past. Once they had conceived the notion that the fairy tales go back to a common mythical heritage at the dawn of time, it was not hard to envision a comprehensive myth (*Urmythus*) that served as a core for all later developments. The mythical component they believed to be the heart of all ancient poetry. Thus they could assume that the tale of "Sleeping Beauty" was a late, folk version of the myth of Brunhilde being awakened by Odin. The similarity of motifs and their appearance in widely separated places and among different peoples—the Grimms were already able to compare English, Scottish, and

Norse tales—were proof to them that their comparative-historical method had discovered the inner relationships of a community of peoples. Their study of the Tell legend and the comparative study of the Siegfried–Perseus fable seemed to confirm both their method and their results. Jacob and Wilhelm, it must be remembered, like all their contemporaries, reckoned with a drastically foreshortened calendar for prehistory, and thought that the creation of the world was but a few thousand years before their time. Therefore their theories with regard to the common Indo-European heritage and to the possible geographic spread of the myth-based tales seem much more plausible. Much later, in 1856, Wilhelm concluded a volume of annotations with the following comments:

> Common to all fairy tales are the remnants of a faith which goes back to the most ancient times and which is expressed in the figurative conception of supersensual things. This mythic element is like little pieces of a splintered jewel that lie on the ground covered over by grass and flowers and only to be discovered by very sharp eyes. The meaning of the mystical element is long since lost, but it is still felt and gives the fairy tales their content while at the same time satisfying the natural pleasure in the miraculous; they are never just the ornamental play of idle imagination.

Quite naturally the brothers started their collecting near home. Wilhelm's first recording took place in 1807 in Cassel, where he noted some tales from Gretchen Wild, who was related to the family of his future wife. Some tales they were able to gather in their own family circle. Soon, however, they were urging all their friends and acquaintances to help. Neighbors were invited to join the cause, and several lasting friendships with the Grimm family were formed in the common enterprise. Philippine Englehard, who lived on the same street as the Grimms, contributed several fairy tales. Malchen and Jeannette Hassenpflug, of the family into which Lotte Grimm married, were approached for help in Cassel. The Friday reading circle founded by the brothers in Cassel was enlisted, and school friends such as Wigand and von der Malsburg were also solicited for help. It is a strange quirk of fate that just one Hessian city, Cassel, should produce so many of the world's most famous fairy tales. The family of the apothecary Rudolf Wild, also a neighbor of the Grimms, was a strong contributor to the collection. In addition to the daughters in the family, the most significant source was "Old Marie," the housekeeper, who seems to have been the informant for nearly a fourth of the tales included in the first volume. Marie is credited with such famous tales as "Little Red Riding Hood," the "Girl Without Hands," and "The Robber Bridegroom." "Old Marie" Müller, a widow in her sixties, was a pious woman who read in her prayerbook every night and kept up memories and traditions of genuine folklore. For many years she was a nurse and housekeeper to the Wild family; an ideal source, she represents just the type one would expect to know fairy tales.

In general women were the best informants as well as the most diligent helpers. But soldiers during the Wars of Liberation contributed, as did shepherds and other country people—the countryside was the real source of most tales—and those who could not recite tales were enjoined to gather them from those who could. Sister Lotte once failed to obtain tales from the *Märchenfrau* (storyteller woman) in Marburg, so that Wilhelm and Jacob found that women assistants were not infallible. Even during his year of severe illness in 1809, Wilhelm scoured Halle for fairy tales. The brothers wrote letters constantly, urging friends such as the Haxthausens in Westphalia to carry on the search. The first contact had been Jacob's acquaintance in 1808 with Baron Werner von Haxthausen, a leading intellectual opposed to Napoleon's occupation of Germany. Relations with the Haxthausen family became more and more cordial over the years. The daughters made trips into the surrounding countryside and generated much enthusiasm in the good cause, their efforts yielding twenty tales for the second volume of the *Fairy Tales*.

Almost as important was the fact that the Grimms then became acquainted with the Droste-Hülshoffs, who were related to the

Haxthausens and lived in the same area. It was during his visit to the Bökendorf estate in 1813 that Wilhelm first met this interesting family that produced the best-known German poetess in the nineteenth century, Annette von Droste-Hülshoff. Wilhelm was captivated by the older daughter, Jenny, but was for obscure reasons rather put off by the personality of Annette. Jacob soon got to know and esteem them, but the dedicated bachelor never developed tender feelings for either of the sisters. Wilhelm, if we may trust the evidence of their correspondence and diaries, fell in love with Jenny, and for the next twenty years they exchanged letters that reveal sensitivity on both sides, a sense of rapport and affinity, and occasional hints of real romance. The correspondence gradually became less intimate, but it continued even after Wilhelm's marriage in 1825. But Wilhelm was an unemployed Lutheran commoner, whereas Jenny was an aristocratic young lady from a strict Catholic family with great pride in its genealogy, so that from the beginning of the delicate and charming affair there were insuperable obstacles to any conclusion such as marriage.

The brothers' collecting experienced failures as well as successes. The lady in Marburg never did reveal her secrets. An old woman in Höxter had allegedly told Brentano many hitherto unfamiliar fairy tales, but Wilhelm was unable to obtain any from her—she claimed that Brentano had drained her memory. Wilhelm had a winning personality and charmed most people he met, but sometimes he had to admit failure in personal interviews. Occasionally the brothers were lucky in fortuitous encounters, as when a chance meeting with a shepherd near Höxter produced several tales or when a Dutch friend of Lotte's repeated some that found their way in translation into the collection. Often they thought they had unearthed an exciting new source only to find that they had a German dialect version of a familiar Perrault tale. In Halle, Wilhelm heard many fairy tales that were obviously local versions of stories from *The Arabian Nights*. Very early in their research Wilhelm and Jacob had to develop critical faculties in order to distinguish the real from the false, the traditional tale from the literary echo. Wilhelm wrote to Savigny in December

1814 that he had been forced to sort and select "what comes from living tradition and what proceeded from impure sources," but that wherever he felt that something was "truly living and popular [*volksmässig*] we did not dare cut into it with a critical knife."

Cheerful as the whole process may sound, there were actually many disappointments. Informants often failed to reveal what they knew, and collaborators frequently garbled what they had heard. The brothers crossed and recrossed their own territory of Hesse, drawing on Hanau, Steinau, and Cassel, but with frequent trips to friends in neighboring areas. In the month of August 1810, Wilhelm went to Marburg, Hersfeld, and Fulda looking for fairy tales, but since he was never single-minded in his activities, he also searched for old manuscripts. There was not a period in all the six years when the brothers concentrated on only one project. Their correspondence reflects the enormous amount of time and energy spent just in gathering material, and as we now know from the Oelenberg manuscript, an equal amount of time must have been spent in sorting, arranging, and preparing for publication. Of the eighty-six tales in the first edition of 1812, only twelve are drawn from literary sources.

The springs of folklore flowed so freely that the sheer bulk of material became a problem. The brothers hesitated to publish, in part because they knew that the undertaking was by no means finished and in part from the pressure of work. We owe the "Christmas edition" of 1812 to the promptings of Arnim, who visited the Grimms in Cassel in March 1812 and helped secure Reimer in Berlin as the publisher. Jacob and Wilhelm meanwhile composed a preface to their Christmas gift which deserves to be quoted at length:

> When a storm or some other misfortune sent by Heaven has knocked the crops to the ground, we find that in some low hedge or bushes which stand by the road, a small spot has remained intact along with individual ears of fruit. If the sun then shines again they continue to grow, quietly and unnoticed. No premature sickle cuts them for the big storehouses, but in the late sum-

mer, when they have become ripe and full, there come poor and pious hands to seek them, and when they are bound carefully ear to ear, they are carried home with more respect than whole sheaves would be, and all winter long they provide nourishment, perhaps also the only seed for the future. Thus it is when we look at the wealth of German poetry in early times and then see that of so much nothing has remained alive, even the memory of it has been lost and only folk songs and these innocent household fairy tales are all that is left. The places at the stove, the kitchen hearth, the attic steps, the festivals still celebrated, the meadows and woods in their silence, and above all the undimmed sense of imagination have been the hedges which protected them and handed them down from one age to another. . . .

In the heart of these poetic tales lies the same purity which makes children seem so wonderful and blessed to us; they have as it were the same bluish-white, spotless and shining eyes (in which children so like to grab), eyes which cannot grow any more while the other limbs are still tender, weak and awkward. Most situations are so simple that many will have surely encountered them in life, but like all true situations they are always new and gripping. . . .

The horizons of this fairy tale world are limited: kings, princes, faithful servants and honest workmen, above all fishermen, millers, charcoal burners and shepherds—those who have staid closest to Nature; all else is foreign and unknown to this world. Also, as in the myths which tell of the golden age, all Nature is animate, and the sun, moon and stars are approachable, give presents, or let themselves be woven into clothes, while in the mountains the dwarves dig metal, the water nymphs sleep in the water, the birds, plants and stones speak and know how to express their sympathy, blood itself calls out and speaks, and thus this poetry exercises rights which later poets can only strive for in metaphors. This innocent intimacy has an indescribable loveliness about it, and we would rather listen to the conversation of the stars with a poor abandoned child in the forest than the harmony of the spheres. All that is beautiful is golden and strewn with pearls, even golden people live here, while misfortune is a sinister power, a monstrous man-eating giant, who can yet be conquered, since a good woman is there to help in some way to ward off the crisis, and the story always ends by opening up endless vistas of joy. . . .

Because this poetry lies so close to the first and simplest forms of life we see in it the basis for its general diffusion, for there is probably no race which lives entirely without poetry. Even the negroes in west Africa amuse their children with tales. . . . The fact that these fairy tales are widespread in Germany, a most remarkable circumstance in itself, can also be explained from this fact. They are not only as widely diffused as the heroic tales of Siegfried the Dragon-Slayer, but even surpass them, for we find the very same tales throughout all of Europe, so that they bear evidence for the close relationship of the noblest nations. . . .

We have taken pains to record these fairy tales as untouched as was possible. In many of them one will find the narration interrupted by rhymes and lines of verse which often even are clearly alliterative, but which are never sung during the telling, and these are the oldest and best tales. No situation has been added or prettified or altered, for we hesitated to expand tales that were already so rich in their own analogies or reminiscences. There is no other collection in this manner existent in Germany, for people have almost always used the tales only as narrative material in order to make larger stories out of them, which, arbitrarily expanded and changed, may still have had some value, but took from children what was properly theirs and gave them nothing in return. Even those who took thought in the matter could not help mixing in mannerisms which were supplied by the poetic mode of the time; almost always there has been a lack of diligence in collecting, and the few, chance tales that were noted were immediately published. . . .

We commit this book to our well-wishers, and in doing so we think of their power to help and hope that those who would deny these crumbs of poverty to the poor and frugal may never get to see it.

The extended metaphors from rural life and the fondness for sustained figures from Nature made the folk-style of this preface unmistakable. Later generations instinctively identified the Grimms with the tales they had told, quite rightly feeling that the brothers were representative of the enchanted world of fantasy and poetic truth opened up by the *Fairy Tales,* and sensing that their enthusiasm and delight were genuine.

The *Fairy Tales* I I

THE SUCCESS of the first volume was immediate. The nine hundred copies printed were sold out in a few months, and the fame of the book far exceeded its sales. The well-wishers, to whom the book was dedicated, helped spread the word throughout the literary world. It is hard for modern readers to visualize how small and close-knit the early nineteenth-century intelligentsia really was. Almost everyone knew, or at least knew about, everyone else; the names of most scholars and authors worth remembering and dozens more worth forgetting occur in the letters of the Grimm brothers. Advance notices in the journals kept everyone informed of everyone else's activities and plans. When Wilhelm was in Frankfurt am Main in 1815 to visit Goethe, he found that "the fairy tales have made us famous everywhere." Wilhelm's delight is easier to understand when one recalls that their early publishing attempts had resulted in so many difficulties. They had enjoyed, up to the time of the *Fairy Tales,* no instant recognition, except by a few generous and open-minded scholars like Benecke in Göttingen and Nyerup in Copenhagen. Their most typical experiences had been with bad reviews, slow and reluctant publishers, and small sales. Since German was then one of the most important languages of learning throughout Europe, especially in the Slavic countries and Scandinavia, European fame spread quickly after the publication of the *Fairy Tales*.

Adverse criticism came from unexpected quarters and from eminent writers like Brentano and Friedrich Schlegel. A professor Büsching in Breslau asserted that the brothers had "obscured" the true nature of the fairy tale. Brentano was one of the first and most severe critics: he found the volume too uncritical and uneven in style, noted the presence of much that was fragmentary, and found too many fairy tales of the same type. He contrasted the brothers' work unfavorably with what he had accomplished in his *Wunderhorn,* and scoffed at the Grimms' claims to fidelity of transmission, something which in his view only detracted from the value of the collection. Although Arnim's praise was sincere and warm, he pointed out to Jacob that the great mass of popular tales and songs was erotically tinged and not altogether free from sexual humor and allusions. "There is a prurient side to human nature," he claimed, and he was astonished at the purity and innocence of the tales. The lack of anything as gross as obscenity, or even anything mildly erotic, was no accident: such elements are very rare and essentially foreign to the fairy tale, and were in any case rigidly censored by the Grimms. Their prudery—they had a horror of dirty jokes—proved in the sequel to be justified, for the consensus of folklorists is that the fairy tale should be just like the ones included by the Grimms in their collection.

Even cruelty, the presence of which psychologists and educators in recent years have found to be the chief objection to the traditional fairy tale, was toned down wherever possible. The tale of the "Girl Without Hands," originally contributed by "Old Marie," was retold in 1815 by another *Märchenfrau* of Zwehren, Frau Viehmann. The brothers kept Marie's opening section, preferring it as the milder, less cruel version. As narrated by Frau Viehmann, the beginning was both cruel and repulsive: a father who wished to marry his daughter had her hands and breasts cut off when she refused him, and sent her off into the world. The oldest English variant, dating from about the twelfth century, gives the legend the same form, proving the great antiquity of Frau Viehmann's opening. The brothers blended the two versions, keeping the continuation of the tale—its proper genre designation is that of legend—in the better-told version of Frau Viehmann. Where, however, a cruel punishment comes at the end of a tale, the brothers let it stand. In the tale of the Goose-Girl the evil handmaid is rolled through the streets in a cask studded with nails; and the wicked queen has to dance in red-hot slippers at Snow-White's wedding. Retributive justice for the forces of evil is one of the striking characteristics of the fairy tale, but the cruelty is a harmonious part of a total world of play with reality and appearance. Snow-White's wedding is no less joyous for the pain of the wicked queen, indeed the contrast, within the whole sphere of credibility, is felt to heighten the sense of rightness and therefore one's pleasure. Curiously, objections to the cruelty in the fairy tales have only been voiced in this century; the Grimms' contemporaries accepted the tales without questioning their possibly harmful effects on the tender minds of young children.

There were, however, other criticisms leveled at the book. Even Arnim, in whose spirit the whole project had been undertaken, expressed regrets at the lack of illustrations. The second edition of the first volume, published in 1819, corrected this obvious failing with engravings by Louis Grimm, and since that time many lavishly illustrated editions have been published. Friedrich Schlegel critized the combination of two mutually exclusive purposes, namely those of a children's book and a record of older German literature. He felt that the brothers should have proceeded more critically in order to produce a scholarly work on literary heritage, or more in the manner of the *Wunderhorn* if their intent had been to appeal to a broad public. The brothers had admired and been stimulated by Schlegel's *The Language and Wisdom of the Hindus* (1808), but were never really satisfied with him as a scholar. By 1809 they had decided that he was not essentially a poet. Schlegel was an imaginative and creative theorist, but he had neither the inclination nor the equipment for the kind of careful scholarship so natural to the Grimms. In 1805 Schlegel offered the public a tale of chivalry "from an unpublished manuscript"; but as Jacob noted in a letter to Savigny, the manuscript had just recently been published.

The most famous and popular fairy tales—"The Frog King," "The Wolf and the Seven Kids," "Hänsel and Gretel," to name only a few—are contained in the first volume, and their success not only encouraged the publication of a second volume, but soon inspired the idea of a second edition. Success made everything easier for the second volume. Informants now came forward gladly and voluntarily, helpers and contributors were eager to submit their findings, and Wilhelm, who had often complained of obstacles in preparing the first volume, noted in his autobiography that work on the second volume was easy and pleasant. Early in 1813 he and Jacob started sifting the material not included in the first volume, and soon new stories began to come in from all over Germany. By the spring of 1814 both Jacob and Wilhelm were busy collecting and arranging, but before the volume could be finished their work was interrupted by the political events of 1814. Jacob, as secretary to the Hessian legation, had to leave for the Congress of Vienna, so Wilhelm continued to work alone, finishing the preface in September of 1814, and the second volume appeared in December just three years after the first one. Plans were soon made for a third volume, but new work interrupted their plans, or rather Wilhelm's, since after the second volume Jacob's part, originally the greater, became less and less. They still shared schemes, projects, and research, watching over and fostering each other's work. Jacob was not entirely satisfied with all that Wilhelm had done with the later editions or with the annotations. For Jacob's original interest was in the material of the fairy tales as evidence of older German customs and traditions, whereas Wilhelm from the beginning was attracted by the poetic character of the fairy tales. Gradually Wilhelm too became more methodical in his work, taking over the technical aspects and becoming a research scholar in his own right, although not always meeting the standards of his stricter brother.

After 1820 Wilhelm turned his main attention to the folk tale, or *Sage,* giving up the idea of further editing fairy tales and contenting himself with publishing the annotations in a separate book in 1822. Originally some notes and indications of sources were appended to the second volume, as a scholarly reference and not for the general public. These notes of the Grimms have provided the basis for all subsequent comparative study of fairy tales.

Of equal importance and of more immediate influence was the preface to the second volume. The prefaces of the Grimm brothers contain not only very significant theoretical statements, but also their most personal and delightful language in attractive, intimate essays, half confessional and half addressed to the public. Although signed of course by both brothers, the final editing was done by Wilhelm:

The country is still rich in traditional customs and songs. One of our lucky encounters was the acquaintance with a peasant woman from the village of Zwehren, near Cassel. From her we obtained many of the stories communicated here, as well as addenda to the first volume, thus they are genuine Hessian tales. This woman, still vigorous and not much over fifty years old, is called Frau Viehmann. She has a firm and pleasant face, a bright and keen look in her eyes, and was probably beautiful when she was young. She preserves these old tales firmly in her memory, a gift, as she says, which is not given to everyone, for many people can retain nothing. She narrates thoughtfully, confidently, very lively and with special pleasure in doing so, at first quite fluently, and then, if one wants, repeats slowly, so that one can copy down what she says. In this way much has been taken down word for word and will be easy to recognize in its truth and accuracy. Whoever believes in the easy falsification of tradition, carelessness in retention, and therefore in the impossibility of long-term memory, should hear how precisely she sticks to the same narration and is zealous about its correctness. She never changes anything when repeating and corrects any mistake, as soon as she notices it, right in the middle of her speech. Attachment to tradition is stronger among people who continue without any change in the same form of life than among us who tend to change can understand. . . . The epic basis of popular poetry is like the green that permeates all Nature in many gradations and satisfies and soothes without ever causing weariness.

The inner value of the content of these fairy tales is to be highly esteemed, for they shed a new light on our oldest heroic poetry in a way which has never been possible before. . . . In these popular fairy tales there is contained a mythic base which had been considered lost, and we are firmly convinced that if people will now search in all the splendid parts of our fatherland, unsuspected treasures will turn into quite incredible finds and will help to lay a basis for the origin of our poetry. It is the same way with the many dialects of our language, in which the largest part of the words and peculiarities, long considered to have died out, still live on unrecognized.

We wanted, however, not merely to do a service for the history of poetry with our collection, for it was also our intent to let the poetry itself have its effect: may it give pleasure to whomever it can, so that a real educational book will result. . . . Anything that is natural can be salutary, and that is what we should strive for. . . . Children point without fear to the stars, while others, according to the popular superstition, insult the angels with such a gesture.

Wilhelm was confident that the second volume was a much better book of fairy tales, and its enthusiastic reception seemed to confirm his judgment. Its success led him to plan a third volume from the abundant material at hand, and collection went on for several years. For the rest of his life Wilhelm continued to rewrite and revise the *Fairy Tales*, although the last edition in 1856 contained fewer alterations than most previous ones. A second edition of the first volume did not appear until 1819, however, since many other projects needed completion and Jacob, then quite engrossed in his *German Grammar*, was able to offer more advice than practical help. Yet even while occupied with his duties at the Congress of Vienna, Jacob did not forget the fairy tales, issuing an appeal in 1815 for the collection of "all the songs, folk tales, and fairy tales that are to be found among country people in Germany."

The genuineness of a true fairy tale is best confirmed by the difficulty in creating an original one. It is almost impossible to invent a convincing tale; Hans Christian Andersen was perhaps an exceptional genius in his ability to do so. The contrived or derivative plot and language betray the modern invention, or the pseudo-simplicity and striving for a folksy tone make an invention easy to recognize. For a basic type of fairy tale in the folk tradition exists that is native to all of Europe beyond the boundaries of states and language; and it contains common elements of character, objects, plot, and style, and tends to stylize everything. The persons found in these tales are usually drawn not as individuals, but as easily recognizable types—all quite sharply divided into good and bad. The style too is relatively uniform, tending to repetitious and formulaic language, although few people aside from Wilhelm Grimm have ever been able to master it. The plot often has a tripartite division, as does the cast of characters. A two-part composition is also quite frequent: the hero must usually repeat his feat and regain his luck, the second and third attempts always increasing in difficulty. Not just the characters are stereotyped, for the situations and tasks assigned the hero are as limited in number as the forms of reward for virtue. The hero of a fairy tale not only has no real, concretely described environment, no personal possessions or everyday problems, but he also lacks inner depth or inwardness—he is usually just good, pure, handsome, and, above all, lucky. Just as in the eighteenth-century period of the Enlightenment, modern educators and child psychologists have objected to the presence of magic in the fairy tales. But the magic of a witch can only alter the sight of the beholder and not the reality of the thing or person seen. Thus the frog-prince is still in reality a prince—children sense this with no difficulty—and the play with reality and appearance changes nothing essential. Magic is so self-understood and matter of fact that its transformations are not cause for astonishment; the response of wonder at the intervention of the supernatural or divine is a characteristic of the legend. The magical, the mythical, the fanciful, and the empirically real all appear in the fairy tale sublimated, stylized, and transformed into imagery. The action is always at least possibly symbolic, and thus may be interpreted on many levels. But freedom in interpretation is not matched by freedom of imagination within the tale; there the fantasy is fettered by old beliefs, old fears and superstitions, and traditional forms of expression which are much easier to parody than to imitate convincingly.

Within this prescribed sphere, the persons who appear in a fairy tale are not only restricted but treated quite differently. Although princes may be good or evil and stepmothers are always bad, the various tradesmen are handled in accordance with the old tradition: shoemakers come off badly, but tailors, although often comically presented, are usually winners. The youngest child, preferably the youngest of three, is sure to be triumphant. Wish fulfillment and an urge to correct wrongs and insure poetic justice play such a role that the ethical element in many tales is not exemplary, in spite of an ending that apparently rewards virtue. Those who are lucky win out in the end, and the proof that they deserve to lies in their winning. Moral tales of virtuous children lead to the form of the legend or moral example. Several tales included in the Grimms' second volume tend especially toward legend. Fairy tales can easily turn into farces; a spoofing attitude toward magic—magic is serious even if accepted as natural—will convert the fairy tale into a farce, a genre inherited from the Greek and Roman tradition. An old tale of genuine folk provenance may have later motifs attached to it and a change of setting and circumstance from the original narrative. There may be accretions from art tales and literary embellishments that have passed into the popular language. But if it is a true fairy tale, it will be characterized by prudery, a totally uncontrived and instinctive naïveté, pedagogical elements, and the avoidance of irony and sarcasm.

The "classic" or second edition of *Grimms' Fairy Tales* appeared in 1819, in two volumes, with engravings by Ludwig

Grimm. Reimer published the first two editions in Berlin; Schlemmer, in Göttingen, the third edition in 1837. The first "Christmas edition" had been dedicated to Bettina von Arnim and her baby son, so Arnim immediately had the book bound in green and decorated with gold; all later editions were dedicated to her with warm words of friendship and appreciation. Wilhelm often spoke of the tales as "belonging to Bettina." The sixth edition appeared in 1850, and the seventh and last during Wilhelm's lifetime in 1857. One of the best modern German editions, with a valuable introduction, was published in Wiesbaden in 1953 by Friedrich Panzer. From edition to edition the number of tales grew: the first volume, the Christmas edition, contained eighty-six; the second volume of the first edition two years later had seventy. By 1856 the total number of tales had risen to two hundred and four, about twenty of these in dialect and therefore untouched by Wilhelm's editorial changes.

It has often been claimed that he who knows Grimms' tales knows the tales of the whole world, yet this fact was not immediately apparent, for the legend persisted for years that a small area in Germany had produced the world's most widely read fairy tales from its private folklore. But within the Grimms' lifetime folklorists studied the *Fairy Tales* with an eye to their ultimate origins and found that many, if not most of them, could be traced in other countries too, often at an earlier date. Some of the very best and most famous tales—and they are also the ones with the best dialogue—are very close to the French source from which they obviously came: "Sleeping Beauty," "Little Red Riding Hood," and "The Wolf and the Seven Kids" may all be found in Perrault's collection. Many of the tales of the Grimms' most celebrated informant, Frau Viehmann of Zwehren, are her versions of stories from Perrault. But Perrault was not the inventor of these tales, which can be traced back at least to the Middle Ages, and often beyond to *The Arabian Nights* and the folk tales of the ancient Hindus.

It is now assumed that the genre we call the fairy tale was not introduced into German-speaking lands until about the tenth

century. In French translation *The Arabian Nights* was introduced to Europe early in the eighteenth century and soon became
part of oral folklore. Not all of the stories included in *The Children's and Household Tales* are in the strict definition of the term
"fairy tales." Many are patently legends, some are farces, some are
moralizing tales of indefinite genre, and some approach the anecdote.

The brothers devoted much of their writing to theorizing about
the origin, spread, and nature of the fairy tale. They were aware
that a tale may pass from popular tradition to literature and back
again to folklore, as for instance occurred with many of the tales
from Perrault. An originally literary invention, such as the tales
of Paul Bunyan in this country, may gradually become genuine
folklore by the process of popular diffusion and the generation of
its own folk variations. This process confused some later folklorists, who felt forced to reject as spurious what may well have
been genuine. The Grimms made allowances for the migration of
tales and trusted their instincts in accepting some and rejecting
others. Although as true pioneers they had no guidelines and no
prior theoretical studies on which they could rely, they had intuitive judgment and the advantage of not being bound by the limitations of dogma. It is true that they overemphasized the mythological basis of the fairy tales, but they possessed too much common sense to indulge in the fanciful mythical interpretations that
became the bane of speculative scholarship in the late nineteenth
century.

All the diverse theories about the origin and diffusion of fairy
tales are at least partially correct. Whether one believes in an
Urmythus, diffusion (or migration), or in the spontaneous origin
of archetypes, one can be sure both that the Grimms allowed for
the possibility and that the theory has at least some merit. The
Grimms knew about the migrations of tales from their studies of
Norse literature with its versions of the original continental Siegfried story. But they also considered a further possibility—poly-
genesis—for they were aware that the common elements among
differing nations and cultures suggested commonality of thought,

feeling, and imagination and, therefore, that there are universal archetypes. But the parallelism with the history and spread of the Indo-European languages was alluring—especially to Jacob—and led to the brothers' emphasis on a body of Indo-European basic myths reflected in the fairy tales. The influence of their thinking, whatever its faults, is still felt in folklore research today, even in the categorizing and classifying activities of the Finnish School. Their most important and most fruitful discovery was the international nature of folk tales and the great antiquity that may be ascribed to many of them.

Many of the best-known fairy tales have a history all their own; there are whole books on the "Cinderella cycle" alone. Perrault's original title was "La Petite Pantoufle de Vair," or the "Little Fur Slipper." But since "vair" sounds like "verre," Cinderella acquired a glass slipper and, thus equipped, entered Germany in many retellings and versions and finally, through the Grimms, became the world's possession. The oldest known version of the tale is a Chinese story of the ninth century. Over seven hundred oral versions have been recorded in Europe alone. The first known written version in Europe is in the seventeenth-century *Pentamerone* of Basile. "Snow-White" also was widely spread throughout Europe in many versions. For historians and folklorists the chief interest in such tales lies in their history, the problems of their origin and diffusion, and the lessons that may be learned from comparative studies—things which parents need know nothing about in order to read the tales to their children.

But often such tales have also undergone further developments that are both informative and amusing. As is generally the case with folk genres, the distinctions among types of tales are often rather tenuous; a few alterations may proceed from fairy tale proper to farce, parodied legend, or humorous anecdote. The most frequently and widely parodied fairy tale in the world is "Little Red Riding Hood." In America the best-known version is James Thurber's "The Little Girl and the Wolf" (in *Fables for Our Times*), with its famous punch line: "It is not so easy to fool little girls nowadays as it used to be." Since the Christmas edition of

Grimms' Fairy Tales the little girl's visits to Grandma have ranged from the hilarious to the obscene, from the bizarre to the absurd. She has had to cross the Brooklyn Bridge while coping with wolves in hippies' clothing, has had to fight for her virtue (or sell it), and has had silly adventures of many kinds. Her famous solicitude for her grandmother has given rise to quite witty dialogues. Even the wolf has become the hero of a musical in this country.

Some parodies are very old, presumably as old as the original tales themselves. Sometimes the parody consists not in altering the narrative thread of the story, but in recasting the language in a dialect or in employing modern allusions in order to produce ludicrous anachronisms. During the Nazi period in Germany, Little Red Riding Hood had many Aryan and non-Aryan adventures, in and out of the SA, the Labor Service, and the resistance movement. The poor girl has had to visit her Grandma in Swiss dialect, in lawyer's Latin, in the patois of Madison Avenue, as well as having her red hood chemically analyzed. The parodies underline the vitality of the basic narrative situations and their many possibilities in hundreds of forms and formulas. But the parodied versions never attain the status of folk literature, and they live their witty but short lives in magazines and journals.

The fairy tale as defined by the best examples of the Grimm brothers has practically disappeared in Western culture outside of printed collections, and no amount of nostalgia will ever bring it back. The genre has been in decline since the early nineteenth century; the Grimms knew they were saving something that would soon be lost forever. Latter-day fairy tales have become mere flower studies, often sickly sweet or cloyingly moralizing and totally lacking in the innocent sense of accepted wonder that suffuses the best tales from Grimm. A more sophisticated and disillusioned society has been able to transform the tradition, however, and recast it on another plane. The form of the "anti-fairy tale," best illustrated by some of Kafka's tales, with their sustained antirealism in a world that is not benevolently magical but demoniacally incomprehensible, has established a new genre that speaks to our condition and to a degree bridges the gap between fairy tale and modern literary style.

For the first time in the preface to the second edition, Wilhelm hinted that the fairy tales as they appeared in print were not stenographically accurate transmissions from the informants: "As for the way in which we collected, our first concern was for fidelity and truth. We have added nothing from our own means and have prettified not a trait or circumstance in the story itself, but rather have reproduced its content the way we received it; that the form of expression comes from us to a large extent is natural, yet we have sought to preserve every peculiarity which we noticed, in order to leave the collection its natural variety in this respect too." Thus they did not arbitrarily alter the content of a fairy tale, but rather reproduced it in a reworked "form of expression" according to their taste and judgment. In a letter to Arnim of 1813, Wilhelm was quite frank about the fact that the final text as printed stemmed from him.

It was not only Wilhelm who felt free to alter his informants' versions, for Jacob agreed with him and cooperated in writing up the accounts they obtained. For Jacob this seems inconsistent, since in dealing with poems from the Middle High German, for example, he was rigidly opposed to any kind of normalization, translation, or reworking for whatever reason. With folk tales or fairy tales, however, Jacob considered the adjusting of a text perfectly natural. As early as the Oelenberg manuscript, Jacob combined various versions as he saw fit, whether from written or oral sources. His sternness in demanding absolute accuracy from collaborators and his unyielding stance on the editing of manuscripts have created the legend, and a popular and long-lived legend it has been, that he demanded scientific, phonographic accuracy from Wilhelm in recording the fairy tales. In practice Jacob had a double standard: he opposed the combining of oral versions as practiced by Brentano and sternly enjoined collaborators to transmit exactly without changes of any kind, yet he would combine and adjust himself.

In a letter to Goethe in January 1816, Wilhelm wrote: "In the *Household Fairy Tales* we have tried to collect the traditions of this kind which are still current. They represent, without any additions by other hands, the characteristic poetic views and attitudes of the common people, since only a strongly felt need was ever the occasion for composing them. . . . We have taken them down as accurately as possible, and have added nothing of our own that would have rounded them out or embellished them, although it was our wish and purpose that the book become one that was poetically pleasurable and impressive on its own merit." The letter to Goethe, with its rather stiff and formal language, is typical of Wilhelm—he commanded several styles and used the one most appropriate to the receiver—and seems to contain a contradiction of what Wilhelm had already changed in the second volume. Quite different is the preface to the 1856 edition, in which the brothers frankly admitted the stylistic changes made from edition to edition and confessed that they had filled out what was incomplete and retold the stories much more "simply and purely" than in the originals. Since they were concerned above all with the spirit of truth in the published material, they said they had not changed the plot or story line nor added anything of importance, but had only carried out stylistic "improvements" which seemed desirable. But near the end, echoing the preface to the second edition of 1819, they admitted "that the expression and the execution of the specific material comes from our pens for the most part is self-understood." In point of fact it was by no means self-understood, since for many generations the legend persisted that the very words of the informants had been faithfully recorded, as if stenographically, by the brothers. It was a fruitful misunderstanding, for it inspired generations of folklorists, long before the tape recorder, to go out into the country with pen and writing block to preserve the oral traditions as faithfully as they could.

Two procedures were used, at first by Jacob, who pioneered in method and research, and later by Wilhelm, in order to reduce varying versions to a single coherent tale: "impoverished" stories were filled out from more detailed ones, and the presumed *Urmythus* was reconstructed by comparison of the variants. Jacob did this with great assurance, for, as he once remarked, he trusted his "rather infallible critical feeling which comes to one by itself through experience." For modern readers the *Fairy Tales* are in fact a carefully reworked version of fairy tales of folk origin; for Jacob they were the faithfully preserved substance of tales that were collected from oral sources. Jacob's experience with oral transmission led him to believe that a story may well retain its identity when retold in other words. For the modern folklorist the collector has no right to do what the Grimms did with such calm confidence. In one area the Grimms felt hesitant about making changes—they sometimes changed the original dialect with great regret to standard High German, but they left untouched the Low German tales of Runge, their original models, and also some in Swiss dialect.

Many of the original tales, even as told by the best sources, had logical gaps and a loose structure. The Grimms often tightened, motivated, and clarified the plot and the narrative in order to obtain a more closely knit story. Jacob especially was interested in complete stories in the belief that completeness was in itself a sign of age and authenticity and that the more details the more likely the tale was to be truly traditional. Stenographic accuracy would have limited the brothers to a single, fortuitous version, or as an awkward alternative, an unwieldy mass of variants making their work as scholarly as legend would have it, but never popular. Jacob especially was apologetic about having published something more popular than scholarly in nature.

Forty-five of an original fifty fairy tales appeared with their titles changed. Modern readers would recognize "Rumpenstünzchen" as "Rumpelstiltskin," perhaps also "Little Brother and Little Sister" as a reasonable title for "Hänsel and Gretel." "Rumpelstiltskin" is one of the most reworked tales in the collection and the only one whose plot was significantly altered. The Grimms were sometimes rather arbitrary in making changes, and almost all stories from literary sources were for some reason given new titles. Some changes were made for romantic reasons: "Snow-White" originally had a normal High German name, "Schnee-weisschen," but Jacob felt that "Sneewittchen" sounded "livelier," probably because of the dialect (Low German) flavor. For reasons which can no longer be determined, "Snow-White" is the tale with the most additions from the hands of the brothers.

Jacob and Wilhelm were right in not fearing contemporary competition. No book since has successfully competed with their masterpiece for very long, although Hans Christian Andersen came as close as any. His tales have won fame and a wide following in spite of the fact that to specialists many of his stories are "art tales" and not "folk tales." Andersen borrowed some of his material from the Grimms, just as they had borrowed from their predecessors. And just as the Grimms' fame spread immediately to Scandinavia, so did Andersen's throughout Germany, a country that seems unusually receptive to folk literature.

Language is the master and matrix of literature, as Dante said. The popularity of the Grimms' *Fairy Tales* beyond the areas where German is spoken has always depended on the felicity of translations. The Grimms were fortunate in being translated early and well. The spread of their tales was not always due to translations from the original German, however—the first Russian translation was based on a French version, the French translation having first appeared in 1830. The first tales translated into Japanese in 1887 were from the English; a complete translation did not appear in Japan until 1928. English has been one of the important mediums for carrying the tales to the corners of the earth. In December 1823, Jacob wrote to Lachmann: "We have been translated recently into English, that is, excerpts from the *Children's Tales,* all neatly printed, and it seems to me, very readable." The translation referred to is Edward Taylor's, entitled *Grimms' German Popular Tales,* of which Volume I appeared in 1823, followed in 1826 by Volume II. Jacob considered the translation very good, and in the same letter to Lachmann wrote: "The tales . . . except for the rhymes are at times more fluent and readable than the German text. The concise, nice

English is basically much better suited for the narrative tone of a children's tale than the somewhat stiff High German. . . ."

The *German Popular Tales* were eagerly received in England and soon competed successfully with native tales. The scholarly impact of the Grimms and their methods of research were slower in being adopted; in general, folklore research in England tended to lag behind that of Germany. Collectors of folk tales in Ireland were the first to follow the Grimms' example, but by the beginning of the third decade of the nineteenth century, the brothers' approach to folklore had made rapid headway in England. The tales of the Grimms had an extraordinary influence on later English tales, so much so that they tended to displace indigenous stories for the reading public. Folklorists began to seek out the tellers of tales, often illiterate, in the borderlands and among the Irish and Welsh, whose folklore seemed less contaminated. Even here, the international tales were found again. Several translations of the Grimms' tales were made during the course of the nineteenth century, a notable one being that by Margaret Hunt in 1884. The latest, and perhaps best, is *Grimms' Fairy Tales, Complete Edition*, based on the translation of Margaret Hunt, revised, corrected, and completed by James Stern, printed in London, 1948, with a folkloristic commentary by Joseph Campbell.

In one form or another, the Grimms' tales have become an integral part of the American heritage. The Grimms themselves have not shared in this fame, since scholarship in this country has generally slighted them. Their tales have long since found their way into popular culture, however, where *Grimms' Fairy Tales* has been a household book since the early nineteenth century. The appearance of the English edition in Taylor's translation undoubtedly had some influence on the reading public here, since an American edition appeared soon after Taylor's second volume in 1826. During the course of the century, both English and American editions—and German editions for German-speaking settlers—were readily available in this country. And for good measure, innumerable parodies have appeared, some of them very early in the period of transmission and assimilation, but more frequently in the twentieth century. The popularity of their work is perhaps due in large measure to the enormously successful films of Walt Disney: *Snow White* and *Sleeping Beauty* certainly reached an even wider audience than the printed versions. In 1962 the Cinerama film *The Wonderful World of the Brothers Grimm* dramatized the life and work of the brothers and made them come alive as people in the popular mind. Proof of the fact that the tales have become part of our living folklore may also be seen in the absence of any nationalistic resentment with regard to their origin—they are not felt to be German any longer, but international property.

❦ VI ❦

The End of the
Napoleonic Era

THE ARMY of six hundred thousand men that Napoleon led into Russia in the summer of 1812 was composed largely of troops from central Europe, some drafted against their will, but many eager to follow the great conqueror on his grandiose campaign in the East. When they came streaming back from the bitter cold of a Russian winter, the survivors deserted by the thousands and spread the news of the disaster to every village and town. King Jérôme was spared the retreat from Moscow: in a fit of petulance he had quarreled with his brother and returned to sulk in Cassel. Jérôme's regime had been able to convert some native Hessians to his cause; the secret police were quite willing to eavesdrop on the citizens of the kingdom. Germans as well as French volunteered for the French army, as long as it was victorious, while others served their own selfish ends in working for the occupation. Denunciations, even an effective spy network, and repressions of a kind not seen in Germany again until the Nazi era were commonplace in Westphalia. Hesse, according to the reports of Jacob and Wilhelm, suffered more than other parts of the kingdom from police arbitrariness and repression. Marburg was the center of attempts to coerce the clergy; Wilhelm was especially incensed by the eagerness with which some Germans there cooperated in the campaign and attempted to ingratiate themselves with the French by oppressing their fellow Germans. Even as late as 1830, he still recalled the occupation period as one of nervous fear: "People looked around carefully when saying even the most innocent things in the street to see if someone behind them had been able to hear. If one put a piece of candy in his mouth, he did not throw away the wrapping, since a policeman might pick it up in the hope of finding a secret message in it."

Jérôme's management of his kingdom had become more and more careless in the days since the Russian expedition. Jacob summed up his judgment on the kingdom of Westphalia in a letter to Arnim of November 17, 1813: "King Jérôme turned out to be unlucky in everything he did, but he was not stupid, rather vain and frivolous and always engaged in a ruinous imitation of the Emperor. He lacked the dignity which probably only a born king has, but what is much more serious, he lacked any sincere love for or even understanding of his subjects—he never wanted to learn German, for example. I cannot deny that he was rather good-natured, and he is said to have cried and uttered some quite touching words when the peasants mocked him on his flight from Cassel. You can scarcely imagine how easily and painlessly the French departed from us without stirring any feelings of regret. . . . Except for the Secretary Bruguière I cannot think of a single soul among all the noble and the humble whom I respected or now feel sorry for." Corruption and flagrant abuses even among the French officials close to the king led to rumors that Jérôme himself did not plan on remaining much longer among his now openly rebellious subjects. From the early months of 1813 on, valuable books, paintings, jewels, and other art objects were packed and prepared for shipment to France. The rumor soon circulated that the royal carriage stood ready in the castle for secret flight. Most painful for Jacob was the packing of the books intended for France.

Jérôme was clearly interested in taking as much booty as possible from Cassel. Jacob, his librarian but a loyal Hessian, tried to save what he could. In his autobiography Jacob describes the events dryly and without commentary: "In 1813, as the war threateningly moved closer to the kingdom, the order was given to pack up the most valuable books in Cassel in order to ship them to France. I went to Wilhelmshöne with Bruguière, who was particularly eager for the copper engravings, and tried at least to represent as unimportant the collection of manuscripts which referred to the military history of Hesse and which began with the Thirty Years' War—there were items written by Gustav Adolf and by Amalie Elisabeth [Landgravine of Hesse-Cassel] among them. They remained unpacked. What had been packed up, however, I did not get to see again until 1814 in Paris, when the same gentleman-usher (he was called Leloup), who had helped pack them, had to hand them over to me for the Elector. The man made big eyes when he saw me."

The summer of 1813 saw the beginning of the end for Napoleon. In February, Prussia and Russia had formed an alliance, and the first edict to establish a militia in Prussia was issued. In March, King Friedrich Wilhelm III of Prussia issued his famous appeal "To My People." In August, the hesitant Austria finally joined Russia, Prussia, England, and Sweden in a grand alliance that was to smash Napoleon's power on the continent. But Napoleon could still fight back, and when the news of his victory near Dresden reached Cassel, Jacob and Wilhelm had to listen with suppressed resentment to the gloating French and their supporters. But in October, the great battle of Leipsic decided the fate of the campaign. The news of Napoleon's defeat reached Cassel toward the end of the month, and a very pleased pair of brothers watched the hurried withdrawal of Jérôme and his retinue. The Russians were the first to reach Cassel, but they had advanced too rapidly and had to withdraw temporarily. Jérôme, who learned slowly, returned and tried to set up defenses for the town. There were some comic-opera aspects to the last days of the kingdom, but the populace was more frightened than amused by the shooting. The Russians finally regrouped and overwhelmed the city, where the citizens rushed out to help disarm the few soldiers still loyal to the king and to greet the Russians as liberators. There was dancing in the streets, jubilant fraternizing with the Russian soldiers, and welcomes of heroic proportions for the Russian officers. Seven Russians were billeted in the Grimms' house, which was hardly equipped for such numbers. But the Grimms did not complain, rather they were astonished at the exotic habits and manners of the Russians, who displayed an enormous capacity for eating and drinking. Jacob and Wilhelm were not only devoted to routine, they were utterly imperturbable, and in the midst of the general joy and excitement in their confused and crowded quarters, they continued their studies. Wilhelm wrote to the Droste-Hülshoffs, who had done so much for the *Fairy Tales,* that he worked to the accompaniment of Russians singing in the next room. For the Grimms, work was a complete way of life that nothing could interrupt for long.

The loyal, quite unpolitical, but intensely patriotic Hessians welcomed back their former hereditary rulers with a fine show of enthusiasm. The prince, the Elector's son, returned in the last days of October 1813 to be greeted by children singing hymns. When the Elector himself returned on November 21, Jacob and Wilhelm were among those who ran into the street to cheer him. Skeptical as Jacob was about the Hessian ruling house, his autobiography years later is frank about his enthusiasm at the time: "The final return of the old Elector, hardly still hoped for, was an indescribably jubilant thing, and my joy was no less great on seeing my beloved aunt [Zimmer], whom I had only visited once in Gotha, enter the town in the retinue of the Electress. We ran beside the open carriage through the streets which were hung with flowers. In those months everything was in excited motion."

During this patriotic period the Grimms donated the proceeds of their latest publication to equip Hessian volunteers for the Wars of Liberation. The work was an edition of Hartmann von Aue's *Der Arme Heinrich,* an epic poem by the Swabian twelfth-century poet and crusader which relates how a worldly knight, stricken by leprosy, is cured by an innocent maiden who volunteers to sacrifice her life to save him. Heinrich refuses the noble offer of the girl and resolves to take the Cross and go on a crusade. Miraculously healed, he marries the peasant girl. The brothers saw in the work a parable for their own times and the upsurge of unselfish readiness to sacrifice for the liberation of the fatherland. They dedicated the profits from this first publication of a Middle High German poem to the Hessian volunteers; but by one of the ironies which pursued many of their publishing efforts, the book did not appear until 1815. They had already sent nearly two hundred thalers, which they could ill afford, to the Cassel Women's Club.

The patriotic fervor of the citizens of Hesse was soon dimmed, however, by the reactionary steps immediately undertaken by the Elector to turn back the clock to 1806, as if the seven years of exile had changed nothing and taught him nothing. Like so many other petty princelings, he tried to pretend the French Revolution was a forgotten nightmare. Both Jacob and Wilhelm, with their great respect for all that had deep historical roots, accepted monarchy rather as a matter of course. But there is little doubt that their questioning of the local system dated from the Elector's return, and that their later republicanism began to form in the years of repression and reaction that followed so closely on the French withdrawal. The immediate result was that Jacob lost his position as court librarian, but he was soon appointed secretary to the Hessian delegation in Paris. Hesse-Cassel was to be represented at the Paris peace negotiations by a certain Count Keller, but Jacob noted in his autobiography that Keller, who was not born a Hessian, "lacked the true Hessian spirit." Nevertheless Jacob was employed again, and he set off via Frankfurt, Freiburg, and Basel, writing Wilhelm detailed accounts of the trip.

Although Jacob was traveling as a member of a diplomatic delegation, the journey was still dangerous, since the war was not yet over. The danger was not all from French soldiers, however, for many of the allied troops entered France as conquerors and felt they had the right to raid and maraud at will. Even before leaving German territory, Jacob had several close calls which he reported to Wilhelm in letters that reveal his anxiety. Early in the winter of 1814 he finally reached France. His observations on the mood of the French citizenry reveal his keen perceptions of people. He noted that the enthusiasm of the French for peace outweighed their dislike of the invading troops and that loyalty to Napoleon had been replaced by resignation. No matter where he was on whatever errand, Jacob constantly searched for old manuscripts and interesting books, and even in passing through pillaged towns he could not resist visiting libraries. Some towns, however, he found totally destroyed, with houses standing empty and unburied soldiers of both sides lying in the streets. Jacob was depressed by the callousness of the allied soldiers, who could march past their dead comrades without a trace of emotion. There was no glamor or romance in war as Jacob saw it.

Equally depressing for a German patriot were the reports of the peace negotiations that circulated as rumors among the allied personnel. France, so it seemed, was not to be punished but rewarded for the years of war and occupation. The boundaries of 1792 were mentioned as the new boundaries for a restored France. This would mean that Alsace, with its many famous cities with German names, would remain French. Jacob had hoped for the return of the disputed province, perhaps to Austria, if not to one of the German principalities. Jacob always considered Alsace a stolen province; he spoke of it as "the beautiful German region." He was still not disillusioned about Austria and Prussia, and he had hopes that their power would restore order to a divided Germany. As the battles leading to the final defeat at Waterloo surged back and forth—Jacob had to join some allied retreats, and his comments on the conduct of the troops are acid—his despondency on account of the final settlement grew greater and greater. Wilhelm could report little from Cassel, for many letters were late in arriving during the confused times, and he had only hope and rumor to sustain him, while he worried about the fate of his brothers. Both Carl and Louis had joined the militia and marched off to war with Hessian regiments. The family could barely afford uniforms for them, and there were delays caused by their efforts to obtain commissions, but both finally joined the campaign. In Paris Jacob was delighted to meet Carl again, who had been serving in the Low Countries. Both Wilhelm and Jacob were very proud that members of the family had contributed to the great and good cause of the Wars of Liberation.

Jacob received the news of the final victory over Napoleon while waiting in Dijon for word that the legation members could proceed to Paris. The period was one of introspection and reminiscence; separated from Wilhelm, distracted by the discomforts and dangers of the journey, and worried about the fate of the nations, Jacob somehow found the strength in himself to start writing recollections of his childhood. He was twenty-nine years old, but obviously felt that the time had come to sum up his youth and take stock of his situation. Both he and Wilhelm wrote autobiographies, kept diaries, and wrote literally thousands of letters to friends. Their ceaseless writing activities were not the result of compulsive graphomania, but rather the irrepressible urge to communicate, to keep accounts of progress in their many projects, to share insights and problems, and above all to confess: the diary and the intimate personal letter were the Protestant forms of the confessional for both. The fashion of confessing in this way—a form of spiritual bookkeeping—was the combined inheritance of eighteenth-century Pietism and the Enlightenment. The letters of the dramatist Kleist reveal both aspects in exemplary form, but echoes of the practice may also be found in Goethe's novels as well as in some of the Romanticists'. Epistolary novels were therefore very fashionable, and in fact represent a kind of realism for the age. The Grimms were more reticent than many of their contemporaries in revealing their feelings and in baring their souls, but their confidential writing represents, even in restrained form, a characteristic trend of the time.

Jacob's second visit to Paris took place under circumstances very different from his first trip, when he had assisted an admired professor in his research. He was now engaged in tedious and tiring duties, necessary but unexciting, and always bound up with the protocol and bureaucratic procedure which Jacob detested yet had to live with for much of his life. He was glad to retrieve the treasures stolen from Cassel by the French, but he was so busy with his duties as secretary of the legation and in reclaiming the stolen property that he did not even observe the pomp and circumstance of the return of Louis XVIII to his capital. What spare time he could wrest from his duties, he put to good use in the National Library in Paris. There he found and set out to copy a Latin manuscript of the beast epic *Reynard the Fox* the most famous and most widely diffused of all European animal fables. In England Caxton had published a version as early as 1481. Jacob estimated that the Latin manuscript dated from the thirteenth century, making it one of the earliest versions known. In 1805 he had found a French account, *Le Roman du Renard,* and in 1811 he had been able to obtain from the Vatican library (and copy by hand with Wilhelm's help) a thirteenth-century manuscript in Middle High German. Until the discovery of the Vatican manuscript, the oldest version accessible had been a Low German one published in Lübeck in 1598. Jacob preferred *Reynard the Fox* to both Aesop and Pilpai, and during the year 1811 had worked with astonishing diligence and devotion in copying out the crabbed and almost illegible text of some twenty-five thousand lines. He was able to copy seven thousand lines in one period of three weeks, and later copied by hand another Latin version during his stay in 1814. There had been literary adaptations made in Germany for many years, the most famous being Goethe's of 1794, based on Gottsched's edition of 1752.

Jacob worked hard and for a long period on collating the many versions of the beast epic. He was already familiar with several popular versions of animal fables, many of which had become part of oral folklore. In the middle of the eighteenth century, animal fables were also a favorite literary vehicle for moralizing and satirizing. Jacob's interest was not purely antiquarian, however—he was reconstructing the ancestry of a living form. By 1817 he felt that he had done enough research to publish, but work on the *German Grammar* interfered and other old versions came to light, so that Jacob, intent on thoroughness and complete coverage, delayed publication until 1834. The result was a fine collection of poems, two in Latin of the early twelfth century, and several in French, Dutch, and High and Low German from the twelfth and thirteenth centuries. This critical edition, dedicated appropriately to Lachmann, the father of critical texts, established reliable versions for the epic and placed on firm philological ground the whole study of the medieval state of the genre. Jacob took great pride in his achievement, declaring it to be one of his best works. Jacob and Wilhelm were usually quite modest, even self-deprecating, about their work, but after twenty years of labor Jacob may be forgiven a little just pride in accomplishment.

No one subject ever totally absorbed Jacob's interest to the exclusion of all others. It was during his stay in Paris that he decided to pursue his studies of the history of law in the Germanic countries—he planned to include Old German, Old Norse, and Old English—in order to show the intimate relationship between older customary law and poetry. Like Wilhelm, he was concerned with the interrelations of all aspects of culture expressed in written form. The great opportunities offered by the National Library in Paris—perhaps also reminders of his Roman law research for Savigny—gave new impetus to an already latent idea. The interconnections of various characteristics of older German culture had intrigued him since the start of his collection of fairy tales; now he felt that he could add dignity to the older period by demonstrating the poetic and civilized qualities of the Germanic tribes in their un-Romanized aspects. The resulting publication, *Concerning Poetry in Law (Von der Poesie im Recht)*, is one of his most charming, personal essays, erudite but graceful, imaginative and scholarly, with many examples to illustrate the homely sense of justice among untutored people and their extraordinarily apt language, often in fixed formulas, to express their very civilized notions of customary law. In December 1813, Jacob wrote to Savigny: "Lately I have been making excerpts of many formulas and customs for a notebook on older German law. As soon as I can read through the numerous Scandinavian laws and work them out, there will probably be much there that is good and useful. Hardly any other jurisprudence was so poetic, and yet at the same time it was sensibly practical to the highest degree, and is related to the Roman law as the epic is related to pure speculation. . . . It is natural that our Germanists failed to understand our oldest and best German law and considered it insipid." Jacob found the metaphorical and picturesque formulas of the old legal customs fresh and poetic; many of them turned out to be identical with the fixed figures of speech used in the medieval epics.

In June 1814, Jacob returned to Cassel, little suspecting that within a year he was to visit Paris for a third time. After only a few weeks at home, he went to Vienna as legation secretary again. Wilhelm meanwhile waited, watched, and worried in Cassel. The return of his Aunt Zimmer and the Electress was cause for joy, and the exotic Russians, with their singing and dancing in the streets at New Year, were a source of entertainment. But money problems overshadowed all other concerns. Jacob sent home some of his salary, since frugal living was a matter of principle, but Wilhelm was still unable to earn a living. To gain a source of income Wilhelm started a periodical called *Old German Miscellany*. But in the troubled times there was little prospect of success in provincial Hesse, and the journal was a financial failure. An application for the post of second librarian in the Cassel library was rejected, in part because the Elector was not really interested in libraries, and in part because Wilhelm, although better equipped than most, had no real claim on the position. After some delays he was finally offered the position of library secretary, an office that carried with it the paltry salary of one hundred thalers. He undoubtedly owed even this minor post more to the friendship of the Electress and the influence of Aunt Zimmer than to the Elector's appreciation of his talents. Although disappointed by the trivial amount of his income, Wilhelm was at last employed and soon began to repair the devastations of the war and the occupation in the library. Most of his real work was in restoring the catalogue, which had not been revised for many years. The library was open to the public for only three hours a day, so that Wilhelm's duties were more boring than demanding. His complaints about the position echo those of Jacob when he was King Jérôme's librarian. During Jacob's absence, Wilhelm also had to manage the move to a new home in Cassel. They had lived in the same house since first coming to the city, but now the expense was too great for their slender resources. In the spring Wilhelm devoted two weeks to moving their household belongings, the most precious of which were their books and manuscripts.

Among the manuscripts were certainly some papers for *Old German Miscellany (Altdeutsche Wälder)*, the unsuccessful publication which consisted of three issues during the years 1813 to 1816. The volumes contained selected essays on many different subjects that interested the brothers: language and poetry, *Parzival*, the *Song of the Nibelungs*, the *Hildebrandslied*, Hindu fairy tales, heroic legends, folk tales, and miscellaneous articles, many of them by Jacob, on problems of etymology and grammar. The Grimms' most likely model was Herder's *Critical Miscellany (Kritische Wälder)*. Appropriately the volumes were bound in forest green. Most of these essays are now available in the *Minor Writings* of the brothers. On the occasion of the last volume in 1816, Wilhelm wrote to Goethe: "In the *Old German Miscellany* we have communicated individual introductory works and some smaller items from our collection of source material, striving for as much diversity as possible. We have intended this periodical strictly for people who are professionals in the field, and see in doing so rather more cause for praise than for blame, since there are enough journals devoted to entertainment in which that which is serious usually gets lost." The enterprise consisted of chips from their workshop and indicates the wide range of their interests and competence. Their main purpose in publishing the volumes was to stimulate interest in the field, to encourage collecting of source material, and to urge qualified scholars to collaborate in a worthy cause. The fragmentary essays and short articles were also intended to serve as the basis for a later general history of older German literature. But Jacob did much more than that. There were then no histories of older German literature worth mentioning; there was no consensus on the dates and works of authors now considered important, the relative chronology was by no means settled, there were no critical editions of the important texts, and there were no reliable grammars for Old High German or Middle High German (these modern designations were in fact coined by Jacob). Up to his establishment of the terms, all literature prior to Luther was referred to as "altdeutsch," and the term persisted well into the century. The whole period from the *Hildebrandslied* to Luther needed scholarly organizing, and Jacob originally intended to start with his contributions in the three volumes.

Many of the essays gathered in the collection represent significant advances in scholarship for their time. But Jacob was never too serious about this series. In 1859, in his memorial speech for Wilhelm, he said: "Today it offers little that is of lasting value; whoever takes a real interest in us and our progress may still perhaps see in some essays the germ of what later was better developed. . . . Quite clear in this journal are the outlines of a later, very successful work of my brother, I mean his book on the German heroic tale, and I do not hesitate to call it the major work of his life."

In spite of some excellent items, however, the three volumes attracted little public attention, and those scholars who responded were by no means favorable in their views. The most important of the adverse critics was August Wilhelm Schlegel, whose criticism of the first volume in 1813 is often considered a watershed in the history of German philology. Schlegel's critique is a long, detailed one, since he refuted almost everything in the volume item by item. He took offense at the Grimms' flexible definition of *Sage*, objecting strongly to the theory that it was "poetry which had composed itself," that is, was a product of the collective "folk." He felt that the Grimms had been imprecise in separating written from oral tradition. Above all he objected violently to their attempts to explain similarities and analogies in theme and

motif by means of a postulated *Urmythus*. He believed that
poetic motifs occur everywhere and at all times as a natural
process of poetic thinking common to mankind, and the phenomenon does not call for the establishment of relations, influences, or the derivation from some basic body of mythology. With
considerable justification, he criticized the Grimms' "ignorance
of linguistic laws."

Much of Schlegel's criticism derives from a fundamental difference in perspective, and the logical result would be the end
of all comparative folklore and mythology. His harsh, sometimes
sarcastic words hurt the Grimms, whose enthusiasm, it is true,
had led them too far, but whose good will and imaginative constructions were to be more important historically than any comparable work by Schlegel. Schlegel considered the whole principle of comparative folklore an aberration; he was quite willing
to explain any similarities as accidental and most parallels as
fortuitous. Wilhelm promptly wrote to Jacob: "Schlegel's review
of the *Miscellany* is three sheets long and contains much that is
silly," and soon afterward wrote to Arnim that he and Jacob were
determined to continue on the course they had chosen. But
really stung by the criticism, Wilhelm published a reply defending in general terms not only the principles of their procedure but
even the daring etymologies.

Jacob did not go so far as to express his pique publicly, but it
is certain that his own methods soon underwent a rapid evolution.
Old German Miscellany represents the last stage in Jacob's early
development. The "pre-scientific" Jacob published his last Romantic and boldly exploratory essays in the three volumes bound
in green. It is more than likely that he took Schlegel's strictures
seriously, for Jacob's next publications are so different in method,
style, and spirit that only a complete change of heart could account for them. The stern rigor of the *German Grammar* (1819)
marked the beginning of a new phase for Jacob's scholarship;
from then on, he curbed his imagination, avoided fanciful combinations, and remained within the strict bounds of the empirically confirmable.

Jacob's work on philological problems was once again interrupted by political events. In the fall of 1814 he attended the Congress of Vienna as a secretary to the Hessian delegation. In the fragmentary autobiography of 1830, Jacob speaks rather dryly and curtly of his stay in Vienna: "In Vienna I spent the period from October 1814 to June 1815, a time passed now without usefulness for my private studies and which provided me with the acquaintance of several scholars. Of especial profit for my studies was the fact that at that time I began to become acquainted with the Slavic language [i.e., Serbian]." What this magnificent understatement means is that he learned to read and understand Serbian, made a start with Czech and Czech folklore, and thus opened up for himself and Wilhelm the whole world of Slavic language and literature. Indeed, German interest in the Slavic world begins with Jacob and his pioneering studies. Naturally Jacob spent as much time as he could visiting libraries and booksellers. But, as he complained to Wilhelm, the libraries had very little of interest and refused to lend books, much less manuscripts. Jacob was equipped with recommendations from several scholars and friends, but still failed to satisfy his scholarly urges in the Austrian capital. He was able to find another version of the *Nibelungenlied,* collect Hungarian and Czech material for the fairy tales and folk tales, issue an appeal for help in gathering such material, and act as foreign correspondent for Görres's *Rheinischer Merkur.* Yet if we are to believe the letters to Wilhelm, he spent all his time copying useless documents for self-styled diplomats who were confusing the state of affairs in central Europe. Jacob was annoyed with the time most of his colleagues frittered away in balls, receptions, pompous and meaningless fulfillment of protocol, and above all in idle and mindless intrigue.

The greed and bitter rivalry of the predatory states of Austria and Prussia; the success of the French in preserving their prewar gains; the contemptible efforts of many petty princes to beg or steal back lost principalities; the general spirit of selfish intrigue, private profit, and aggrandizement; and the frivolousness in the sacred concerns of greater Germany—all contributed to a general mood of depression and despair at the Congress of Vienna. At one point Jacob was really alarmed when the suggestion was made that Bavaria be compensated with the city of Hanau. He was able to express his outrage in the *Rheinischer Merkur* just before that periodical was shut down by the censors. A constant source of irritation was the attitude of the French, who did not assume the humble pose proper for a defeated nation. His own work as secretary was trivial and routine, often interrupted and never praised; and a general feeling of frustration overcame him whenever he described his condition to his brother or to Savigny.

The beginnings of Jacob's distrust of the Prussians may be seen in the period of the Congress. All his life he had an ambivalent attitude toward the state destined to lead the German states to unity—and to be his home in the last years of his life. Jacob assigned Prussia the dual role of preserving its own special political characteristics and at the same time guiding the rest of Germany toward union, but he often felt that Prussia was too rigid and selfish to fulfill the second part of its role. Jacob's resentment of Prussia and its official silence reached its height later when, in 1837, he and Wilhelm were dismissed from Göttingen for political reasons. Then he became convinced that Prussia strove only for political power without providing spiritual leadership: "If Prussia is German and connected with the rest of Germany, then it must protect justice, otherwise all is folly and nonsense." The brothers never forgave Prussia for not helping them in their time of political trouble. When the great dictionary of the German language was being planned, Jacob wrote to Bettina von Arnim: "We want to accept nothing from Prussia, which has acted unjustly and in our opinion unworthily in the affair [dismissal from Göttingen] which concerns us." Even after years of residence as honored citizens of Berlin, Prussian politics and diplomacy remained suspicious to them: in 1848 Prussia failed in its task; in dealing with the Danes, the Prussians vacillated and gave in too easily. One of Jacob's genuinely Hessian comments was that Prussian territory contained too many unassimilated Slavs. For the brothers, only Hesse was ever really home.

Jacob's political views were a curious combination of historical perspective, majestic thinking, and forward-looking idealism tinged with a conservatism that was almost medieval. He preferred the so-called "Greater German" (*Grossdeutsch*) solution to the problem of German unity, that is, a confederation of the German states that would include Austria. But Prussia seemed to be an obstacle to this solution. Germany, at the time of course an abstraction, was not given its due at the Congress. Jacob had hopes for the restoration of the Holy Roman Empire—one of Napoleon's positive achievements had been to abolish it—and believed that the dignity of imperial status was necessary if Germany were to maintain itself in the concert of nations and not lose out in negotiations. "A German *Kaiser* is not simply an empty noise, like a Russian or Turkish one, which could just as well have some other name, but has in itself a certain holy power greater than that of Kings and Princes, and its force lies in this very fact. It is the best means of holding Germany together." Jacob shared with many of his contemporaries a hearty dislike of the division of Germany into petty principalities—Prussia he considered a "Great Power" and excepted it from his references to small states—and looked to the Congress for a solution. By the winter of 1815 the politicians had succeeded in reducing the number of sovereign states to thirty-eight. Woodrow Wilson would have approved this observation: "The distribution of lands without rulers must take place according to the inner need of the people involved and not according to the desire of those who wish to engage in partition."

But the Congress danced. It had no great goals other than turning back the clock as far as possible and redistributing various pieces of land. To Savigny, Jacob made the shrewd comment: "The recent time of greatness [the Wars of Liberation] now matters nothing for the course of events, and it is as if it had never been, for people cling to its successful outcome instead of to that which caused it." Jacob was an astute political observer, even if often rather idiosyncratic. Prussia's incorporation of Saxony, at first a rumor and then a confirmed fact, made Jacob doubt his own views of a solution to German unity. He soon reported to Savigny the growing discontent in the lands newly acquired by Prussia, and his complaints that Prussia violated the little states continued in his correspondence for years. In the days of the Congress, he found harsh words for the Prussian spirit: "The Prussian way is unfriendly, unneighborly, and often lapses into the hated French tone. The nature of the Prussian government is a certain humanized and benevolent despotism . . . and a kind of arrogance and sternness, so that I can imagine living much more naturally in Austria, which is otherwise much less tolerable."

Jacob's view of his contemporary world was usually pessimistic, for his mind was constantly turning to the glories of the past. A keen observer of what went on around him, he rarely felt content with the present course of history. He greeted innovations and inventions, however, with boyish enthusiasm: he celebrated the development of steam transportation by taking a ride on one of the very first railroads, from Berlin to Potsdam, and he welcomed photography, which he thought was great fun. But in general his impression of progress was that it was actually a process of dehumanization and a loss of ancient values. Wilhelm was of like mind, once writing to Savigny: "What is most depressing is the thought that if industrial development and striving for commercial success everywhere get out of hand, then an ever greater contempt for higher, spiritual, and scientific development will take hold and a splendid barbarism, such as prevails in America, will predominate."

Napoleon's return from Elba put a temporary end to the fancy balls of the Congress of Vienna. Soon Jacob was on his way to Paris for the third time. The trip was brief and businesslike. His main assignment was to recover manuscripts looted from Prussia and to manage a few affairs for the Elector of Hesse-Cassel. The recovery of the stolen manuscripts brought him into conflict with the librarians in Paris, with whom he had previously had good relations. He was therefore unable to do much private work, but could at least return home in December of 1815 with a note from Prince Hardenberg of Prussia attesting to the satisfactory discharge of his duties.

The return to Cassel marked the beginning of what Jacob referred to in his autobiography as the best years of his life: "From now on began the quietest, most industrious, and perhaps also the most fruitful period of my life." In April 1816, he became second librarian at the Elector's library in Cassel with a salary of six hundred thalers. His job was really a sinecure, his relations with his superior, the first librarian Völkel, were friendly enough, and he was able to devote himself wholeheartedly to his studies. His most telling comment on the period was that "the years passed quickly."

These quiet, fruitful years saw Wilhelm and Jacob develop into mature scholars with an ever-growing international reputation. Meanwhile it was astounding that with all Jacob's official duties as secretary to the Hessian legation during the year 1815, he was still able to cooperate with Wilhelm in several projects; Wilhelm, of course, was busy with the preparation of the *Fairy Tales* and the final editing of the folk tales. Their publishing activities in the midst of the general turmoil are incredible: *Concerning Poetry in Law, Collection of Old (Spanish) Romances (Silva de Romances Viejos), Songs of the Elder Edda,* and Jacob's last speculative, pre-scientific venture in wild etymologies and wide-ranging thematic connections across cultures, the much-criticized *The Route and Votive Columns of Irmen (Irmenstrasse und Irmensäule),* were all published in 1815, while the third and last volume of *Old German Miscellany* was being prepared. The *Spanish Romances* appeared in Vienna, in Spanish and without translation, since Jacob believed that any educated person should be able to read Spanish. As a first-rate Latinist himself, he thought that the Romance languages hardly needed study, since one could just naturally read them.

❧ VII ❧

The *Folk Tales*

THE PUBLICATION of *German Folk Tales* (*Deutsche Sagen*) in 1816 is an event in the history of folklore second in importance only to the publication of the *Fairy Tales*. Few books have been so influential in popularizing a nation's treasury of tales. Quite naturally the spread of the localized folk tales beyond Germany's borders has never been as great as that of the *Fairy Tales,* but the book is certainly the best-known and most widely read collection of folk tales in German-speaking lands. From the beginning the task of collecting ran parallel with that of the fairy tales; the folk tales might even have been published first had it not been for Arnim's advice and the Grimms' belief that the fairy tales were more poetic. In March 1808, Wilhelm had written to Savigny: "We are now engaged in a big project. We both agree that a history of poetry is not possible until one has before him the folk tales out of which our poetry has developed, for all its ramifications go back to a folk tale root, just as a stream may flow through the country in many branches. We are also convinced that one must treat poetry the way one does mythology, namely by giving back to each country that which is its particular property and then determining the modifications which it has undergone in each nation." Although the planned general history of literature was never written, the Grimms were laying the basis for comparative folk tale study.

Jacob and Wilhelm dedicated the first volume of 1816, containing almost four hundred tales, to their brother Louis. The project was again a collective one, with many contributions from among the Grimms' friends; again it was published "by the Brothers Grimm." As with the *Fairy Tales*, Wilhelm's part was often considered to be the greater, but both the process of collecting and the theoretical considerations were a joint undertaking in equal measure by both brothers. They obviously enjoyed the work on the tales, as their preface indicates: "The business of collecting, as soon as one seriously sets about it, is soon worth the trouble, and when one finds something, the pleasure is much akin to the innocent childhood joy of surprising a brooding bird in its nest among moss and bushes; here too in the case of the tales there is a quiet lifting of the leaves and a cautious bending of the branches in order not to disturb people and to be able to peer into Nature in its strangely and modestly snuggled state, redolent with leaves, meadow grass, and fresh-fallen rain. For every communication in this spirit we shall be grateful and herewith thank publicly our brother Ferdinand Grimm and our friends August von Haxthausen and Carove, who have diligently supported us."

Jacob was at first not very sanguine about the chances of the book's success. In October 1814, he wrote to Wilhelm: "A real fashion for folk tales has arisen, and the poor collections will harm and hurt the good ones." J. G. Büsching, their severe critic from Breslau, published *German Folk and Fairy Tales* (*Sagen und Volksmärchen der Deutschen*) in 1812; Friedrich Gottschalk published a book with the identical title in 1814, and in 1815 two other books with similar titles and contents appeared. Folk tales had become a discernible fad by the time the Grimms published their collection, but they turned out to be right in their confidence that their methods assured them greater quality than their competitors.

The first volume contained what the Grimms called "local

tales" arranged thematically as far as possible. The second volume, published in 1818, contained about two hundred of the so-called "historical tales" in chronological sequence. The distinction between the types is only a working one and is now no longer considered a satisfactory form of categorizing. The two volumes contain several international favorites whose fame has spread beyond Germany: the Pied Piper of Hamelin, Lohengrin the Knight of the Swan, Wilhelm Tell, the Emperor Barbarossa sleeping at Kyffhaüser while his beard grows through the table, Tannhäuser at the Wartburg, Bishop Hatto, and the Seven Sleepers. Many others are famous throughout Germany, such as the tales about Henry the Lion, Frau Holl, Kaiser Karl (Charlemagne), and the legend of the Mummelsee. Once again the nation was presented with a wealth of fascinating folklore, as rich and varied in its themes as the fairy tales, yet connected much more with popular history and local legend. The folk tales were drawn from oral tradition to a lesser extent than the fairy tales. Oral variants were collected vigorously, of course, but especially in the second volume written sources predominate. The brothers reached back to the first reports about the Germanic tribes, drawing on such Roman authors as Tacitus, and continued their search in written sources down to the seventeenth century. They listed their sources, thus aiding immensely later folkloristic research; they even planned a third volume with annotations in the manner of the *Fairy Tales,* but their work on the *German Mythology* interfered decisively.

Patriotic motives were just as important in the publication of the folk tales as the *Fairy Tales.* Similarly, the brothers hoped that the book would have educational as well as entertainment value:

Around all that which seems extraordinary to men's minds that lies in the nature of a region or that is recalled by its history, there is gathered an atmosphere of *Sage* and song, just as the far line of the sky becomes blue and delicate, and fine dust collects about fruit and flowers. From living and dwelling together with rocks, ruins, lakes, trees, and plants, there soon arises a kind of relationship which is based on the specific nature of each of these objects and at certain times empowers one to perceive its wonders. The bonds that are thus created are shown by the heart-rending homesickness that unspoiled people suffer. Without this poetry which accompanies them, noble nations would pine away and die; language, customs, and usages would seem to them vain and stripped of value, and in all that they possess a certain protective enclosure would be lacking. This is the way in which we understand the essence and virtue of the German folk tale, which deals out fear and warnings against evil and joy in what is good even-handedly. The folk tale still reaches places which our history no longer can, or rather, they both flow together and intertwine; only at times the folk tale, now no longer separate, can still be recognized, just as in streams the greener water of another river can.

The distinction between fairy tale and folk tale, as the titles of their competitors' books indicate, was not established before the time of the Grimms. Neither term was invented by the brothers, but later usage was determined by their specific use of the word *Sage,* or folk tale. The folk tale is often bound to a real place and a specific time, may have an historical or legendary figure as its hero, and aims at credibility. There is often a miraculous event at the core, but it is essentially believable, and the interplay of the miraculous and the everyday elements make up its character. The true legend, however, is a genre which demands faith of a religious kind; the fairy tale moves in a sphere where individual personality and location in time and space are indifferent or lacking. The fairy tale, a form which developed later than the folk tale, lacks the latter's connection with historical events and personages; unlike the folk tale, it floats freely in a pure world of fantasy, where its truth is wholly that of the poetic imagination.

These differences were first analyzed in an oft-quoted passage from the preface to the first volume of folk tales: "Every man is given a good angel who accompanies him in the familiar form of a fellow-wanderer when he sets out into life; whoever does not suspect how much good he derives from this may yet feel it when he crosses the border of his home land, where the angel leaves him. This benevolent companion is the inexhaustible store of fairy tales, folk tales, and history, which all stand together and strive to bring our past closer to us as a fresh and enlivening spirit. Each of these has its own sphere. The fairy tale is more poetic, the folk tale more historical; the former stands complete within itself and its innate flowering and perfection; the folk tale, of a lesser variety of color, has the special property of clinging to something known and familiar, to a place or to a name known from history. . . . The fairy tales are therefore destined partly through their diffusion, partly by their inner nature, to contain the pure conception of a childlike view of the world; they nourish directly, like milk, gently and lovingly, or like honey, sweetly and satisfyingly and without cloying heaviness; in contrast, the folk tales are a stronger food and wear simpler, but all the more distinct colors and require more seriousness and thought." They continue by discussing the historical value of the folk tale, pointing out that it is a legitimate form of popular history. The popular memory may change and modify what it receives, but it always retains what is congenial and suitable—a faculty which the Grimms considered "one of the most comforting and refreshing gifts of God."

Jacob and Wilhelm made clear their criterion of fidelity in the preface, first noting that the tales, as living poetry, were essentially true. They believed that all genuine poetry was "true," and that changes and growths in a tradition were justified as a process of Nature. "No human hand can invent the basis and course of a poem. . . . Poetry can only be created from that which the poet has truly felt and experienced in his soul and for which the language has revealed the words to him half consciously, half unconsciously. . . ." This view of the poet as the mouthpiece of the collective consciousness of his race and time makes the folk tale a precious thing, permitting no tampering or alteration: "Therefore its innermost nature may not be violated even in details, and facts and situations must be collected without falsification. . . .

For us it was as far as possible a matter of retaining the words, but not of clinging to them." With this last statement, they allowed the possibility of their own rephrasing and recasting within the narrative framework. Since they had translated from other languages, notably Latin and older German, in the end the folk tales were presented to the public as much restylized by the Grimms as the *Fairy Tales* had been.

Wilhelm took the background research for the folk tales every bit as seriously as Jacob, whom later generations have usually considered the theoretician of the brothers. In March 1808, Wilhelm had written to Savigny that he intended to read *all* existent folk tales before continuing his work in collecting local German versions: the Bible, Homer, Hesiod, *The Arabian Nights,* all Norse sagas, and then the older German tales. At this point he was planning to cast a wide net and gather in tales from all over the world to show their mutual relationships and cross references, connecting, for example, the stories of Till Eulenspiegel with the adventures of Odysseus and the Hindu tales ascribed to Pilpai. The publishing of Old Norse sagas in prose in the original and in translation was a first step in the larger project as originally conceived. But the magnitude of the task and the enormous amount of research required soon made the brothers plan a work of more modest scope. By January 1811, they could write confidently to Savigny that many folk songs and folk tales of a purely epic nature usually had their historical basis in the period from the twelfth to the fifteenth century.

Jacob entered into the research for the folk tales with as much enthusiasm as Wilhelm. His first great insight into the nature of the problem had come in 1807, when he noted that certain motifs, motif complexes, and even whole plots appear in all world literature and that, although the manner and style may change, the narrative core remains unmistakably the same—the so-called *Urmythus.* That the narrative basis remains constant and intact through many guises became the guiding thought of their research in folklore. Their enormous influence on all subsequent thinking about folk traditions stems from this, and by organizing as well as collecting great amounts of source material, they laid the basis for all later comparative studies of themes and motifs in literature. The triumph of the comparative-historical method in literary studies goes back to the efforts of the Grimms in folklore.

As early as 1809 Jacob too began a concordance, or index, of motifs from many sources, including the Bible, the Edda, Herodotus, Thucydides, and Hindu legends. This was arranged alphabetically by key words and represents in both intent and method a remarkable anticipation of the later motif-indexes made famous by Antti Aarne and Stith Thompson. Work on the concordance continued until 1811, when Jacob began to realize the impossibility of ever completing it as planned.

The concordance was prepared for the private use of the brothers, although Jacob often spoke of it as a prerequisite for any history of poetry. By poetry both he and Wilhelm meant primarily epic or narrative poetry; lyric poetry was for private pleasure and never became a field of research. Jacob used the jottings in his concordance to attempt to arrive at the origins of the folk tales, or at least to ascertain their relation to some supposed *Ursage*. During their search for "epic" material from the European literatures, all questions of literary or aesthetic value were secondary to this quest for the original theme. Widely read as they were and masters of a dozen languages and literatures though they might have been, they still did not feel properly equipped to establish firmly the historical development of the folk tales and all their variations and mutations. But they were able to achieve a great deal that was of lasting value. As early as 1812 Jacob had sorted out and arranged the different strands of the complex Tristan legend and had set up the main branches and interrelations of this ramified epic material. Subsequent research has confirmed his findings, for although Jacob did not have the resources modern scholars possess, his good judgment prevented him from falling into many traps and becoming ensnared in details. The brothers' contribution in method and organization can be estimated at its true value in the study of the folk tales even more readily than in that of the *Fairy Tales*. Their openness to possibilities and their lack of dogma prevented them from making systematic errors or achieving one-sided results.

Later scholars without the Grimms' overview tended to fasten on one or more aspects only. Thus the search for the *Urmythus* had vexatious consequences. For Jacob and Wilhelm it had been an important consideration, but only one strand in a complex fabric. They believed myth, epic, and history to be descending stages which succeed each other in the course of a man's life on earth. The epic period is followed by the historical period, but the epic era is more interesting, more lively, and more closely connected with an emerging from a long tradition—we would now say mythopoeic age—whereas what happens in the bright light of historical times, according to Jacob, "appears so cold, lifeless, and indifferent. There is truth in epic times too, and also divine truth, and thus I claim that all the data which the epic supplies are factual truth." His criterion for truth or accuracy was very subjective—he proceeded on intuition in all their work—but essentially in tune with the Romantic times: "That truth seems to me the most splendid where I see the greatest emotion of the soul in what is related as happening. . . . Without imagination the knowledge of the deed is impossible. . . ." The myths behind history are also "true," a thought that in its context was a fruitful one for the brothers, whatever its consequences for later research. History too they considered to be equally sacred and inviolate, insisting that "the main thing is that we give the nature of each its due and at the same time realize that they interlock."

Living history, to use their term, is true and meaningful because it is really existent and may be observed and recorded. Tales with an historical basis may renew themselves and undergo changes, so that eventually they become fiction. Once again one can observe the importance of their knowledge of Norse in their studies. They were able to compare the Norse sagas with the *Song of the Nibelungs,* as few of their contemporaries could do. They believed that the Edda was older than the *Nibelungenlied*—a debatable point—but that the latter had preserved very old historical elements better than the former. In the *Nibelungenlied* Etzel is obviously the historical Attila, King of the Huns; in the Norse version Atli has become a figure of fiction. Thence they drew the conclusion that only comparative study, buttressed by a genetic approach and combined with total coverage, could ever hope to establish a satisfactory assessment of authenticity.

As an older and simpler form of literature than the fairy tale, the folk tale may be more flexible in its variations. Not all contemporaries of the Grimms accepted the view that the folk tale was "nature poetry" as opposed to "art poetry," and friends such as Arnim objected that the lines between the classifications were fluid and that each could partake of the other. Modern critics agree and point out that the Grimms themselves included tales that tend toward the riddle and even the fairy tale. Jacob was quite firm in defending the basic distinction between folk and art poetry, whereas Wilhelm tended to side with Arnim in discounting the differences and in noting the interrelationships. Jacob's view of the history and origin of the tales made him esteem them far more than modern literature: "Poetry is that which comes pure from the heart and becomes word, and therefore always arises from a natural urge and innate ability to comprehend this urge—folk poetry proceeds from the heart of the whole; what I mean by art poetry comes from the heart of an individual. That is why modern poetry names its poets and the older poetry can name none. . . . I cannot conceive that there ever was a Homer or an author of the *Nibelungenlied*. . . . Thus the old epic poetry—the *Sagen* and the mythologies—seem purer and better (I won't say nearer and dearer) to me than our witty, that is knowing and finely composed poetry, in which I feel the urge for knowledge and learning. The old poetry is innocent. . . ." Jacob prized innocence and purity above all skill and sophistication or even depth of understanding and intellectual range. He and Wilhelm were still profoundly imbued with the Romantic spirit and world outlook when they published their *Folk Tales*. This is fortunate for their heirs and successors, for otherwise the brothers might never have bequeathed their precious legacy to posterity.

❧ VIII ❧

Creative Years in Cassel

THE YEARS AFTER Jacob's return from the Congress of Vienna until his departure for Göttingen in 1829 were for the most part good years that passed peacefully and quickly. The two brothers, both librarians, held positions that were undemanding, they had a wide circle of friends, and their reputation, now established by the *Fairy Tales* and the *Folk Tales*, brought them into contact and correspondence with foreign as well as German scholars. Recognition from learned societies became a source of pleasure that entailed no extra duties. Jacob had become an honorary member of the Académie Celtique of Paris in 1811; in 1813 he became a member of the Dutch Society for Literature, followed by Wilhelm in 1816. They both became members of the Frankfurt am Main Society for the German Language in 1818, and both received honorary doctorates from the University of Marburg in 1819. Their sponsor at Marburg was a certain Professor Rommel, with whom they had carried on several disputes, so that recognition from an opponent was doubly welcome. Denmark, the country that Jacob was later to attack for political reasons, was generous in recognizing the merit of the brothers, with Jacob becoming a member of the Icelandic Society of Copenhagen in 1823 and receiving a diploma from the Nordic Society of Copenhagen in

1825. Wilhelm, whose first works had been in Scandinavian studies, became a member of the Academy of Science in Copenhagen in 1829; Jacob also received membership later in the same year. The University of Göttingen followed Marburg in recognizing the brothers, making Wilhelm a corresponding member of the Society of Science at Christmas 1824, and offering both brothers full memberships in 1830. At the instigation of Lachmann, the Royal German Society of Königsberg honored Jacob in 1825. The Westphalian Society for History and Antiquity offered Jacob membership in 1827 and accepted Wilhelm in 1828. The University of Berlin, at the suggestion of Savigny, gave Jacob an honorary doctorate in 1828, and Breslau followed in 1829.

These honorary doctorates and the memberships in learned societies afforded the brothers great pleasure, and they took frank delight in their recognition. They were by nature modest, even self-effacing, but a justifiable pride in their achievements led them to accept honors more as recognition of their accomplishments than of themselves. Jacob had mixed feelings about academies and societies for the advancement of learning. He considered the Berlin Society for the German Language disastrously ineffectual and avoided contact with it as much as he could. On the occasion of one honorary doctorate, Jacob wrote to his brother Ferdinand: "The honor gave me great pleasure, and how glad our father would have been at the thought. The whole affair may be very useful to me some time." The honors might have been more useful if the brothers had wanted to enter upon academic careers. As early as 1811 Savigny had persuaded the newly founded University of Berlin to offer Jacob a professorship, but the times were not right, and Jacob felt no call to teach. Both he and Wilhelm preferred scholarly routine and quiet research. They did not want to leave home, nor did they want to lecture, although during the next few years Breslau, Bonn, and Marburg offered them professorships. In Cassel they had their large common study well stocked with books and manuscripts, and there they shared thoughts or worked quietly side by side. Although they continued to cooperate and participate in each other's enterprises, they also began to turn more and more to their own special interests, with the result that their paths gradually diverged. Wilhelm continued the collecting and editing that led to the *Heroic Tales,* while Jacob turned to the history of the Germanic languages. Outwardly nothing changed, and in fact their intimacy and mutual support grew even greater, but Jacob's progress on the *German Grammar* was the turning point.

Their paths remained parallel and complementary. But they were different people, with different personalities and temperaments, even though they often seemed to write with the same pen. Wilhelm once found himself in a ground-floor apartment in Cassel, which he considered quite advantageous "because I can shake hands with friends out the window," a notion which would never have occurred to Jacob. Jacob was conscious of his faults and limitations, especially in social relations, but he did little to change them and expected tolerance from others. He possessed the ability to see himself with irony, however, and did not always take himself too seriously. To Lachmann he once wrote: "I grant everyone some vanity, and admit that I am not always free of it, but it is its own punishment anyway." Jacob, who was short of stature and not an imposing figure physically, spoke in a rough voice with a strong Hessian accent. Herman Grimm, his nephew, recalled the voice but was much more impressed by the studious habits of his father and uncle:

> That is the first thing I recall when I think of my father or uncle: that silence was their real element. . . . I remember how as a child I slowly walked about in the studies of my father and "Apapa," as we children called Jacob Grimm. Only the scratching of the pen was audible, or perhaps Jacob's frequent little cough. When writing, he bent down close over the paper, the ends of his quills were cut off short, and he wrote quickly and eagerly. . . . My father left the goose quills unplucked to the end, and he wrote more deliberately. The facial features of both were constantly in slight movement: their eyebrows went up or

down, at times they stared into empty air. Often they got up, took out a book and turned the pages. I cannot conceive of anyone's daring to interrupt this sacred silence.

The brothers' mutual tolerance for each other's foibles did not prevent them from sometimes seeing one another in a critical light. Jacob once confided to Savigny: "Wilhelm is often superior to me in tact and a feeling for generalities, and is also able to express himself more gracefully, but to compensate for this I am more daring and go deeper into detail; in the main we agree." He later admitted that Wilhelm was more moderate and restrained than he, but lacking in endurance and ardor in pursuit of ideas. Yet he appreciated his younger brother's qualities, especially those that he felt he lacked himself. In several letters to Lachmann, he emphasized that Wilhelm surpassed him in many respects, notably in versatility and the social graces; of himself, he explained: "I am lonely and silent as the result of long habit." As time went on and Wilhelm's children grew up, Jacob could say: "We grow more taciturn with each other, Wilhelm and I, without impairment of our community; in our work only details are discussed and at the table the children now do the talking." Many years later, after Wilhelm's death, Jacob confessed that he had dominated Wilhelm and reproached himself for having forced him to do work for which he was not suited by nature. But Jacob did exert immense moral influence over his younger brother. Once when Wilhelm was sick with a fever and could not be prevented from trying to climb out of bed, Jacob was called from his study. He came silently, sat down on the bed facing his feverish brother, and gazed at him long and seriously. The feverish chills subsided, Wilhelm sank back into the pillows, as docile as a lamb, and fell blissfully asleep.

Jacob was generally cheerful in the self-assessments he made to friends. In 1822 he wrote to the Haxthausens, describing his routine in Cassel: "I am what they call here a homebody; yet I go walking every day and know by heart all the footpaths and bridges over brooks; I don't consider myself happy, but God has given me a basically serene disposition that immediately mends any defects. Work is proceeding well, and that comforts me and gives me pleasure." Such frankness combined with a fine sense of irony about himself makes it easy to believe that Jacob's modesty was quite genuine. His reaction to praise was to find the suitable form of expression that would not make him appear ungrateful, yet would also not seem immodest. Effusive praise was more embarrassing for him than sharp criticism; he was after all his own severest critic, and he loved honest assessments. He valued work more than success in the marketplace, and his concern for his brother Wilhelm took precedence over all else in his life. Wilhelm's death, as he wrote Lachmann in 1831, would destroy his life.

Meek and mild Jacob was not, however, when he had once entered the polemic lists. His vexation could be expressed as eloquently if not as elegantly as his modesty. When he felt that a manuscript was being unrightfully withheld from him, or that he had been deliberately misrepresented in intent, he commanded a fine store of invective. He wasted considerable energy in quarrels and forensic jousts with unworthy opponents, some of whose names are known to posterity only because he dignified them in combat. The corollary of his ferocity in polemics was the ready courtesy with which he apologized for errors. In correspondence with friends, his reaction to criticism was usually gentle; public criticism that seemed unwarranted or unfounded led to wrath. His generosity in giving others credit was sincere and adequately expressed in forewords and dedications. One area which he reserved for intimate talk at home (or struggled with in letters to people whom he trusted) was that of the direct expression of feeling where loved ones were concerned. He was offended by gratuitous frankness in confession by others, and considered the baring of one's soul in a published book in unforgivably bad taste. All the more striking are the letters in which he comforted Wilhelm, finding warm words of solace and tender expressions of affection. But this was evidently difficult for him, and he had to make a special effort to express himself in this way. After their mother's death he wrote to Wilhelm: "It is hard, even impossible for me to talk about things which concern my feelings with someone whom I love." Even though he was usually frank and open in his correspondence with Savigny, he once wrote him: "My confession looks strange on paper, and it is hard for me, because I cannot pour out my feelings any further, neither to you nor to others."

Wilhelm was as aware of their differences in temperament and personality as Jacob, and in general it was he who yielded in personal matters. In questions of principle, however, he could be just as stubborn in his quiet way as Jacob. To Arnim, Wilhelm once confessed:

> Since I have given into him in so many things where I valued doing him a favor more than having my way, he is spoiled and thinks it must always be that way. All his errors are so closely connected with his character that the more he expresses his personality, the more rigid his errors become. I know that for my sake he would burn the whole Edda without hesitation, but he will never be convinced that another opinion can exist besides his own. . . . He has a great tendency to bury himself in something, and yet he can also be quite lively; if that is indeed his nature, there is nothing to object to, but it is bad that he considers his tendency to be the only right one and indulges it too much. Because he is without a sense for social activity, he lacks to a degree a sense of community. . . . Therefore he exceeds the limits in all his judgments, in my way of thinking, and he doesn't like the fact that I don't do likewise.

A dozen years later, in 1822, Wilhelm explained to Arnim why Jacob was not suited for an academic career:

> He has neither the desire nor the serenity for communicating and presenting in class. Altogether he is always excited and belligerent and thus not well suited for communal things where one person has just one place. He tends by nature to constant criticism, and he has nurtured this tendency, so that he always sees the worst side first and thus is repelled or bored by the larger

side of man's life, which after all is mixed with natural defects and faults. . . . I often worry about this condition of his, but then he is also extremely sensitive, often believes he is abandoned and neglected and is sad at the fact, whereas in fact he has alienated people by his prickly nature.

Wilhelm's own sensitivity enabled him to appreciate his brother's positive qualities, which he often praised to friends, while defending Jacob's whimsies and emphasizing Jacob's sense for poetry and fondness for the finer things. Even if Jacob preferred to "withdraw and look at life historically, finding no social gathering quite right," he could still communicate his love in this way, and Wilhelm never questioned his loyalty or his good heart and noble intentions. But it is also abundantly clear that it was generally up to Wilhelm to make the concessions, to adjust, be tolerant, and make allowances. There is no doubt that he did this gladly, but evidently his flexibility of character made their unusual partnership possible. Jacob was the dominant personality and although well aware, could not help imposing his will. Wilhelm accepted this, just as he accepted Jacob's superior gifts: "I am conscious of my slight powers and really consider Jacob as the main person and gladly submit my will to his in the matter. He will always surpass me in learning and in industriousness." But he added that he liked work, once he got started on it. Wilhelm had very modest demands on life; he was content with very little—if he could have the books he needed and the leisure to work with them. Just a few years before his marriage in 1825, he wrote to Arnim: "I have no desire to become an aristocratic and distinguished man, my wish is only to be able to live in simple and natural circumstances as before, and I have enough honor from this form of life. . . ." Each brother knew his own worth and yielded very little to the other. Wilhelm often had dreams at night, mostly sad ones, and some of the dreams reported speak eloquently of his relation to Jacob. On the second anniversary of his mother's death, he wrote from Halle that he had dreamed of Jacob, who had looked at him with blood-red eyes and reproached him, "which made me cry horribly in indescribable fear." The letter was not sent to a psychiatrist, however, but was written to Jacob, who surely understood.

The Grimm family was always worrying about sickness and ill health. Wilhelm was the chief sufferer; at times his illness robbed him of the ability to work, at others it merely made work more difficult. In 1815 his health improved remarkably, and for a few years he seemed on the way to complete recovery. But respiratory trouble continued to plague him. In 1823, for example, he went to Marburg for two weeks to recover his strength; and many of his short trips during this period were convalescent vacations. Both he and Jacob had periods when they were convinced that they would die young, as their father had done. Such periods of the consciousness of imminent death were not necessarily total gloom, since they accepted the possibility of death in faith and with a certain resigned cheerfulness.

Love, Wilhelm once wrote to Jacob, was the only basis of their lives. He considered love the "only real thing that we possess on earth that endures when other trivia have passed away." Even in literary criticism, he believed in the primacy of love: "All criticism consists for me in distinguishing what is true and what is false, and this necessarily leads to love." He had great faith in truth and love, and believed in people and their good will. His first criterion was sincerity: "Everything that a man does with conviction, that is, if there is no falseness in him, has an inner necessity, and what occurs in accordance with this is right, before God and then too before men. . . ." Wilhelm was fortunate in being surrounded at home by gentle people who loved him and believed in him and his sustaining ideals of home life.

Life in the Grimm household in Cassel was ordered, regular, and studious except for family festivals. Christmas was the greatest event of the year, but birthdays were taken very seriously and celebrated heartily. Friday nights, when the reading circle of about twenty-five people met, were often gay affairs. Wilhelm seems to have been the sponsor of the reading circle, but Jacob participated too. They could be festive at social events and would savor them with pleasure, if not with abandon. During the war years Jacob missed two birthdays at home. Wilhelm wrote immediately to describe the events in detail—how they had remembered the day and drunk to his health in absentia and prepared gifts for his return. But Wilhelm also had sad news to report to Jacob, for early in 1815 Dortchen Wild's father, Rudolf, the apothecary in Cassel, had died, leaving the children without support. Wilhelm's grief at the father's death was overshadowed by his concern for Dortchen, the playmate of his childhood and his future wife. "I felt sorry for her with my whole heart, she is such an honest, good soul and so sincere." Only three months later he had to write again to Vienna to announce the death of their beloved Aunt Zimmer. At this point the brothers became the beneficiaries of one of the few positive sides of late feudal aristocracy —the Electress paid for the funeral. Wilhelm's letter is full of tender, loving appreciation of the woman who had done so much for them. It was an emotional blow which struck them at a time of uncertainty and worry in their own lives, but Jacob's answering letter is a touching eulogy of Aunt Zimmer. Their sorrow was deep and genuine, but their inner spiritual resources enabled them to find comfort in God's ordering of the world. Sustained by their faith and love, they found words of solace and support for each other, for every loss in the family served to join them even closer. When Wilhelm wrote describing his aunt's funeral, Jacob's first concern was for a gravestone, since she could not be buried next to her sister, the brothers' mother. He felt especially sad that the things she had loved in life would now be scattered and lost. Jacob loved the objects of everyday life, his books, the flowers he tended, and all the little things of daily association. He admonished Wilhelm to let the other relatives take what they wanted, especially the more valuable things, "so that no quarrel will arise and because after all our aunt has done so much more for us all these years."

The younger brothers, except perhaps for Louis, who gradually established himself as an artist and successful illustrator of books, caused the older, more responsible brothers much worry. Louis married a wealthy peasant girl, but this step was taken only after some wandering about and a rather long stay in Cassel from 1817 on. In 1832 he became a professor at the Art Academy in Cassel. Ferdinand, the *Sorgenkind* about whom they worried most, began to work for Reimer, the Berlin publisher, in 1815, and for twenty years continued off and on at this job, to the great relief of Jacob and Wilhelm. In 1835, however, he gave up his position and came to live with the brothers in Göttingen, much to their embarrassment, since he made no attempt to gain employment again and was apparently a contented parasite until he died in Wolfenbüttel in 1845. Their kindest judgment on him was to remark that he never was lucky in life. While he lived, however, complaints in their letters to each other freely expressed their annoyance. Wilhelm himself had long been unemployed, but never lazy; he was irritated by Ferdinand's weak and witless ways, and sometimes reproached himself for not having taught him industry and a sense of order. In describing him to Lachmann, Wilhelm said: "He has the equipment for being a philosopher, for he views everything according to a preconceived opinion and is awkward in naive observations." Jacob sometimes felt that Wilhelm was too harsh in judging Ferdinand and said that this came from "a certain pride in your nature, which you should not get rid of but which has seemed wrong to me." However, they could never understand a person who was not diligent all the time, and Ferdinand was a true test of their forbearance. Jacob could write calmly to Savigny: "By nature I am light-hearted and adjust to the inevitable; the younger brothers cause me restlessness, although not distress—for that we are too fond of each other—because they do not behave in the way that would be best for their success in the world."

Carl returned from the Wars of Liberation without any firm goal in life. He too was a cause for worry, although he was helped financially by Savigny, who at one time or another subsidized all the younger brothers. Jacob, as the oldest and the head of the family, took his responsibilities very seriously, perhaps too much so. He once wrote to Wilhelm that he sometimes felt he should go away for a while so that the younger children would like him better. Jacob saw his own weaknesses very clearly; it was just that he could not be any different than he was. Carl finally went into business and showed his true Grimm inheritance by writing a book and teaching French and English as a tutor. The book, however, was on double-entry bookkeeping—not quite in the tradition established by the older brothers. But Carl was neither fortunate nor successful. Wilhelm was annoyed by his hypochondria and his pedantic judgments. Like Ferdinand, Carl seemed to be capable and honest, but Wilhelm felt that he lacked a central focus in his life and did not really fit into the world.

Lotte, the only sister, was a pampered favorite as a child, but she too did not develop along the lines that Jacob had hoped she would. When she married Hans Ludwig Hassenpflug in 1822, the brothers were happy for a time and glad to see her well settled. But they soon became disillusioned with her husband, who was a petty politician in the petty state of Hesse. He curried favor with the Elector, had great ambitions and dreams of glory, and later made many enemies as minister of the interior for Hesse-Cassel. Her marriage left only Jacob, Wilhelm, and Louis at home in Cassel, although Louis soon left to marry. Lotte remained loyal to the brothers in her way, but after her marriage the relationship was never as cordial as before. For a time, however, the formalities were carefully observed; Lotte and her husband visited the Grimms on Saturday evenings, and the brothers returned the call on Sundays. When Lotte fell ill later, she preferred the care and nursing of Dortchen, Wilhelm's wife, to that of anyone else. Thus at times of crisis, the family always came together again.

Family reunions were celebrated whenever the opportunity presented itself. In 1818 a reunion brought together all six members of the family. Carl was unemployed, as usual, which cast a slight shadow, Ferdinand was as always in trouble with his employer, and Lotte became ill. An idyllic picture of family bliss does not emerge from Jacob's letter describing the event. Jacob tended to communicate his worries and woes more than his joys to Savigny, but even allowing for this it is obvious that the brothers' good nature was being tested. Loyalty, comforting words, financial help, and advice were always available from Jacob and Wilhelm, who consciously set a good example, yet the younger children seem to have taken advantage of the situation without appreciating the qualities of the pair. Only Louis appears to have been grateful and appreciative. Perhaps the others were grateful in their way; perhaps they were simply unable to meet the high standards set for them.

For Christmas in 1820, Jacob presented the family with a "family book" in which the dates of birth and other data for each member were printed. It was to be a family chronicle that would record all the important events affecting the brothers and sister. Jacob wrote a charming preface, assuring the family that their concerns were nearer to his heart "than all the stuff that goes around in my head." As a special touch and a characteristic one, he included Dortchen Wild, by addressing her as a sister, and he asked her forgiveness for being so bold, "but I love you as much as my own family."

The greatest family event of the 1820's was the marriage of Dortchen Wild and Wilhelm Grimm. Until 1825, when they were married in May after announcing their engagement at Christmas in 1824, Dortchen had been busy helping with her ophaned family, and Wilhelm's small salary had to be shared with the younger brothers. Jacob greeted the engagement with a joyous announcement in a letter to Lachmann, repeating what he had so often said that Dortchen was really already one of the family. "The marriage can have only good consequences for our household, since it is founded on the old and steadfast agreement that we brothers will continue to live together. Therefore you can congratulate Wilhelm, although it is I who write, since he is too modest to speak of it." Wilhelm, who had been an apparently contented bachelor until he was thirty-nine years old, was very happy as husband and father, and took to married life with enthusiasm. As he wrote in his autobiography, "I have never ceased to thank God for the happiness and blessedness of the married state." His happy letters sang the praises of Dortchen, and the bliss of wedlock was from then on a constant theme in his correspondence. Like the hero and heroine of a fairy tale, they lived happily ever after in love, trust, and understanding through the tragic loss of children, ill health for both of them, and constant lack of money. Dortchen never complained, though both she and Wilhelm had their full share of sorrow and chronic problems.

Wilhelm's special intimate ties to Jacob were accepted by Dortchen as a matter of course, and externally at least nothing changed in the brothers' lives or manner of working together. Jacob for his part welcomed her into the family, admiring and respecting her and appreciating her role in the household. Dortchen mothered Jacob a bit, cutting his hair, keeping him content in his chosen routine, and helped to create an atmosphere of love and intimacy. Jacob became a devoted uncle, beloved by the children of Dortchen and Wilhelm, to whom he was tolerant and kind in a charmingly avuncular way. It was Jacob who announced Dortchen's first pregnancy to Savigny with "ineffable joy," since "it gives our household a new firmness and makes our prospects for the future secure." Jacob in his own way was tenderly and protectively fond of Dortchen. The confirmed old bachelor believed "that women have a warmer and more receptive imagination than men," which is a flattering reflection of his knowledge of women such as his mother, Aunt Zimmer, Bettina von Arnim, and Dortchen. In his *Mythology* he admitted that it was difficult to distinguish among the Germanic goddesses and demi-goddesses, for he considered them of minor importance. He was conservative in his social relations, as in his preference for quaint old towns over large cities; similarly his love for the older Germanic law rather than the impersonal modern law reflected the warmth of the family or the clan. In his relations with those outside the family and a small group of friends, he commanded respect more than love, deference rather than warm admiration. Within the family circle he flourished and found spiritual fulfillment; he wrote tender and concerned letters to Dortchen when she was ill during one of his journeys, and "Apapa" was a favorite baby-sitter for Wilhelm's children.

The routine of the household suffered in no respect from the marriage. The coming of children also did not interfere with any of the habits which the brothers had acquired over long years of working together. Wilhelm, who was an early riser, often started the day by reading in the Greek New Testament. In mid-morning he drank coffee with Jacob and Dortchen, then went with Jacob to the library. In the afternoon they were both free from their duties and pursued their studies, taking an hour or more off for walks. They usually did not walk together, since Jacob liked to set a pace too fast for the frail Wilhelm, but they often came together in the course of the stroll and were glad to meet. Jacob strode along vigorously, slightly bent over with his hands behind his back, observing everything, and enjoying the communion with Nature even in bad weather. Wilhelm's health prohibited such a strenuous approach to exercise, but he too loved his solitary strolls and counted them a precious part of life.

Social life was an unavoidable nuisance for Jacob, who often felt irked at being disturbed in his work. "Where many people are gathered together, I am awkward and stupid. The most annoying thing in the world is the unavoidable visits of people who are indifferent to me." During the period of preparation of the *German Grammar,* Jacob became a real recluse and worked with so much zeal that Wilhelm feared for his health. After Lotte's marriage, there were social events which he could not escape. He preferred serious conversation with friends or correspondence with people such as Arnim, Savigny, and Lachmann. All his life his letters were an important part of his thinking, feeling, and way of living, almost a substitute for sociability. His correspondence records his personal life and private problems with all the traits and characteristics that make him an appealing personality. Wilhelm welcomed interruptions in the day's routine more cheerfully than Jacob. Also a great letter writer who could even gossip at times, Wilhelm's correspondence is nearly as rich and rewarding as that of Jacob.

Travelers passing through Cassel often came to visit the Grimms, who entertained many guests, both distinguished and humble, well known to them or strangers. Some were famous scholars and diplomats like Wilhelm von Humboldt, who called on the brothers in 1828. Wilhelm reported to Paul Wigand that Humboldt was a very distinguished and learned man of affairs with great skill in philosophical study and an astonishing knowledge of languages. This favorable report of 1828 may be contrasted with earlier, less friendly accounts of him. Jacob had been very critical of Humboldt during the Congress of Vienna, disapproving of his actions as Prussian minister and disliking his personality, which he considered cold and not "hearty in the German way." Lachmann too was distressed by Humboldt's "chill and condescension." But Jacob and Humboldt had great respect for each other as scholars. Jacob was enthusiastic about Humboldt's writing on the comparative study of languages, and Humboldt greeted Jacob's *German Grammar* with quite unexpected enthusiasm and warmth. Thus the personal contact in Cassel finally made for friendlier relations between two of the great scholarly families of Germany.

Less famous people were more important in the daily life and contacts of the Grimms. Georg Friedrich Benecke, at the neighboring Göttingen library since 1789, was a fine Germanist and a great help to the brothers, who drew on Benecke's knowledge of bibliography and older German. Benecke they often referred to as "our true friend." Not everyone with whom the Grimms came in contact, however, turned out to be a friend. Varnhagen von Ense, a well-known gossip and memoirist of Berlin best remembered for his wife's salon, was intensely disliked by both brothers, who considered him a talkative old aunt who loved to spread malicious gossip. Wilhelm was disgusted by him; Jacob met him in Paris in 1815 and reported: "He is a very self-seeking, coldly calculating person who treats everything with a clever but one-sided wit." Every chance encounter with Varnhagen reconfirmed their low opinion of him.

More important although more complex was their relationship with one of the founding fathers of Romanticism. August Wilhelm Schlegel's adverse criticism of *Old German Miscellany* had shown Jacob the straight and sober road of scholarship. Schlegel had always been an innovator and inspirer, much like his brother Friedrich the philosopher, and he opened up new fields which others then learned to harvest more carefully. By 1818 Jacob could write confidently to Savigny that Schlegel was not really scholarly in his knowledge of Old High German. A year later he scoffed at Schlegel's mannerisms and affectations as a professor in Bonn. Wilhelm met him occasionally—Schlegel also visited in Cassel—but, put off by his personality, he did not find him attractive. Lachmann was even more severe than the Grimms, making fun of Schlegel and using him as a target for quite sarcastic wit. Jacob was moved by his spirit of fairness to defend Schlegel from Lachmann's jibes, agreeing that he had many foibles and mannerisms, but asserting that he was essentially a man of good will and pleasant in conversation. But the most telling remark from Jacob is: "I am still grateful to him for the inspiration I received from him in my youth."

Loyalty to friends was a cardinal virtue of the Grimms, who could remain closely bound by ties of friendship even when careers and interests became widely divergent. Paul Wigand was born in Cassel in 1786, attended the Gymnasium with the Grimms, and went to the University of Marburg the same year as Wilhelm. King Jérôme first offered Wigand the position as librarian which Jacob eventually received. Wigand later founded a society for the study of the history of Westphalia, and achieved a great deal for the cause of local history. Over the years his study in legal history enabled him to share some fields of interest with the brothers, whose literary and philological studies he in turn followed sympathetically. The Grimms' letters to him continued in trust and friendship over many years, although they made no attempt to maintain contact with most of the others they knew from their youth and the university.

Some friends, like Savigny and Arnim, came with their families and visited as honored guests with old and special ties. Others visited for a variety of reasons, while some came to escape the unwelcome attention of the Prussian police. In 1819 Schleiermacher, the religious philosopher, visited the brothers in Cassel while he was under Prussian surveillance. Lachmann greatly admired Schleiermacher, and his stay may well be due to a recommendation by Lachmann.

Personal visits in Cassel were not, however, the only form of contact for the brothers. Their correspondence with foreign scholars, already quite extensive before the *Fairy Tales,* became wider after 1812. In April 1814, Sir Walter Scott wrote to Jacob, informing him of Old English studies in England and sending him a copy of *Tristram.* Cordial letters were exchanged for a while; Scott said that he had studied some "ancient German literature" and was aware of what Jacob had done for the field. The correspondence was carried on in English by Scott, in German by Jacob, who wrote German in his letters as a matter of principle. Wilhelm was fond of Scott's stories, and to an extent Jacob shared his liking for the writer, who was then very popular in Germany. In the end Jacob came to believe he had discovered a lack of scholarly depth in Scott, and he let the correspondence die out without much regret.

Goethe was the revered idol of the Grimms from boyhood to the end of their lives. They exchanged several letters with the great German poet, receiving answers that were usually couched more in a tone of correctness than cordiality. Wilhelm wrote to Goethe in a serious, carefully expository style, justifying his undertakings and explaining the purpose and principles of his projects. In assessing Goethe's works, the brothers maintained their independence and freedom of judgment, worshiping the man and his reputation, but reserving the right to be selective among the works. They admired *The Elective Affinities* and the poems of *West–East Divan,* were enthusiastic about *Faust,* criticized *Wilhelm Meisters Wanderjahre,* and maintained a rather cool distance to the latter parts of Goethe's autobiographical *Poetry and Truth.* As the crowned head of German literature whose voice meant more than that of all other persons combined, Goethe was the object of many solicitations for prefaces, favorable reviews, and other forms of free promotional writing. On several visits to Weimar, Wilhelm found Goethe agreeable in personal conversation, but was unable to gain much help from the interviews. The Grimms sought support for their studies in older German literature; Goethe's responses were never quite the recommendations for which they had hoped. They in turn were often critical of Goethe's attitude toward Romantic art and literature and believed that he did not fully appreciate the forms of older folk literature. Most surprising of all was the fact that they considered him too caustic and rather unjust in his anti-Catholic stance, although at the same time the brothers were incensed by the wave of conversions to Catholicism. Goethe welcomed the *Fairy Tales,* but did not review them in the detail or with the enthusiasm with which he had greeted Arnim's *Wunderhorn.* Nevertheless Goethe was the writer they most admired and respected. Even their severest criticism was mixed with reverence; when Wilhelm declared that Goethe's *Rheinreise* was cold and stiff and in places ridiculous, he hastened to add that it was most difficult to understand its coming from the same heart as *Faust* and *Werther.*

Like-minded friends who could help in professional fields were not numerous in those pioneering days. Karl Lachmann, professor of German language and literature in Königsberg (from 1826 on, in Berlin), a famous scholar and exemplary editor of medieval manuscripts, was one of the few friends bound to the Grimms by ties of mutual affection and respect who could also enter into their problems of research. During Jacob's period of intense concentration on the *Grammar,* he gave Lachmann a running account of his progress and was much encouraged by Lachmann's answers. Only Savigny and Arnim also received such letters that were both personal and professional in content. When Wilhelm was very ill in 1822, it was Lachmann in whom Jacob confided. In 1826, after Wilhelm's first child had died when only a few weeks old, he turned to Lachmann for solace, and his friend's answers were a great comfort. Jacob and Wilhelm differed in several important matters of principle with Lachmann. They rejected vehemently his theory of the origins of the *Nibelungenlied* from the amalgamation of several ballads, but as with Arnim they sharpened their own critical views in such discussion. Lachmann did not visit the Grimms in Cassel until 1824, when their friendship, established by exchange of letters, had already become intimate. Jacob's impression of this visit was expressed in a cool understatement that concealed his real affection: "I have the greatest respect for his scholarship in older German. He is also a pleasant, good man." In professional matters the three formed an alliance of friendship and mutual trust in opposition to hostile colleagues.

As they grew older, the Grimms and Arnim tended to move apart in interests and activities, yet they remained close personally until Arnim's death in 1831. Arnim, four years older than Jacob, had at first been the leader and guide. As Jacob gained more confidence in his work, he became the expert and relied less and less on Arnim's judgments in matters that were not aesthetic or purely literary. Even here he became critical of Arnim's writings —he was primarily a creative writer without scholarly pretensions —and in 1819 noted that Arnim seemed confused and planless and was squandering his poetic gifts. He took too much pleasure in complications and digressions to satisfy the standards of the Grimms, who somehow expected more organization from a Prussian nobleman. Yet Arnim was received cordially in their home in 1820; four years before, when he was very ill, Bettina had written requesting a visit from one of the brothers, claiming that he needed their presence to help in his convalescence. So Wilhelm, who was always temperamentally closer and more congenial to Arnim, went to Wiepersdorf, Arnim's country estate, and stayed for several weeks.

Arnim had good, calm common sense—a valuable asset for the Grimms in their polemics and feuds with other scholars. He was usually a soothing influence and could cool the brothers' tempers. At least once he persuaded Wilhelm to maintain a dignified silence rather than continue a pointless feud in a scholar's teapot. He took Wilhelm's side in the problem of translation, supporting reason and common sense against the strict claims of Jacob. Jacob was very frank with Arnim, and more than once his negative criticism of Arnim's creative efforts depressed the hopeful author. Jacob was quick to apologize, but clung to his views even while tempering his tone. When Arnim's complete works were being prepared in 1838, Wilhelm visited the widowed Bettina and wrote the preface to the first volume, paying tribute to the person whom they had considered "first among friends."

Over the years connections at court proved to be as much a nuisance as an advantage. The politics of a petty principality are depressing. As Aunt Zimmer had been a lady-in-waiting for the old Electress Caroline, whom the brothers liked and respected, they were often invited to the Electress's table in the evening. Wilhelm was frequently asked to read aloud to the company, preferably the works of Sir Walter Scott, the favorite author at court. In addition Wilhelm was for about a year, from November 1820 on, a private tutor for Prince Friedrich Wilhelm, the Elector's son and heir. He tutored him three times a week and was paid twelve thalers a month for the privilege. History was supposed to be the main subject of instruction, a subject surely more to Wilhelm's taste than to the prince's. Wilhelm considered the prince a youth without real substance, lazy and sensual and completely devoid of all intellectual interests. The young prince had not long succeeded his father as Elector when Jacob wrote to Lachmann: "The governments of our time are best served by mediocre people who submit to everything. Striving for individual, independent learning is not favored but feared. Among the untutored servants of the state, hopeless cowardice prevails of a kind that would not have been possible twenty or thirty years ago." The brothers did not wish to be identified with such types, nor were they eager for work or play at court. Wilhelm's tutoring was a frustrating task that bore no fruit; his final pronouncement on the interlude was, "Much work and little pleasure."

The old Elector, Wilhelm I, became seriously ill in 1817, causing Jacob great concern for the future of the principality. He did not grieve very much for the old Elector, but he feared the consequences when the young prince became Wilhelm II. After the death of Aunt Zimmer, the brothers had maintained cordial relations with the old Electress Caroline, and Wilhelm was often summoned to read to her. She was the brothers' patroness and for years their one true if not very influential friend at court. Her death in 1820 was a cause for mourning and sincere sorrow. The old Elector's death in February 1821 was an occasion not so much for sadness as for speculation on the future of Hesse-Cassel.

The citizens did not have long to wait for changes. Wilhelm II immediately introduced some improvements, abolishing the official pigtail which Jacob so detested, loosening some of the more antiquated forms of court protocol, and raising the pay of the older officer corps. The salaries of other state servants were not increased, however, and the librarians, traditionally the poorest paid state officials, were the only group not to receive a subsidy for the new state uniform. The greed and ambitions of the new ruler soon made him detested by the citizenry. He set out to impoverish his state with riotous living and wasteful enterprises. His private life was a scandal even in an age that was tolerant of the affairs of ruling houses. His wife, the Electress Augusta, was relatively well liked by the citizens, but Wilhelm II soon installed his mistress in the palace and raised her to the rank of countess. The Electress promptly moved out, creating a division into two camps in the ruling family.

The brothers made the tactical if very understandable mistake of siding with Electress Augusta, a cultured lady of good taste and manners, quite in contrast to the coarse brutishness of her husband. This partiality did them no good with the Elector, who never raised their pay or promoted them during the nine years they were in his employ. When the Electress finally left Hesse completely after a few years, the Grimms lost what little support they had enjoyed in high places. Even more vexing to them in their positions at the library were the changes under the new regime. The budget, never generous or even adequate, came under the management of the Court Chamberlain's office in the early 1820's, provoking Jacob's comment: "Whether the service of the Elector gained by this, I shall not judge; this much is certain, that through this all payments were held up and the librarian's hands were tied and he was prevented from making advantageous purchases." In addition the administration demanded that the entire catalogue of seventy-nine or eighty folio volumes be copied "to help in supervision." Old Völkel, who was still the first librarian, and Jacob and Wilhelm copied the catalogue by hand over the next year and a half and spent, according to Jacob, "the noblest hours in this copying whose purpose we could not see. One works gladly at everything that has some usefulness, but this business, I confess, was the sourest in my life and ruined my disposition for hours and days at a time."

The unpleasant contacts with the court helped focus the brothers' attention on the deteriorating political conditions in German lands after the Congress of Vienna. "Now we can see what the Holy Alliance leads to—it is a baseless idea which only has a negative effect and no power to act. It paralyzes Europe's natural strength. . . . The abstract and hollow nature of the Holy Alliance paralyzes the natural course of all affairs." Jacob, who had never thought highly of the efforts of the diplomats in Vienna, was sorry to see his fears well founded. He reported little that was positive in the period of political reaction which swept over Austria and Germany. Absolutistic tendencies, frustrated by the turmoil of the Napoleonic era, came back stronger than ever after 1815. The preservation of the status quo was enforced by armed intervention of Austrian troops in Italy and of French troops in Spain. The Holy Alliance was successful in maintaining peace among the states, but it suppressed all political strivings for reform or liberalization. Demands for constitutional government among its members were summarily denied, and censorship, imprisonment or exile, and political persecution were the order of the day. Görres, whose *Rheinischer Merkur* had been closed down by government order in 1816, had to flee to Strassburg in 1819. That year there was great political excitement in Berlin: Prussian reforms were brought to a complete halt, Humboldt was dismissed, liberalism in general was driven from office, and a wave of persecution poured over the land. Görres's fate touched Jacob's soul, and he wrote to Savigny of a "system of government through fear, distrust, accusations, and shameful attacks by police."

Student unrest is hardly an innovation of a later day. The Wars of Liberation had raised hopes for a united Germany under constitutional rule; as the general reaction in the age of Metternich became more and more stifling, students began to express their displeasure and voice their demands for reforms. Some were trifling and fuzzily romantic, but their aspirations were also those of the intelligentsia, and legitimate in an historical sense too, since much had been promised by the princes in the fervent days of the war. The liberal fraternities were now persecuted, with severe censorship being felt in the universities themselves. Jacob could not help but share in the student associations' hopes for a united Germany, but he did not sympathize with their rhetoric or their posturing. The fraternities, or *Burschenschaften,* Jacob detested, as he confessed to Savigny, and he imagined that they must be deadly boring. Just as put off by Jahn and the gymnastic movement of the period, he hoped this craze would not spread to Hesse.

Although the atmosphere was not healthy for people sensitive to political affairs and as devoted to the cause of freedom as were the Grimms, the brothers never suffered directly from anything but official neglect and disapproval. They were discreet in their utterances, although their letters to confidential friends were full of complaints and resentment of the repressive atmosphere. They often fled from the disorder of the contemporary political scene to the coziness of their common study, where they could explore the past and rediscover the ancient glories of the nation. For both Jacob and Wilhelm, the study of Germany's past in language and literature was a more or less conscious form of escapism. Wilhelm was inclined to speak of political ups and downs in terms of the weather, admitting that his studies were a comfort in times of stress. Yet he was just as patriotic as Jacob, although less interested in politics and less given to theorizing about it. Like Jacob, he longed for an end to the division of Germany into many petty states: "We Germans are one body and all the limbs demand and need only one head." The brothers saw only one positive aspect to the system of loose federation that prevailed in the German states—the republican spirit which they attributed in part to the many divisions and the local patriotism they engendered.

Their attitude toward monarchy, the "one head" that the nation needed, was full of contradictions and fluctuations. In 1819, writing to his legal friend Savigny, Jacob had proposed the establishment of estates (social classes) with legislative power to offset the power of the princes and hereditary rulers. Constitutionalism was generally in the air; leading statesmen of the stature of Stein, Hardenberg, and Humboldt were proposing and urging a constitution on a reluctant Prussia. But Jacob was never constant in his political views. He was at heart a conservative who looked back to the golden age of the mid-eighteenth century as a model for the 1820's. He was not impressed by liberal innovations, especially those which seemed to break the continuity with the past. "Everywhere statesmen are desirous of new, broad constitutions and laws, while the people are concerned only with a few simple paragraphs the reform of which could be well carried out within the framework of accustomed and beloved institutions." He really wanted as little government as was possible, for "the state cannot know what each person wants, it should only demand of its servants enough so that they can cultivate their own inner development."

Although interested in curbing the privileges of the nobility, Jacob was by no means a complete democrat. "I am by nature and from my childhood faithful to the monarchic and princely form of rule; all my studies and experience teach me that it affords the most security and tranquility and that it has provided the people with happiness, at least for long periods of time." This statement seems clear and unambiguous enough, yet Jacob was also opposed to monarchy. He was very critical of princes who were out of step with the times, and he felt that there were "moments when one must act without regard for the past or the future." From this we must not infer that he was a republican ready to renounce tradition, for his political views, never simple or obvious, rested on a profound knowledge of German history, a deep sense of human justice, and an instinctive love for traditional forms. Sensitive to the stirrings in the *Volk,* he could appreciate the emotional urges of the people and sense their frustration at the denial of reforms that were practical and touched their daily living. He was quite capable of deriding the princes who "think they have to carry out a kind of perfumed monarchism which won't permit the slightest or most honest objections and which scoffs at the nature of human feelings and rights."

Jacob's inconsistencies extended into all his political attitudes. He favored freedom of the press, but wished that some form of censorship would inhibit the flow of nonsense. He had great contempt for political journals, clubs, and the like, yet wanted his own good, true, and faithful Hessians to be more politically conscious. He was anti-French in a bitter way, harboring resentment of that nation all his life. He was at times an admirer of the English, at others rather anti-English: "I would not want to be an Englishman; their much praised freedom has something crude and insensitive about it." He was always upset by any form of political unrest and commotion, since it hindered the calm and objective study of history, yet he was concerned with reforms and advocated change. Most of all, he believed in moral forces directing society and government, and he was more interested in reviving these forces than in changing the external forms of governance. He was very enthusiastic about the Greeks' struggle for independence in 1822, but was pleased at the humbling of the Belgians in 1831. In 1832 he could complain to Savigny: "Miserable politics spoils all our days now and thrusts itself into all our thoughts and occupations." For like Wilhelm, what he resented most about politics was its intrusion into their private lives.

❦ IX ❦

The German Grammar

THE DISCOVERY of the great Indo-European family of languages by Jacob was one of the most exciting and stimulating intellectual events of the early nineteenth century. A whole new aspect of the past, a vast common heritage and tradition, and a new view of the interrelations of many cultures were recognized and greeted with an enthusiasm which it is hard for us today to imagine. The thrill that came with the certainty that Latin, Greek, Germanic, Slavic, Celtic, and Sanskrit were all members of the same linguistic and cultural family cannot be recaptured. Vague relations had been noted much earlier, but there had been no proof that Germanic and Greek, for example, were really connected. The establishment of the true relationships among the members of the family meant that a whole community had been discovered, a community united by linguistic affinity over many centuries and across all of Europe and much of Asia. From the western margins of Ireland to the plains of India, from the fjords of Scandinavia across the steppes of Russia to the cradle of Western civilization in Greece, branches of this linguistic tree could now be welcomed into the family. Modern dialects—the vulgar tongues of everyday use—gained enormously in respectability, for they were now recognized as full-blooded relatives of the esteemed classical tongues, Greek and Latin. The gain in prestige was obviously more important for languages such as Germanic and Slavic, which could not claim descent from Latin, as French and Italian could. The wave of enthusiasm ran highest among the status-conscious Germans, whose inferiority complex stemmed from French dominance in all things cultural, as well as from the prestige of the classical languages. Jacob's monumental *German Grammar* of 1819, with its demonstration of the language's long, rich history and tradition, helped German to replace Latin at the German universities.

For years the notion of a linguistic family that included Persian, Greek, and Latin had been popularized in Europe, but mostly on a speculative basis. There was no system in establishing relationships, fanciful etymologies hindered more than helped, and the belief that Hebrew, as a sacred language, must somehow be brought into the picture impeded progress for generations. The discovery of Sanskrit by western European scholars gave a tremendous impetus to language study at the end of the eighteenth century. Its relation to Latin and Greek was immediately noted. The age and venerability of the language, its exotic literature and great wealth of mythology, and the romantic associations with distant India captured the imagination and stimulated study. Friedrich Schlegel's *The Language and Wisdom of the Hindus* (1808) had an influence that is difficult to comprehend today. The ensuing burst of energy and the rapid progress in discovery made this the most fruitful and grandiose period in the history of language study. Goethe welcomed the new literature from the East; he modeled the prelude in the theater in *Faust* on the prelude to Kalidasa's *Shakuntala*. The surge of enthusiasm for the newly discovered Eastern relative led to renewed efforts to describe more precisely its position and relation in the family tree. At the foundations of modern philology lie many Romantic dreams and exotic urges.

Romantic features may be found in the first edition of Jacob's *Grammar*. His constant quest for the oldest and most genuine in every field finds its expression here as in all his works. There is no lore without language, he believed, and the search for language was a concomitant of his research into folklore. He dedicated the book to Savigny with warm words of appreciation, writing a eulogy of his admired professor and inspirer. The success of the first edition, which sold out within a year and was widely acclaimed, encouraged him to start reediting it almost immediately. He felt that every book, as soon as it was published, was ready for a revision. Sometimes he could do this rapidly without further study by simply drawing on his vast store of knowledge. Thus the second edition appeared in 1822, for Jacob continued to write while the first pages were at the printer's. In rewriting the book he severely "pruned the lush growth" and what he considered Romantic elements. Jacob had the habit of writing by inspiration, without plan or program, filling in gaps by means of addenda and appendices. He developed his thoughts as he wrote, which meant that his style often revealed less organization and care than one might expect from a scholar fastidious about details. After the *Grammar* had appeared, he wrote to Lachmann: "I like to learn my concepts for the first time from the objects of study in which so much is still obscure. With time, objects and general concepts will become clearer." The primacy of subject matter over abstract or *a priori* ordering of concepts is a distinctive feature of all Jacob's work. He generally did not impose a conceptual scheme on his material, but rather let it emerge from the evidence. Much later, in 1835, he wrote Lachmann, describing his procedure: "My persistence in working through material I have started may have some advantages, but also dangers. To be sure, nothing gets lost, but improper material may be added. I can only survey the whole when I have finished."

Jacob much preferred metaphorical language to dry, expository prose. Sometimes his tendency to express his ideas in comparative and analogical thoughts led to obscurity, so that Wilhelm had to interpret and formulate more precisely for him. Pictorial language with many figures drawn from Nature mark his style throughout his life. The language of imagery and metaphor is more a visualization of thoughts than a rational explication. Jacob realized this, submitted gladly to corrections from his brother, but could not change his style, which after all was an integral part of his personality. He tended to personify language and ascribe nearly human attributes to it:

> The old poetry is like the old language, simple and rich within its own resources. In the old language there are nothing but simple words, but these are capable of such inflection and modification that they perform miracles. Modern language has lost its innocence, and it has become outwardly richer, but through composition and accident, and therefore needs much effort in order to express a simple sentence. Since in all metaphors there is a part of a secret, greater truth than that which is conceded for the sake of the external dissimilarity, let me make a comparison with the following legend, which is obviously true: At first men begat children through merely gazing at one another (God works with the mere thought), afterwards however kisses were used, and finally an embrace and physical union.

This was written in 1811 as a defense against criticism from Arnim, but it reveals a constant and typical trait in Jacob's thought and style. Jacob drew his figures of speech from everyday life and from his observations of natural phenomena. His metaphorical language was not empty rhetorical embellishment, but the form he needed to express his thinking: as he once wrote Arnim, he used metaphors only when the picture was clear and firm in his mind.

The *Grammar* was properly a "Teutonic Grammar," since it included Gothic—an extinct ancestor of modern German—Scandinavian languages, English, and Dutch, as well as the standard High German then used. The first volume contained only the formal inflections of these languages; the really revolutionary phonology appeared in the second edition of 1822. The *Grammar* was epoch-making in method and form of presentation, since it was not a prescriptive book which attempted to regulate the language. For the first time ever, an historical and descriptive grammar of all the known Germanic dialects was presented. The growth, forms in historical and comparative perspective, and the

development of all the Germanic languages from the fourth—
when Gothic was prevalent—to the nineteenth century were
authoritatively recorded and systematized by Jacob. Comparative
grammar was not a new field, since the classical languages had
invited such treatment and Bopp's work on the verb system of
Sanskrit in comparison with Greek and Latin had already appeared in 1816. But the combination of historical approach and
comparative method in one great overview made Jacob's *German
Grammar* a basic book for generations to come.

The reception of the first edition was immediate and enthusiastic; the scholarly world acclaimed it as a masterpiece. Benecke
in Göttingen wrote such a laudatory review that Jacob was genuinely embarrassed. Wilhelm von Humboldt paid the book warm
tribute, and appreciation from such a source was doubly dear.
Even August Wilhelm Schlegel greeted the volume with praise
both for its historical approach and for its erudition in detail.
From the first it was clear that it represented a landmark. The
path of Germanic philology was set for the nineteenth century.
The University of Marburg responded by making Jacob a doctor
of philosophy. The Elector took the book calmly; if he noticed
it at all, he failed to recognize it officially.

The vast amount of material was superbly organized; the sheer
weight of information made it a valuable reference book, but
the volume would not have become revolutionary without the
formulation of many important philological discoveries. Most
famous of these is "Grimm's Law," the rules by which the correspondences between the consonants of Germanic and its sister
languages in the Indo-European family may be determined. Jacob
coined the term "sound shift," which has persisted to this day,
to show the change in Germanic consonants. If all that Jacob had
done was to systematize the phonetic correspondences between
Germanic and its sister tongues, this would indeed have been an
epoch-making achievement. But Jacob noted that the shift or
change continued, apparently in a coherent direction, to produce
the differences between High German and all other Germanic
dialects. The "Germanic Sound Shift" was the prehistoric proc-

ess whereby almost all the consonants of Germanic became differentiated from the corresponding consonants in the common ancestor—primitive Indo-European. It is now assumed that almost all languages of the family differ in some respects from the postulated parent tongue, but this was not a certainty in Jacob's day, nor was there any agreement that the existence of a single parent tongue could be reconstructed in theory by comparison of all the offspring. The "Old High German Sound Shift" is the term used to describe the phonetic changes which make modern standard German different from the cognate English and Scandinavian forms. It was Jacob's genius to combine the two complex processes in the light of one principle and to show the second as an analogical continuation of the first. With his great discovery, he brought order into the chaos of resemblances which had confused all earlier scholars.

The *German Grammar* also had polemic tones. Jacob was hard on those predecessors who had written grammars in the stuffy, school-text style which he abhorred. He was emphatic in his rejection of prescriptive grammar; Jacob stressed that he was describing, not setting up norms and standards, and that the natural growth of a language, like that of a beautiful flower, should not only be recorded and respected but also left unspoiled by academics' rules. The purists such as Adelung, Campe, and Jean Paul, who wished to reform and purify the language, were anathema to Jacob. He enjoyed laughing at some of the absurd coinages they made in trying to substitute German words for French and Latin. The language societies and all they stood for aroused Jacob's contempt: "These people do not want to follow modestly the profound spirit of the language," he wrote to Lachmann, "but wish to overthrow this spirit and replace it with a miserable idol."

Some adverse criticism of the *Grammar* was inevitable. Jacob understood the inadequacy of the first edition, but he was, as always, slightly touchy and on the defensive when others saw his errors. To one of the common reproaches that he had devoted too much attention to petty details, Jacob countered: "I am more convinced every day that the spirit of language extends from its heart to all of its limits and fingertips, and that therefore every single letter offers an incalculable certainty which we must not abandon for the sake of some favorite theory. This certainty must come to us slowly and gradually, and then it will seem simple and wonderful like everything in Nature."

Jacob did not treat language as much like living Nature as his metaphors would suggest. He was interested in arranging and bringing order into the vast chaos that lay before him. Therefore he set up the ordering principles for declension and conjugation which on the whole still obtain, and in so doing he made several important contributions.

The preface to the second edition of 1822 was even more emphatic in its insistence on pure observation of linguistic phenomena: "I am hostile to notions of universal logic in grammar. They apparently lend themselves to exactness and firmness in definition, but they obstruct observation, which I consider the soul of linguistic science." With such statements Jacob also rejected the speculative, philosophical grammar represented by Wilhelm von Humboldt. Jacob was interested in the organic growth of language and its changes, and not in the psycho-linguistic aspects which formed the basis of language study for Humboldt. The split between *linguistics,* as the study of the nature and structure of language, and *philology*, as the study of the history and forms of language, is presaged here in the divergent approaches of Wilhelm von Humboldt and Jacob Grimm. Jacob became the father of Germanic philology, with profound influence in method on all later study of Indo-European philology; Wilhelm von Humboldt continued in the Cartesian philosophical tradition.

Not that Jacob did not speculate, too, in his own way. Some of his comments sound like reversions to his pre-scientific period: "From one point of view the sound shift seems to me to be a barbarous aberration from which other quieter nations refrained, but which has to do with the violent progress and yearning for liberty found in Germany of the early Middle Ages, and which started the transformation of Europe." Such remarks combined evidence or assumptions from several disparate fields in an inexcusable manner, along with the invidious suggestion that the Germans yearned for freedom more than other nations. Jacob came to language study from poetry, and therefore his views were always colored by poetic attitudes. While busy revising the first edition, in 1821 he wrote Lachmann a half-serious comparison of the vowels in German with colors, equating *a* with white, *i* with red, *u* with black, *e* with yellow, *o* with blue, and finished by remarking that this was all quite clear and obvious. Several of his whimsies stemmed from his fascination with triads—the three persons of the verb, three numbers (singular, dual, plural), three genders in nouns—and led to theories that were quite unfounded in fact and as purely fanciful as those of his predecessors. Thus he believed, for example, in the primacy of the three "real" vowels *a*, *i*, and *u*; *e* and *o* he considered weakened or debased forms derived from the original triad of genuine vowels. What is astonishing about this is that Jacob knew Greek very well, and in that language the alternation of *e* and *o* is basic to the verbal system. But Jacob's starting point was Gothic, the oldest recorded Germanic language, in which *e* and *o* play no significant role. The evidence of Sanskrit seemed to corroborate his thesis, for Sanskrit shows a predominance of the vowel *a*—and *a* is the oldest, noblest, and best of the vowels in Jacob's Romantic view.

Many other Romantic notions, appealing in their imaginative formulation but quite unscientific, may be found scattered through the *Grammar,* not as part of the factual information, but as sideline commentary. One theory which Jacob espoused was that of the decay of modern languages when compared with the older tongues. The older languages, notably Latin and Greek, had much fuller inflections than the modern tongues, and this ability to inflect Jacob considered a sign of vigor. Since Sanskrit had even more luxurious inflections than either Greek or Latin, it followed that it must be the oldest, purest, and greatest. Gothic, much more inflected than Old High German and still preserving many "real" vowels in its endings, was a "richer" language, just as the endings of Old High German were superior to those of Middle High German, and so on down to modern, decadent times. Loss of inflections, in Jacob's view, was hardly compensated for by clarity of structure and ease of expression. This view was widely held at the time, largely because of the prestige of the highly inflected classical languages, and it did not die out in the minds of many philologists until recently. Another whimsical notion was that the vowels are feminine, variable, capricious, and not to be trusted. The masculine consonants are the firm structure of the language, and if they change, well, then one is dealing with a serious sound shift. This is a quaint notion, but all thought in a subtle mind is interrelated; perhaps Jacob would never have hit on his great observation of the consistency in the sound shifts if he had not believed in the masculine superiority of the consonants.

The core of his revolutionary discovery is that the consonants in Germanic keep consistently to the same areas of articulation as the corresponding consonants in other Indo-European languages. Thus, for example, Latin *d*, a sound made with the teeth, corresponds to English *t*, also a dental; or Latin *f*, as in *fero*, remains a lip sound in the English *bear*. This sounds reasonable enough today, but it must be remembered that only a few years before Jacob himself was willing to equate any consonant with any other if it served his purpose. His contemporaries, especially those who wished to keep Hebrew and other non-Indo-European languages in the running, were equally arbitrary. But from 1822 on, the principle of correspondences as established by Jacob Grimm triumphed for good, and the new historical-comparative method of research in languages dominated the entire nineteenth century.

There were, understandably, errors in Jacob's results, since not all the requisite data were available for his scrutiny, and much that was remained mysterious to him. He was quite content to let anomalies survive as such even in the second edition of the *Grammar,* knowing that he could not answer all questions or solve all problems in a pioneering work. One of the famous omissions in his *Grammar* is the failure to explain in terms of the sound shift the changes in verb forms in the plural of the past tense. An apparent irregularity such as English *was–were,* a phenomenon to which Jacob gave the name of "grammatical change," was not explained until 1875, when the Danish scholar Karl Verner showed that the influence of the old Indo-European accent produced such irregularities. On the other hand, Jacob's study of dialects anticipates many modern views and conclusions. He saw the dynamics of dialects, their changes and modifications in proximity to each other, and his theory of shifting boundaries suggested the first criteria of dialect geography.

It is a typically Romantic inspiration to refer to verbs as "weak" and "strong"—because the so-called strong verb is capable of changing its vowel, as in *sing–sang–sung,* whereas the weak verb has to add an ending to indicate change of tense. *Ablaut,* or vowel change, is the change of the vowel in verbs to indicate tense, and also functions in nominal derivatives of verbs (*sing–song*). Jacob was greatly intrigued by the phenomenon and called it "the soul of our language." The term *Ablaut* had been used before Jacob, often in a derogatory sense, for vowel gradation; *Umlaut* had also been in use, but these and many other terms became the technical—and respectable—terms for Germanic philology from that time on. Jacob did not have to invent a whole new vocabulary, but a good dozen words became established through his use of them, and he coined many neologisms now standard. In his letters to Karl Lachmann he complained about the necessity of coining new terms, worried about the possibility of their acceptance, and was in general diffident in many matters: "I am really ashamed when I see a term I have coined being adopted and used." The tone of the second edition of 1822 was firmer and more confident than that of the first. The rapid acceptance of most of what he proposed confirmed his good judgment.

The first edition left many loose ends that Jacob felt he could tie together. As fast as he could write, Jacob sent off new pages to the publisher. Printing of the new volume began in 1820, and for the next months the pages went from Jacob's pen to the printer in a steady flow. It was not until April 1, 1821, that he coined the term "sound shift" and achieved his final insight into the total process. A third edition of the first part, now swollen to eleven hundred pages, was published in 1840. Meanwhile the second part of the grammar, dealing with word formation, appeared in Göttingen in 1826; the third volume came out in 1831 (dedicated to brother Wilhelm), and the fourth and final volume in 1837. The monumental size and wealth of the material and information would have been enough to insure Jacob's fame even if he had discovered no new principles for organizing the vast new field. For in 3,854 pages the Germanic languages were documented in their historical growth from the fourth century to the nineteenth.

❧ X ❧

The *Heroic Tales*

WILHELM'S SCHOLARLY PURSUITS during the years in Cassel covered a wide range of subjects. First in priority, naturally, was the work on the *Fairy Tales,* with the long-promised third volume containing the annotations finally being published in 1822. The year before Wilhelm had published a smaller work, but one of the guiding texts for several years in the study of the oldest Germanic inscriptions: *On German Runes.* A greatly expanded version with much larger coverage was published in 1828 under the title *On the Literature of the Runes.* Runes were still something of a mystery at the time; there were no other reliable treatises on the subject, and the differences in the form and shape of the letters were not yet fully explained. Carvings on helmets, votive tablets, rocks, and wood were known, but the information and sources were scattered and haphazard.

Wilhelm's interest was aroused by a unique opportunity in his own neighborhood. At Willingshausen several burial mounds of uncertain date were excavated in 1817–18. Among the objects, presumably artifacts, were some stones marked with strange symbols. Wilhelm, a friend of the Schwertzells, on whose estate the excavations had been made, was able to study the findings *in situ.* Although Wilhelm was not yet a full-fledged expert in the field, he decided that the strange markings were not runes.

Into the picture came Professor Rommel of Göttingen, a man with no scholarly scruples; he represented the type of scholar the Grimms detested most—the kind that rushes into print before even the bare beginnings of real research have been undertaken. His claim that the markings on the stones were probably made by some priest and had some deep religious significance turned out to be quite incorrect. Modern research has ascertained that the symbols were inscribed by a special type of sandworm.

Wilhelm's calm good judgment was thus vindicated in the case of the runic inscriptions, but work in the field was secondary to other concerns at the time. The brothers collaborated in publishing *Irish Tales of Elves* in 1826. It may seem odd that Jacob would cooperate in a translation, but he had long since abandoned his rigid position on the subject, and was charmed by Crofton Croker's *Fairy Legends and Traditions of the South of Ireland* of 1825. Jacob had great spurts of energy that enabled him to accomplish prodigious things in a brief span of time: he wrote his *German Legal Antiquities* from May 11 to July 25, 1827, although he had been collecting material from sources for many years. Wilhelm's attention turned again and again to the Middle Ages. In 1828 he published the fragmentary poem of the Crusades, *Count Rudolf,* collating existing sections and piecing together what could still be found of the medieval epic.

As early as 1823 Wilhelm was contemplating a history of medieval German epic poetry. The project, never completed as planned, was to occupy him for years. Besides the *Nibelungenlied,* he planned to include *Gudrun,* an epic that was, as Wilhelm put it, hardly known to a dozen people. His main interest was in the origins and development of the epics and epic cycles; his intention was to show the Germanic origin of the epics, thus excluding all works of the Arthurian cycle and others that had come from France. The attempt to find the earliest forms and trace the interrelations calls to mind the similar approach to the *Folk Tales* and *Fairy Tales.* In essence, all the brothers' work was part of one consistent quest.

Jacob always referred to Wilhelm's *German Heroic Tales*

(*Deutsche Heldensage*) as his greatest achievement; later critics tended to concur. Much of the material for the book had been gathered and published in the three volumes of *Old German Miscellany*. The arrangement there had been according to the contents and narrative bases of the tales. In reworking them for publication in book form, Wilhelm chose to order them chronologically. In 1827, Wilhelm's most intensive year on the epic collection, he felt much more certain of his relative chronology and could assign dates with confidence. The main body of the book, called "documents," contained the retold plots of tales from the sixth to the sixteenth century, with excerpts of the original texts. At the end Wilhelm included an essay on the origins and development of the heroic tale that summed up his wisdom and experience in the field.

The critical reception was favorable for the most part. Several reviewers, however, took issue with Wilhelm's theoretical musings even while welcoming the wealth of material and the manner of editing. A second edition was prepared by Jiriczek in 1867, and a third by Reinhold Steig in 1889. A fourth edition was not published until 1957. The work bore fruit in a variety of ways— writers were as interested as scholars, and the book found acceptance with a broad reading public. Uhland, for example, used the material for his work, and many others, some less interested in the scholarly aspects, also found a rich field to harvest. Research in scholarly form was stimulated by Wilhelm's opus; some of the continuation of the plan by scholars such as Müllenhoff was in opposition to Wilhelm's theoretical views. Müllenhoff took up the position upheld by Lachmann in his correspondence with the Grimms: he sided with Jacob against Wilhelm and Uhland, believing that the heroic epic is mainly poetic in character, infused perhaps with elements of old myths, but basically in its finest medieval expression a work of art and therefore to be judged primarily as such. Wilhelm's views are sufficiently well known from the discussion of the *Folk Tales* and the *Fairy Tales*. He was less insistent on mythic content and historical elements, however, since his main concern was with the problem of how various legends merged, expanded, and varied over the centuries. Subsequent research has rejected many of Wilhelm's theories, agreeing for the most part with Müllenhoff. The historicity of the main heroic epics is no longer a matter of debate. But their poetic quality might have been lost or forgotten if Wilhelm had not laid a foundation on which later scholars could erect their own research and theories.

Most heroic epics are in content and basic format quite closely related. Epic cycles sometimes reflect the combination of several tales, sometimes a common origin in history or legend of the basic narratives. By the early nineteenth century it was difficult to determine exactly how the epics had grown and changed, and thus Wilhelm inevitably made some errors which later scholars have been pleased to point out. Wilhelm could not believe that Dietrich of Bern (Verona) of the *Nibelungenlied* and its related tales could be identical with Theodoric the Great: there were simply too many historical anomalies. He set up a quite ingenious but totally incorrect hypothesis to explain the situation because he refused to believe that historical material could be so completely reshaped in the epic. Since he believed in the "truth" of folk poetry—and for him heroic epics were folk poetry—he found it impossible to accept the poetic changes he observed. In another respect his belief in the folk origin of the epics slanted his analysis: since he knew that a genetic approach to the epic was eventually self-defeating—one would have to go back to Adam and Eve—he helped himself out of the dilemma by postulating a common origin in an *Urmythus* for those epics that seemed to share content and themes. Such a thesis precluded the question of literary influence, although later students of the problem agree that epic style was a formal style shared by most bards and that cross influences are the most striking feature of both the early and the medieval epic form.

Wilhelm's views of the origin and growth of the *Nibelungenlied* nevertheless anticipated many modern conclusions. By 1821 he was certain of the German origin of the epic, rejecting the thesis that it arose in Scandinavia, and had worked out to his own satisfaction the relationship to the Norse versions. This alone would have been an important contribution for the time, since the whole epic period in Germanic history was shrouded in mystery and uncertainty. Previously he had shared the general view that the Norse versions were older and more original, even though less historically accurate. He had come to realize that the sober and unembellished style of the Norse sagas had its own unique originality; the sagas depicted real people, not imaginary or legendary heroes. He was ahead of his time in recognizing that what the heroic epic seemed to have borrowed from the fairy tale was not complete narrative elements, but only motifs or motif series. Wilhelm's genetic approach made him aware of the fact that sagas could continue and be renewed over the centuries, but he was uncertain about the transformation of historical events into literary form. Since the epic in its essentials is the traditional property of a whole people, the bard is bound to recite his tale to reflect popular beliefs and expectations. But the popular imagination, Wilhelm believed, usually transfers historical events and persons into the realm of the timeless and may even invert the true relationships of historical fact, as in the case of Theodoric and Odoacer. The hero becomes an idealized representative of his people as the heroic legends draw material from history, the national life, the invention of individual bards, and what is available in fairy tale and folk tale. Myth and religious cult practices may even be embedded in the heroic epic, but the hero's life and deeds follow a restricted path with very few choices and a standardized type of career.

The very term *Heldensage* (heroic tale) was a coinage of Romanticism that was based on a false analogy with the folk tale and the equally erroneous assumption that there was no single poet or author. The Romanticists—and both Jacob and Wilhelm must here be considered members of the movement—thought that the epics had a long oral tradition behind them. The true heroic epic, however, does not exist outside of written poetic traditions. The historicity of an heroic epic is based mostly on just names; relative chronology is usually ignored where other interests conflict, so that in the *Nibelungenlied,* for example, Theodoric and Attila are contemporaries. Such distortions are usually ascribed to tribal interests, and it is assumed that facts from history were recast to fit the personal, tribal, or local demands. Gradually, however, in the heroic epic the hero ceases to be truly tribal and fights for himself and his own glory, not for a tribe or cause. This theory might be refuted if more epics had survived from the Great Migrations or if Gothic tales had come down to us in their original form. Norse sources must be consulted as corrective and control at every step—here was one advantage Wilhelm had over most of his German contemporaries —otherwise it is impossible to reconstruct the German epic in its variants and evolution.

Wilhelm's patriotic pride was as evident in his book on the heroic epic as in his earlier works. He could point to a tradition of over a thousand years, with great works like the *Nibelungenlied* as crowning achievements of the German genius. Jordanes, the Gothic historian, was writing saga and not history according to Wilhelm, and this insight alone is evidence of his critical acumen. In many other cases he anticipated modern research based on much wider material, refuting, for example, the theory that the heroic epic originated from tales of the gods. Some of his theories are now forgotten, but his great contribution in its time has had enduring value.

❧ X I ❧

The Move to Göttingen

IN 1829 VÖLKEL, the first librarian at Cassel, died. Jacob expected to succeed him, and of course Wilhelm also hoped for advancement. Both had been satisfactory librarians, and had worked conscientiously if not enthusiastically at their duties. But their labors had not endeared them to the Elector, who was not a patron of the arts and sciences. When Jacob presented a copy of the first volume of the *German Grammar* to the Elector, he was greeted by the remark that it was the Elector's hope that he was not neglecting his official duties for such unessential work. The brothers' applications for promotion were filed on February 2, and returned rejected by the Elector himself on February 5. To make their disappointment complete, the man appointed as first librarian was Professor Rommel, a favorite of the Elector and already Court Archivist. Rommel knew little about runes, but he knew how to insinuate himself into favor. The Grimms were promised a salary increase of one hundred thalers each, a sum which they felt was insulting.

In the fall the situation suddenly changed when an offer from the University of Göttingen, in the kingdom of Hannover, opened up an alternative to the life of drudgery in Cassel. Jacob was invited to come as professor and senior librarian, Wilhelm as librarian; Jacob was to receive one thousand thalers and Wilhelm five hundred a year. A Professor Reuss would be their supervisor as head librarian. Their chief assignment was as librarians, although both were invited to give lectures at the university. Their sense of injustice and the prospect of new salaries and financial security overcame their apprehensions about teaching and their deep and sincere regret at having to leave Cassel. After much debate and soul-searching, they sent in their resignations in November 1829. The Elector's sarcastic remark when he found out that the two most distinguished Hessian scholars were leaving has become an oft-quoted classic: "So the Grimms are leaving. What a loss! They have never done anything for me."

Wilhelm considered it his duty to inform the Electress Augusta of their departure. He assured her that it was not lack of loyalty to Hesse that made them go and expressed his sorrow at leaving "Hesse, which our family has served with unstained honor for centuries." But the Electress had no power over her husband, and from her they expected no favors and no help. As they were about to depart, however, an unexpected event occurred which might have made their stay in Cassel possible after all. The Elector gave a dinner to which he invited Professor Rommel and a Major von Lützerode, the Saxon ambassador. The ambassador commented on the Elector's great good fortune in having such learned men as the Grimms in his employ and suggested that Saxony was interested in inviting the brothers to come to the University of Leipsic. The Elector, whose interest in intellectual matters was as slight as his learning, was genuinely surprised and turned to Professor Rommel to ask if the brothers' reputation was indeed so great. Rommel, whose intrigues had much to do with the Grimms' departure, had to agree. Jacob was especially irritated by Rommel, because the man, although of solid bourgeois origin, had let himself be ennobled. The "von" in front of his name was an affront to Jacob, who believed in being above all a *Bürger*, a citizen, and who disliked both the nobility and its medals, orders, and ritual.

The Elector was interested in prestige, if not in scholarship, and now that it was too late began to reconsider the loss of such apparently famous men. The brothers' market value had obviously increased in his eyes, for he offered them the positions they had applied for and even raised their salaries to a figure greater than that offered by Göttingen. In addition he promised them complete independence from Rommel. But now it was a matter of honor for the brothers; they had accepted at Göttingen and had already painfully completed the process of severing their ties with Hesse. They made preparations for departure in a depressed mood, clearing out the house at Christmas time, a season that was usually their happiest festival of the year. Dortchen fell ill on Christmas day, so that the celebration had to be limited to a little tree set on a traveling trunk. Some form of festivity they felt they had to offer Herman, Wilhelm's son, who had been born only a little over a year before. The brothers set out in bitter cold on December 27, full of sorrow at leaving home, and worried about Dortchen, who had to stay behind. They arrived by nightfall in Göttingen and spent the next two weeks in the home of Professor Benecke, their friend and admirer of many years.

Göttingen was by no means an obvious place for the Grimms to find refuge. In 1816 Jacob wrote Savigny that he had only gone to Göttingen because of the library and its rare books—"otherwise one had an uncanny feeling about the place." To Lachmann he confided in 1820 that he had never liked the town or the people or the area. In 1827 Jacob had refused an offer from the university for the following reasons: devotion to his fatherland—"although it could hardly attract a foreigner, it does hold me here. Inseparability from my brother and his fate; the secret presentiment that I have only five or ten years to live; my father died when he was forty-five." Jacob dreaded going, since he had forebodings about the whole idea of entering Hannoverian territory. But Savigny among others urged them to accept, and the call itself had come through the mediation of their friend Benecke. For Wilhelm it meant leaving a sick and pregnant Dortchen in an unfurnished house in Cassel at the coldest time of year. All the omens were evil. Wilhelm caught pneumonia

during the first year. This illness had an odd consequence—
Wilhelm let himself be named professor at Göttingen in order
to give his widow, should he die, some security. Everything they
did seemed somehow anxious or wrong. Jacob's first lecture in
Göttingen was on the subject of homesickness. He had to comfort himself with the thought that the same stars shone in Hannover as in Hesse.

Meanwhile, in Cassel, Herman had fallen ill, so that Dortchen's arrival was postponed until Easter. The brothers had an
uncomfortable apartment in the town, too small for the whole
family and poorly heated. They lived among their baggage and
packing boxes for over three months. Even the contacts with the
university that had so generously invited them had a dark side—
the hospitality of the local residents was overwhelming. Their
colleagues' welcome was cordial, but formal of course, so that
the brothers had to make visits, return hospitality, and keep up
a social routine quite beyond their means and totally at variance
with their interests. Even the library work was more demanding,
since they had to put in six hours a day, thirty-six hours a week,
or about twice what they had done in Cassel. The work was
not really onerous, however, and their complaints might have
been more muted if they had not had to contend with Professor
Reuss. As head of the library he did all the book ordering, but
he had his own odd methods. He read the learned journals,
selected those books which were favorably reviewed, and then
kept secret what he had ordered. If a book was not reviewed,
or if he failed to see it, it did not exist for him and he would
refuse to order it. New acquisitions took about three years to
appear on the shelves, so that even if the brothers found out what
Reuss had ordered, there was no reason to hurry to the archives.

Jacob's complaints about the loss of his precious leisure did
not concern only his increased library duties and his troubles
with Reuss. Jacob had to start a career as a professor, an experience which he had always dreaded and put off. Lachmann's
letters on the conditions in Berlin, especially in teaching German
language and literature, discouraged him before he started. Lach-

mann claimed that there were few students and mostly lazy ones; he noted that the study of German was amazing and novel for most students, who could hardly believe it a proper subject for serious university study. In addition there were the academic feuds and vendettas; there were three full professors of German literature at the university, and Jacob had to agree that this was absurd. Before Jacob had even moved to Göttingen, his apprehensions had reached alarming proportions. After accepting the offer from the university, he wrote to his old school friend Meusebach: "I don't even know if I have sufficient breath to lecture; I felt very little desire to. Whatever I have learned I like to communicate down to the smallest detail and not just skim off the top as must be done for students—it will be hard for me until I get used to it. . . . The town and the area are far inferior to our native soil, and there is something disturbing about the fact that the faces of the people one comes most in contact with, namely the students, change every year, which does not appeal to me." Jacob went prepared to dislike every moment of it. Actually he had eight hours of public lectures a week, a difficult chore for him; and he grumbled about the assignment for most of his stay at Göttingen.

As a professor of German language and literature, Jacob was very conservative. He did not want to change the lecture system, believing that students learned by taking notes. Seminar methods did not suit his style at all: "Is the teacher to ask questions and have himself answered? Is the work to be a collective effort under his guidance? That would easily weaken the teacher's authority, which is so beneficial to receptive minds. Changes in a form of instruction which has for so long splendidly proved its worth are most questionable. . . ." But he found lecturing tiring, demanding, and not wholly satisfactory either: "Lecturing gives me little pleasure and much trouble; I have to consider what the students can use from the stuff I offer, and arrange and order it for them. I learn nothing in doing this. Stepping up to the lectern at a set time has something theatrical about it and is repugnant to me." Even lecturing on his favorite subject, German grammar, gave him little satisfaction. He considered his own learning more important than that of the students, and he descended to their level very unwillingly. He studied and wrote for himself, for scholars, and for the fatherland.

Nevertheless Jacob made an impact as a professor, students remembered him, most colleagues seem to have respected him, and not all aspects of life were gloomy for him. Karl Goedeke, the well-known literary historian, recalled his study under Jacob:

Jacob lectured on legal antiquities, grammar, literary history and diplomacy, explicated some older German authors and sometimes the *Germania* of Tacitus. Many will still remember the small, lively figure, the rough voice with its strong Hessian dialect. He lectured without notes, and a small card with a few names, words, and numbers was sufficient for his incomparable memory. But the lecture did not come up to expectations. To be sure there were often beautiful and striking figures of the kind in which his writings are so rich, but orally they did not have the same effect as when written, for they were cast out abruptly and interrupted in an odd manner the never-failing richness of factual information, whereas in his books they were set pertinently in the proper place and not only presented his thoughts differently but also developed them in their figurative form: "Thought is lightning, words are thunder; the consonants are the bones, the vowels the blood of language." It was touching when in the middle of a factual lecture there came a pause which was then quickly excused: "My brother is so sick." And Wilhelm was often sick, but Jacob never. Although his external appearance was one of slightness and delicacy, he had in him something very akin to the old warriors who took off their helmets and cooled off in the air in order to start the battle with renewed strength. He himself made this comparison. Just as the warriors gained strength in battle, he gained it in work. His work proceeded smoothly and easily, for he had everything at his fingertips and wrote for publication without making changes. But when he saw what was printed he would have liked to reject it altogether in order to write it again more fully and better. He said, almost with amazement, of Wilhelm: "My brother reads through again what he has written before having it printed."

Students did not flock to Jacob and Wilhelm in Göttingen. Their fame was by this time well established in Germany, and indeed in most of Europe, but primarily as the editors of the *Fairy Tales,* the *Folk Tales,* and the *Heroic Tales.* The study of German literature did not have much prestige at the universities, where the classical languages and literatures were considered more important and elegant. Although Jacob's *German Grammar* eventually helped to restore the balance by showing the long and noble tradition of German and German culture, the status of German was still in doubt in the 1830's. In 1830 Jacob had to cancel a series of lectures on Otfried (an Old High German Bible translator) because only seven students were listed for the course and Jacob felt that twelve was the minimum. On the other hand, too many students meant too much work; he once complained because he had twenty-four in one class. He lectured on the *Nibelungenlied* to only eight students, complaining all the while to Lachmann that the number was too small and that some of those who did come were lazy. In 1835 he had thirty-five students studying Tacitus' *Germania,* but Tacitus after all wrote in Latin. Jacob was hard to please—even recognition and honors were not necessarily something that made him happy. In 1832 he was made a corresponding member of the Academy of Sciences in Berlin, but wrote Lachmann: "I am genuinely ashamed at such occasions, and long for the old, quiet times when everyone considered me as insignificant as I feel myself to be—in Göttingen I still have an uncanny feeling. The most precious thing for me is the attitude of those who have initiated the honor."

Wilhelm was ill almost from the first days in Göttingen. The visits and receptions which courtesy entailed wearied him, and his worry about his family did little to make him feel cheerful. In 1831 he became desperately ill, so apparently near death that for months Jacob's letters were full of worried references. After his recovery, Wilhelm also lectured at the university, where he became a full professor in 1835. He complained less than Jacob, but he too was not really excited by his teaching duties. He shared his brother's skepticism about the quality of the students. Twenty-two regular students signed up for his lectures on the *Nibelungenlied,* but this did not appease Wilhelm, who noted that many were there only because they had to pass examinations in older German —and Jacob was in those years the examiner. Wilhelm had a low opinion of the students' initiative and imagination: "They know nothing of the happiness that comes with seeking the solitary paths on which one climbs higher and higher to where the air is pure, the prospects refresh, and the soul remains youthful." Like Jacob, Wilhelm was homesick for Cassel, found Göttingen boring and strenuous, and longed for his former leisure. His Hessian patriotism never slumbered; his pride in his native corner of Germany was a constant theme in his letters during the restless years in Hannoverian territory. Honors came to Wilhelm too during his stay, however, and the recognition of the Academy of Sciences in Berlin, which also made him a corresponding member in 1832, was an indication of his acceptance in academic circles. Wilhelm's inaugural lecture was not scholarly in the usual sense, however; rather it was a poetically stated view of the relation of poetry and history. The general tendency of the lecture follows lines of thought already familiar. It contains some fine and typical formulations: "Poetry is the first, simplest, and at the same time the most grandiose means which man has been given to express a lofty feeling or a sublime insight. It is the treasure-house in which a nation stores its spiritual wealth."

The year 1833 was an unusually melancholy one, even if marked by Jacob's being made a Court Councillor in recognition of his prominence in his field. It was an honor he did not seek or value very highly. Wilhelm's son Herman was, like his father, often sick and in need of special care. In March 1830, a second son, Rudolf, was born, and in August 1832, a daughter, Augusta. The family was now large enough so that the illness of one person could upset the whole routine. 1833 was a year of illness;

Dortchen became very sick, and for a time they feared for her life. The Grimms' only sister, Lotte, died after an attack of pneumonia following the premature birth of a child. Wilhelm hastened to Cassel, where Dortchen had gone to nurse Lotte, and took care of Lotte himself in her last days while Dortchen and the children were also confined to bed with illness. Wilhelm's health suffered as a result of his nursing care and many worries, so that the period of 1834 to 1835 was one of constant concern for his condition. Jacob's letters during this time were full of references to the ups and downs in Wilhelm's life, and for the first time in years Jacob noted that Wilhelm's good humor and usual cheerful disposition had been affected. Wilhelm's illness lasted well over a year; several times he was believed to be dying, but he recovered and gradually resumed his work at the library. But his mood was one of deep depression, and Jacob complained that he could not even persuade him to take a short vacation trip. For a time Wilhelm seemed possessed by fixed ideas, melancholy, and an aversion to all social contacts. At the library he worked mechanically, and to Jacob's great sorrow he seemed to take no pleasure in his research at home. He was able to work sporadically, starting to edit the *Rolandslied* and finishing *Freidanks Bescheidenheit.* This *Wisdom of Freidank,* a moralizing medieval text, was based on the collation of several fragmentary manuscript sources, and thus was a real challenge to Wilhelm's powers of reconstruction.

Jacob meanwhile had written Lachmann in 1832, saying that he intended to write a book on German mythology, excluding Norse mythology and tracing the development of the continental German tribes. The publication of *Reynard the Fox* in 1834 cleared the way for Jacob's final work, *German Mythology* (perhaps, Teutonic or Germanic would be a more accurate title). His interest in the field went back to the first years after his study in Marburg. Mythology attracted both brothers, and Wilhelm's work with the Danish ballads and the Edda as well as his own Norse studies had led Jacob to appreciate the central importance of mythology in the study of folklore. For years Jacob kept up with the literature on the subject, admiring Görres's book on the history of Eastern myths for the parallels drawn with Western mythology. He viewed partly with admiration, partly with skepticism, the speculative work of people such as Friedrich Creuzer. Even in his wildest period Jacob was not a mystic; he always looked for established sources and documentation. The *Old German Miscellany* contained remarks on mythology, some of it already systematic and foreshadowing the results of 1835. As early as 1811 he discovered what he believed to be a principle of interaction between the names of gods and heroes in mythology: names give rise to etiological explanations, but the names also arise from the body of myths. Jacob strongly believed that people cling tenaciously to traditional beliefs and are converted very slowly to new ideas and forms. "Everything that made my works fruitful I owe to the early conviction that what continues to live in popular language, saga, and song cannot be newly invented but can only have arisen in antiquity." Important here is the analogy with language and its historical development. Jacob opened his book in 1835 with a recounting of the spread of Christianity among the Germans, but in the firm belief that much pagan custom and religion was only overlaid and not entirely lost. Well aware that people influence people, he did not confine his research to Germanic alone, but included the neighbors of the Germanic tribes, such as the Celts, Slavs, Balts, and Finns.

German Mythology, dedicated to the historian F. C. Dahlmann, was every bit as revolutionary as the *Grammar* had been. The study of Germanic mythology may be conveniently divided into "before Jacob" and "after Jacob." His purpose, as in all his works, was mainly patriotic. In the preface he stated his aims: "From a comparison of the old and the useful recent sources I have attempted to demonstrate in other books that our ancestors, even back into heathen times, did not speak a wild, rough, unregulated language, but rather a fine, well-forged, and articulate tongue, which lent itself to poetry in earliest times. Our ancestors lived not in disorderly, untamed hordes, but rather nurtured ancient and traditional, meaningful law in free union according to vigorous custom. By these and no other means I would like to show now that their hearts were full of faith in god and gods, and that happy and grandiose, even if imperfect ideas of higher beings gave soul and sustenance to their lives. . . ." Jacob's joy at discovering that the old German beliefs and practices were not gloomy and bloody, or decadent like some Hindu beliefs in his view, is easier to appreciate if one considers the stereotyped notion, widespread in Jacob's day, that the hairy and unwashed Teutons were a rude, crude people awaiting Roman law and custom to lead them to the threshold of civilization. Jacob had already done much to demonstrate the high level of cultural achievement among the old Germanic tribes: *German Legal Antiquities* and *Concerning Poetry in Law* were written with just this purpose in mind. Together with the *Grammar,* these works helped to make the German language and the history of German customs respectable; even the universities, the citadels of conservatism then as now, began to show interest in a national past that was slowly becoming prestigious and entering into competition with the accepted studies of ancient Greece and Rome.

The height of Jacob's early labors in mythology were the years 1813 to 1816, which saw the publication of *Old German Miscellany.* This was a formative period for Jacob, who clung to many of his basic beliefs while correcting his errors and improving and refining his methods. All of his works are valid documents of his personality. The speculative epoch of his development in the second decade of the century produced some of his least successful, least convincing writing. He took surviving mythology as evidence of an original divine revelation, but this did not prevent him from manipulating what he found for his own human purposes. In some of the early flights of fancy in the field, Jacob was as guilty of egregious errors as any of his contemporaries. In one article he used the equation of straw and gold from a German children's story and the equation of corn and gold from an Old Norse kenning to explain the Turkish name for the

Milky Way. He isolated and made absolute certain motifs chosen at random from totally different contexts, invented mythic correspondences, and arrived at astounding and absurd combinations. To buttress his arguments, he stooped to some hilariously wild etymological inventions.

In the early nineteenth-century mythological study involved uncontrolled speculation that offered boundless scope to the imagination. Until Jacob's serious work in the 1830's, there was not even a sure understanding of the most basic questions. There was no methodology, and information from Germanic, Celtic, and Slavic sources was confused and considered interchangeable. The use of Greek and Roman mythology did more to muddle than clarify what little was known, since the classic examples were taken as models of how it should and must be. The sources of Germanic mythology were either obscure, secondhand, or misleading, and in fact there was no competent collection of sources prior to Jacob's *Mythology*. Even in Germanic mythology alone, the preponderance of Norse evidence and the scant, fragmentary continental sources combined to make reconstruction very difficult. The discovery of Hindu mythology was of dubious help, since it led mostly to fanciful attempts to establish parallels without any systematic understanding of the problems involved. In 1813 Friedrich Rühs, an ardent opponent of the Grimms, published a book in which he attempted to prove that Icelandic poetry was at least derived, if not directly translated, from Anglo-Saxon. In 1816 a certain Trautvetter published a "key" to the Edda in which he treated the Edda as an enciphered textbook of chemistry. The folly of such absurd books makes Jacob's merit all the more striking. Jacob not only had to place the sources on firm ground—a remarkable achievement in itself—but also had to clear away an incredible amount of rubbish. His work became the basis of all later mythological research because it was careful and methodical. Very little systematic error mars his book, since his opinions were usually stated only parenthetically and unemphatically: the main focus remains on the sources which he discovered, ordered, and presented.

Jacob started with the premise that Norse and German mythology are essentially identical. He then proceeded to connect the oldest documents of the Wotan cult with the reports of Tacitus, describing the most ancient beliefs in the pagan gods. But his coverage extended also to the "lower" mythology, and in addition to the gods and goddesses he treated swan maidens, forest females, wights, elves, and dwarfs as legitimate parts of popular beliefs. These quaint ideas are as important to folklore as the establishment of a pantheon or a cosmogony. He noted the gradual conversion of old pagan gods into devils and demons as the Christian religion replaced older beliefs. From his legal studies he could identify mythological remnants in legal language and oaths. As one might expect from the author of the *Grammar,* his starting point was often linguistic; the first chapter is devoted to the word "God" in all its Germanic forms. Where possible he noted the connection of Norse and German, yet in general he paid little attention to the possibility of borrowing and interchange between Norse and German. His indifference to distinctions between original common Germanic property and later mutual influences has been cited as a flaw by critics, but given his prime purpose it is very understandable. Jacob liked to use folk tales for comparison because of the supposed pagan reminiscences they contained; for this reason some of his material on superstitious beliefs about elves, nixies, and the like was derived from popular tales, many of uncertain date and origin.

The use of fairy tales and folk tales as sources for mythological material stemmed from Jacob's poetic view of the whole problem. Years before he had written to Savigny, explaining his feeling for myths and folk tales: "Myths are for me the pure water that waters the world from the beginning, and again and freshly with every rain. . . . The truth in every folk tale is very perceptible, it touches us like the pressure of a sunbeam which we cannot grasp at its source." Jacob also overestimated the possibility of reconstructing German mythology. The continental Germanic tribes lost their old religion without leaving behind enough material to enable later generations to recapture it except in fragments.

Yet Jacob believed that he could reconstruct it on the model of Norse mythology, but in the attempt he used material of dubious provenance, often drawing on German poetry of the thirteenth century and even later for pagan echoes. He was curiously inconsistent in discounting foreign influences on Germanic beliefs on the one hand, while on the other emphasizing the possibility of interchange within neighboring tribes.

For later scholars there remained some of Jacob's tacit assumptions to overcome, such as the notion of the gradual decay of mythology or the thesis of early creativity in primitive innocence. These Romantic ideas, so dear to Jacob, are not useful to modern folklorists. Later generations of scholars have lived happily on the capital he amassed, gradually refining and improving the modest conclusions he drew. The enthusiastic reception of the *German Mythology* by writers as well as academic scholars helped to spread knowledge of older German beliefs among Germany's intelligentsia. It never became a household book like the *Fairy Tales*, but it was the standard reference book for many years. A second edition appeared in 1844, a third in 1854, and the fourth edition, edited by E. H. Meyer, was published in Berlin in 1855. James Steven Stallybrass published an English translation in London from 1883 to 1888, wisely translating the title as *Teutonic Mythology*. The edition was reissued in England in 1900, and in America in 1966. Stallybrass translated from the fourth edition, which included an appendix originally only in the first edition of 1835, and a supplement collected from Jacob's posthumous notes by E. H. Meyer. Phototyped reprints of the fourth edition were made available in Germany in 1953. Other works on the subject of Germanic mythology have corrected many of Jacob's conclusions and have retreated from his view of a specifically German myth-tradition, but no single work has ever replaced it as a source book. Even the work of Jan De Vries, now considered the most authoritative scholar in the field, is a correction of Grimm, to whose pioneering work De Vries pays tribute.

Jacob found pupils and followers almost immediately. The general interest in Germanic mythology, already great and stimulated by works of Wieland, Simrock, and other popularizers, found an outlet in journals of mythology which began to appear in the 1840's. Jacob's assumption of a common Indo-European mythology, long-questioned and disputed, gradually became an article of faith among scholars; Jan De Vries states categorically that there was a completely developed system of deities in common Indo-European times, and that the various migrating tribes took this along as part of their heritage. Most Indo-European tribes thus developed their own variations of a common inheritance. This is most important in considering the Germanic tradition, where the individual tribes from the time of the Great Migrations had their own special deities whom they worshiped even while recognizing the existence of others. Jacob, as is so often the case in his work, was deceived by his foreshortened calendar; one must go back to the time of the Great Migrations to find, or rather to postulate, a common religion shared in detail by all the Germanic tribes. All these corrections and amendments to Jacob's work do not diminish its merit; rather they confirm its value as the first foundation of scholarship in the field.

❦ XII ❦

The Seven of Göttingen

In 1833 THE KINGDOM of Hannover acquired a new constitution, replacing the one reluctantly agreed to in 1819. The political storms that arose in France in 1830 were reflected in German lands, generally in the milder form of demands for constitutional government. Since William IV was both King of England and of Hannover, the new constitution was based on that of England. All state officials, among them university professors, had to swear an oath of allegiance to the king. At the time it must have seemed a routine formality to Jacob and Wilhelm, who took the oath with their colleagues without suspecting any adverse consequences. In May 1837, the king died, and the personal union between England and Hannover lapsed. Princess Victoria, then only eighteen years old, came to the throne of England, but since Salic law forbade the succession of a woman to the throne of Hannover, her uncle, Duke Ernst August, became King of Hannover. Ernst August, the Duke of Cumberland, was the fourth son of George III and from his youth had been known as a dissolute person involved in many scandals. He was disliked in his own family and unpopular with the English public. He came to Hannover in June 1837, a thoroughgoing reactionary and a throwback to the age of absolutism.

Ernst August's first act upon arriving in his new kingdom was to prorogue parliament; three months later he dissolved it. Meanwhile, in September, the University of Göttingen held its centenary celebration, not suspecting that the political steps taken by the new king were soon to threaten its freedom. On November 1, 1837, Ernst August revoked the constitution of 1833 and released all servants of the state from their loyalty oath to the constitution. The king was preparing to reign as an absolute monarch without the restraints of a parliament or a constitution, and was but little concerned with the reactions or sentiments of his subjects. He was probably quite honestly astonished when seven professors from the University of Göttingen objected in writing. The university had been founded by George II and nominally the King of Hannover was always rector of the university. On November 14 all professors were required to swear a new oath of allegiance. By taking such an oath, normally a routine occurrence on the accession of a new king, the professors were by implication renouncing allegiance to the constitution and revoking their earlier oath of 1833.

These political problems found the brothers deep in their usual scholarly work. They had been alert to the political unrest of 1830, since they habitually kept abreast of the news, but their family concerns and their research meant that their private interests outweighed political ones. Jacob was completing the fourth and last volume of his *German Grammar* and composing the preface:

When a wanderer over desolate heaths has borne the burden of the sun and the day and is going home in the twilight through narrow and winding garden paths, he takes his final steps, wiping the dust of his feet on the dew of the grass, with refreshed limbs and freed from care. Epilogues, which we like to set at the beginning of our books, are written in such cool comfort in order to give an account of what has been achieved, to make excuses for what has gone wrong, and to make up for general omissions. Often it is only between the hedges on the road home that we remember the reader, of whom I have meanwhile been thinking in silent meditation: let him now judge whether I may once more enjoy his tolerance. . . .

Filled with such modest and gentle thoughts, the brothers were psychologically unprepared for the blow that was to strike them. But the oath of allegiance to the king clearly implied disloyalty to their previous oath. Both had been trained as lawyers in Marburg, but they were concerned primarily with the moral problem, believing that no mortal man could release them from a sworn obligation. They reacted immediately and forcefully. Dahlmann, the professor of history, led a group which consisted of the brothers Grimm and professors Albrecht, Gervinus, Weber, and Ewald in drafting and signing a protest document which was delivered to the king on November 17. It reaffirmed their loyalty to the constitution of 1833 and rejected the implication that the king could absolve them of their pledge to the constitution. The document opened with "most humble remarks of some members of the national university concerning the royal decree of November 1." It was by no means an insolent letter, but rather a calm, firm statement of fact. As Wilhelm wrote just two days later to Ernst Freiherr von Canitz, the whole problem turned on the king's arbitrary action in revoking the constitution: "It is in the nature of the matter that a king cannot unilaterally revoke a basic law and release people from the oath to it with mere despotic power."

Wilhelm did develop some legal arguments to defend the protest, although he also admitted that the material sense of the constitution itself did not interest him. Jacob was more outspoken, writing Savigny that he was protesting as a matter of conscience, not for political reasons at all. He claimed that he did not care a whit for the constitution itself, and that he found "all modern liberalism repulsive"; but the honor of the university, and indeed of the whole of Hannover, was at stake. More than that, it was a matter of principle for *all* Germans—*tua res agitur*—and he reproached Havemann, who subsequently accepted Dahlmann's vacant chair, with his failure to see the moral and humane principles involved above and beyond personal advantage and political expediency. Wilhelm too insisted that he had not joined the liberals, and that he would not go over to those who supported "some liberal political party." All the brothers' letters of this period breathe a true conservatism in politics, reinforced by their attempts to place the whole emphasis on the moral aspects of the affair.

The famous protest, the "most humble remarks," was drawn up chiefly by Dahlmann, who emerged as the leader and prime mover during the initial protest and its first consequences in Göttingen. Jacob Grimm and the literary historian Gervinus were his principal supporters who helped draft the document. For a time there was no response and no action was taken. The king must have been puzzled at the rebellion and the tenor of the protest, which had made a moral issue out of what seemed to Ernst August a trivial matter well within his autocratic rights. Not only Ernst August but also all of Germany was surprised at the quarter from which the protest came—professors traditionally lectured, collected their stipends, and published learned articles while maintaining a profound political silence. On December 11 the king finally reacted, issuing an edict according to which all seven were relieved of their positions at the university. Dahlmann, Jacob Grimm, and Gervinus, as the ringleaders, were ordered to leave the kingdom within three days.

The court officials in Hannover had obsequiously submitted to the king's caprice. No citizens objected, and most of the faculty of the university acquiesced. The king, the court, and most of the faculty were astounded that seven professors—not by any means the most prestigious of the state's officials—should dare to question a royal edict. The faculty remained silent and passive; those who agreed in principle with the seven concealed their support. Some professors were even outraged by the actions of the protesters and publicly reviled them. The king had earlier made the pronouncement that he considered "eight hussars more valuable than the whole university."

The response of the students stands in cheering contrast to that of the community in general. They came out almost to a man in support of the seven professors, sensing the symbolic significance of the action better than their teachers and elders. Göttingen was put under martial law to prevent disorders; troops filled the city, and about fifty students were arrested. The pro-rector Bergmann, whose cowardice was unfortunately typical of most Hannoverian state officials, declared himself unable to cope with the situation. The university senate, failing to see the issues, could not act honorably. From his hunting castle of Rothenkirchen, the king suggested to Bergmann that he was expecting the homage of the university. The deans of the de-partments and the pro-rector hurried off to Rothenkirchen, where they were met by the demand that they take a stand toward the protest of the seven. With obsequious sycophancy they not only congratulated the king, as requested, but also gratuitously gave their monarch to understand that they opposed the protest. The university senate tacitly approved their actions, although it had empowered them only to bear congratulations.

Up until December 10 Dahlmann tried in vain to persuade the senate to correct the impression of supine subservience which had been created at Rothenkirchen and reported in the press. On the eleventh, the seven professors reaffirmed their protest. Since they had no support from any official quarter and troops stood ready to quell any student riots, the king had a free hand. He expelled the seven without appeal. Jacob, even more than Dahl-mann or Wilhelm Grimm, was incensed by the cowardice of his colleagues. He could neither understand their obtuse failure to see the principles at stake nor comprehend their flaccid moral stance. And he was especially bitter because of the silence in the theological faculty: "As guardians of faith and conscience, they are the ones who should have forcefully poured out their wrath and conquered their stupid doubts in mindfulness of Lutheran courage and constancy."

On the evening of December 15, several hundred students met in secrecy outside Göttingen to discuss developments. Clearer in their concerns and bolder in their actions than the feeble faculty, they adopted the following resolutions: that they would send an address of respect and approval to the seven, that they would boycott all lectures, that they would not reclaim lecture fees from the seven, and finally that the three who were being exiled should be given a triumphal farewell as they left Hannoverian territory. During the meeting the chief of police sent a message to warn the students against entering the town in large groups and stating firmly that he was prepared to use force. The dismissed professors for their part announced that they were willing to return lecture-fees to any students who so desired. Only six students, all from aristocratic families in Hannover, demanded repayment from Dahlmann. He never revealed their names, but the story became known, and the students in question suffered opprobrium for the rest of their Göttingen days.

The role of the pro-rector during the crisis was especially shameful. To avoid disturbances to protect his own compromised position, he suggested to Dahlmann that he leave Göttingen secretly and misinform the students as to the time of his departure. Dahlmann's famous proud answer was that his last words to the students would not be a lie. December 17 was the day when the three ringleaders were to leave; the police forbade the renting of horses and carriages to students on that day. Nevertheless about three hundred students walked the twenty miles to the border town of Witzenhausen. Here they greeted the three professors with cheers, although mounted police had arrived to keep watch. The students unharnessed the horses of the professors' coach and dragged it across the bridge over the river Werra into Hesse. Once across the border, they put on a festive lunch for the exiles, drinking toasts, singing songs, and wishing the three Godspeed.

The students did not forget the incident for months. The Christmas holidays were a quiet interlude, but when the university reopened there were demonstrations and protests by the students, who let the administration feel their displeasure. Bergmann, whom the students blamed for sacrificing the protesters to protect his own position, was their chief target. The windows of his house were smashed by stones, as Wilhelm reported with satisfaction, and he was made to feel his folly for some time to come. He vigorously denied that he had ever denounced the seven, and this may well be true. But his role was infamous, and his protestations were never accepted by those who stood on the side of the seven. Wilhelm was able to report in a letter to Jacob another episode that gave the exiles some comfort. A professor named Mühlenbruch gave a reception during the winter of 1838 at which he became angry at his guests' obvious sympathy for the seven protesters. He rose to his feet, reviled them, and gave a toast to their ruin along with all those who honored the *Dummkopf*. On the following day Mühlenbruch's lecture was filled to overflowing. As soon as he spoke to inquire what was going on, the room exploded with shouts, whistles, stamping of feet, and a general uproar. With cheers for the seven, the students drove Mühlenbruch from his lecture room.

Not all professors shared Mühlenbruch's views. Jacob noted with deep satisfaction that there were six "late protesters." The government received the news that the exiles had left along with the report that six professors had publicly declared that they did not wish to share the shame of the Rothenkirchen episode. Jacob praised their courage in taking a step that was sure to gain the hostility of the king, and he considered this late protest "our finest exoneration and splendid evidence of the university's spirit."

Moments of satisfaction and solace were rarer than times of depression and anger. Jacob's indignation, which for years never really ceased to burn within him, was based on moral considerations more than political principles, and he tried in vain to persuade not only his friends but the nation at large of his convictions. He did not entirely lose his sense of humor, however, and once wrote Wilhelm (who was still in Göttingen) during the winter of 1838 from Cassel that his main problems were the bitter cold and the lazy housemaids: "Altogether exile would have been more proper in the summer time." He did not always take himself too seriously, since he knew that man's fate is to be forgotten, and he realized that life would go on in Göttingen without him. But he never ceased to insist on the correctness of his moral choice in response to the voice of his conscience: "I shall not cease to love and respect Dahlmann, for whom his political conscience is the highest thing, but for me my private life is just as sacred or even more so. In the end our public purity and virtue are based on our private lives." Ugly rumors were circulated by government circles in Hannover in an attempt to denigrate the protesters. Wilhelm wrote in February about the rumor then being propagated that the basis of the dismissal was a quarrel over salary—the protesters had asked for an outrageous raise in pay. A Countess Münster spread the tale that Dahlmann had been promised ten thousand thalers for a book on the constitution and had protested in order to protect his fee. The Grimms' own sense of purity and virtue was not shared by everyone; their motives were questioned by many colleagues in Göttingen, probably, as Wilhelm suggested, in order to ease their own bad consciences. For Jacob it was entirely a matter of conscience: "Never, from childhood to now have I, nor has my brother, ever received any support from any government. This independence has steeled my soul, and it resists demands which would besmirch my conscience."

Sympathy for the exiled three came from all over Germany; funds were gathered and sent to them from private persons and from special committees formed to aid them. The response was so heartwarming that Wilhelm later wrote that it was the happiest period of his life. This is all the more significant since Wilhelm, still in Göttingen, had to bear the separation from his beloved brother. Jacob felt proudly independent, desiring no help in the form of funds but rather recognition for his principles. Dahlmann had difficulty in persuading Jacob to accept three hundred thalers from a committee in Leipsic, finally appealing to Jacob on the ground that his refusal would mean stifling an upsurge of patriotic fervor and rejecting well-meant help. While pledges and money came from all over Germany, the rulers of the many sovereign states viewed the dismissal from the university with coolness or silence. Saxony was an exception for a time, but even here promises were unfulfilled. Committees to help the exiles were formed in many cities—Leipsic, Königsberg, Kiel, and Hamburg being the most important. But German officialdom took the attitude that insubordination against a ruler should not be rewarded. For generations Prussian tolerance had made that state a refuge for people persecuted in their own countries, so that it was only natural to expect Prussia to help at this time. At first the Electress of Hesse requested a visit from Jacob, but apparently without offering aid of any kind. The King of Saxony announced that he was willing to receive all seven professors. This seemed a way out for them, since Hesse had allowed only Jacob Grimm, but not Dahlmann and Gervinus, the right of asylum in Hessian territory. Dahlmann and Gervinus spent the night after their dismissal at a tavern in Cassel, but had to leave the next day. Hesse, after all, was no less autocratic than Hannover.

Jacob wanted to exercise his rights as a member of the Academy of Sciences in Berlin, where he hoped for a brief time to be able to give public lectures. Jacob was hurt when Savigny did not suggest Berlin, where he had many friends and contacts and much influence in high places. But Savigny had suggested Munich, to which Jacob answered: "I wouldn't live in Bavaria at any price and they don't want me in Prussia." Savigny's suggestion sounded almost like an insult to the sensitive Jacob, who wondered why he was not wanted by his friends in Berlin. Savigny also seemed to take a cold, objective view of the whole affair, citing section and paragraph of law rather than warmly endorsing Jacob's moral courage. "He doesn't praise us and he doesn't blame us," Wilhelm wrote to Bettina von Arnim in dejection over Savigny's neutrality. Jacob's excited reactions threatened the longstanding friendship during the trying period of exile in Cassel. Savigny thought Jacob was too severe in his condemnation of his colleagues. He once referred to the brothers as "people innocently seduced," and his refusal to take sides—although he kept reassuring them of his constant friendship—irked them most of all. His coolness contrasted unfavorably with the fiery and fervent efforts of his sister-in-law Bettina von Arnim. For the next two years the brothers were confused and disappointed that their old friend and legal historian did not support them. In May 1840, Jacob wrote to Lachmann, complaining still that Savigny refused to take a stand. In July of the same year, he wrote Bettina, assuring her that he "had never ceased to believe in Savigny's continuing friendship."

Their friend Karl Lachmann, who had gone to Berlin from Königsberg, also failed the brothers. To Jacob's astonishment, Lachmann wrote him not to go to Berlin. Since Lachmann also taught German literature, and especially medieval literature and language, the ugly fear of professional competition crossed Jacob's mind. Von der Hagen, Bopp, and Graff also were in the same field, but their opposition made sense, since they had long been at odds with the Grimms. Lachmann felt the coolness of the brothers, especially of Jacob, and delicately referred to the "cloud" that had come between them, and apologized if it were his fault.

The timid and lukewarm responses of Jacob's friends in Berlin were all that was needed to reinforce his ingrained dislike of Prussia. Its official silence in the affair of the protest made him rather embittered about the state which he had hoped would lead Germany morally and spiritually toward union. In August 1838, he wrote Lachmann that he believed Prussia was doing nothing but trying to paper over and ignore the whole matter: "There must be an incredible degree of narrow-mindedness and selfishness among the Prussian officials, and I am content not to come any closer to them." He knew, of course, that Ernst August was the brother-in-law of King Friedrich Wilhelm III of Prussia. A Swiss friend, Lassberg, tried hard to get Jacob to go to the University of Zurich. Jacob had visited there in 1831, liked Switzerland, and much preferred Zurich to Berlin. He tried to persuade Wilhelm to join him in accepting, but was unable to convince him. Jacob's letter of refusal gave as the only reason his desire not to be separated from Wilhelm.

Dahlmann preferred Leipsic in friendly Saxony. He received an offer to give lectures at the university there, but just as he was writing to accept, he received a letter withdrawing the offer. In January 1838, the University of Kiel informed him that he was not wanted there either. Soon the exiles had to face the bitter fact that the ruling princes and kings preferred solidarity within their own ranks to the appointment of a protesting professor. It looked like a conspiracy on the part of the rulers. Ernst August hoped that the success of the conspiracy would force the seven to repent and come crawling back to Göttingen. After a few months he offered them an opportunity to return as guest lecturers, but on the condition that they recant and renounce any notion of publishing pamphlets of justification. Wilhelm weakened for a moment and considered the possibility. He had not left Göttingen, Dortchen and the children needed medical care, and his attitude throughout was less adamant than Jacob's. But Jacob wrote him immediately: "We must demonstrate steadfast agreement in the matter. The right of lecturing as social members of the university could be arbitrarily withdrawn and limited and gives us no security." It was clear that Wilhelm, who stayed in Göttingen until October 1838, needed security for his family. Jacob was not moved by any considerations, and was even proceeding to find a publisher for *Concerning My Dismissal*.

The historian Friedrich Christoph Dahlmann and his wife Luise had been a great comfort to the Grimms in their early days in Göttingen. They were among the first to welcome them, and they remained loyal through all the trials and tribulations of the years to come. Wilhelm once characterized Dahlmann as follows: "He is a little difficult to get started, but he has a free, lively, and individual mind and an open and honest heart." Jacob referred to him several times as his "most appealing and closest colleague." During the years of exile, the brothers were as concerned with his fate as with their own. They wrote Bettina in 1840 that Dahlmann needed an appointment as professor more than they did, "for he is made for teaching." Jacob had to wait almost three years, until November 1840, before he held a teaching position again. Later established in Berlin, the brothers' first thought was to secure a call to Berlin for Dahlmann, and they were most depressed by their failure. Dahlmann had responded to the conditional amnesty of Ernst August by demanding a restoration of his honor in a public declaration. This was patently impossible, and the King of Hannover made no further offers. So Dahlmann, "the soul and the leader of the protest," had to wait the longest of the seven for an appointment; it was 1842 before he obtained a professorship at the University of Bonn.

Georg Gottfried Gervinus, the third of the ringleaders, was a literary historian. Born in Darmstadt in 1805, he had been an instructor at Heidelberg before coming to Göttingen in 1835 as a professor. Jacob had reservations about him as a scholar when he first came to the university, believing that his history of German literature was good, but too "aristocratic," that is, that it neglected folk poetry. But he liked Gervinus personally, found him "of a good mind and lively spirit," and became quite intimate with him, although never so close as with Dahlmann. Jacob wrote Savigny in 1837: "He is modest in society, somewhat withdrawn, and has something in his face and voice that touches me. In the long run I think I shall like him better and his writings less." Gervinus's lectures on German literature represented competition in the Grimms' special field, but he was careful not to give offense and his behavior was always correct, even deferential. He had dedicated his literary history to Jacob, and years later Jacob dedicated his *History of the German Language* to him. His actions following the dismissal of the seven did not win the approval of the brothers in at least one episode. In March 1838, he visited the University of Heidelberg and addressed enthusiastic students and some townspeople, receiving an ovation in return. The police broke up the meeting, several heads were cracked, and sensationalism colored the whole event. In his address Gervinus stated: "It is true that we seven have sacrificed much in the eyes of the world. But it happened with cheerful courage and out of the purest convictions. My conscience made me take the step and will never regret it." Wilhelm's comment was that Gervinus had caused the trouble and should have avoided a university town like Heidelberg. Only two of the seven ever did return to Göttingen, Weber, the physicist and assistant of Gauss, and Ewald, although the last named had also written a protest at his dismissal.

The dismissal of the seven protesting professors from Göttingen was a political act of the greatest significance. Never before or since have German professors stood in the limelight to such a degree and received favorable reactions for their courage and their convictions. The whole affair is famous partly because it is unique; the right to protest against arbitrary authority is not generally considered a prominent civil right in German history. From Luther's "honor authority" to Bismarck's "calm is the first virtue of a citizen," the tradition of acquiescence has been fostered by intellectuals as much as by politicians. Jacob had high ideals for a university: it must be open to all intellectual currents and must deal openly and freely with all issues. For a time, until disillusionment set in, Jacob hoped that his experience at Göttingen would be a moral lesson for the nation: "To have had martyrs can help the university later more than restitution and a general forgetting of the matter now." Posterity did not share Jacob's sublime view of the university. Succeeding generations squandered the heritage of the Grimms in the field of academic freedom. Hitler was able to subvert the universities with almost effortless ease in the 1930's. But for many years every act, every publication by the brothers (and by Dahlmann and Gervinus too) was a political deed of the highest order, attracting attention in all the German states. They had a representational value like none possessed before or since by members of the German academic community. Even a birthday reception could become an affair with political overtones, as seen in the Grimms' life in Berlin. Neither brother enjoyed publicity, and both strove to avoid attracting attention from any source. Their essential lives were lived at their desks, and the privacy and silence of their study meant more than the praise or blame of the public. While in Göttingen Jacob had complained to Lachmann that he wished he were still a "private person" and not before a public every week. But from 1838 on, whatever they did or said was news.

Jacob started to write a document in defense of his stand in December 1837, but his *Concerning My Dismissal* was not finished until January 1838, when he had settled down in Cassel. It is the most aggressive, polemical diatribe he ever wrote. His complaints about the hardships of lecturing should not deceive the reader about his lofty concept of the teaching profession: "German universities, as long as their tested and excellent establishment remains, are exceedingly sensitive not only because of the students who come and go but also because of the carefully calculated qualities of the professors, and they respond easily to all that happens in the country, whether good or bad. If it were otherwise, they would cease to fulfill the purpose they have had hitherto. The open, unspoiled minds of youth demand that the teachers at every opportunity trace every question about conditions in life and the state back to its purest and most moral source and answer the question with honest truth. . . ."

Feeling injured and insulted as well as wronged, Jacob turned his wrath on his critics: "I neither lusted after applause nor did I blame when I acted as I had to; but raised against me are hateful voices which deny me wisdom and arrogant voices which note my lack of good sense and scoffing voices which are determined in advance to impute base and unworthy motives to me, just as the crows come flying to pick out the eyes of someone they consider to be dead." These are not the tones usually associated with state-appointed officials, whose main duty is to stay calm and worship authority. Jacob's pamphlet breathes anger, outrage, and resentment on every page. "Only the truth will endure, and even evil-minded persons or those who are weak and do not confess the truth aloud feel it secretly pulsing through them. The world is full of people who think what is right and teach it, but as soon as they must act are afflicted with doubts and faintheartedness. . . ." Jacob possessed a rich store of invective and commanded a prose of savage irony. His moral rigorism, lofty idealism, consciousness of purity of purpose, and righteous indignation are all eloquently expressed in what is perhaps his finest and surely his most impassioned prose. But even in his wrath he could not suppress his tendency to poetic figures and homely metaphors, so that the full scope of his marvelous control of language is brilliantly evidenced in the document. In the middle of a bitter diatribe, there are idyllic passages: "With inner joy I have drunk at the silent springs of our middle ages, and they seemed no swamp to me; I sought to enter the rude forests of our ancestors, harkening to their noble speech and pure tales. The old freedom of our race did not remain concealed from me, nor the fact that it nurtured an ingenious and heartfelt faith before the blessings of Christianity came to it. . . . I feel that I am part of all that exists. . . ."

In private letters the same tones may be heard. Religious notes occur often in his references to the affair in the first months of exile in Cassel: "We acted deliberately and as far as this was possible for us intelligently, but with the determination which the feeling of being right gives one. . . . God in Heaven and our conscience challenged us to do it. But whatever decision God may finally permit in this affair, no one will come out free from guilt." There were those who blamed the seven for the troubles the university experienced in the following years. The university's reputation was damaged by the loss of the seven and the student riots. Official slander failed in its purpose, since the truth was so easily accessible. When the pamphlets of Dahlmann and Jacob were finally published in 1838 in Basel, they sold well all over Germany. They were banned in many states, but this did not prevent their spread. Student enrollment at Göttingen dropped quickly from nine hundred to seven hundred, and many foreigners stayed away. For a time only second-rate professors could be appointed as replacements.

Publication of Jacob's document was delayed for months. Since others wished to publish in order to justify their act, a common document was considered for a time, but the suggestion was dropped in view of the difficulties with the censors. Dahlmann, who kept in touch with Jacob almost daily during the weeks after their dismissal, encountered the same obstacles. When both finally succeeded in having their documents published in Basel, their feelings with regard to German politicians were but little assuaged. They were, however, both surprised and pleased to see their pamphlets sell so rapidly and well throughout Germany, and they felt that this was a blow to the conspiracy of silence maintained by the state governments. Friendly responses came in from Austria and Switzerland, the aid committees continued to support them, and there were many encouraging and heartwarming incidents.

Jacob never really recovered from the events of 1837–38; all his remaining years he had to live with the disillusionments he experienced. Scars appeared in his friendships with people such as Lachmann and Savigny, and even with the ever helpful and zealous Bettina. As late as 1848, he recalled the events with bitterness, harking back to the days of exile, the failure of friends, and the hostility of governments. Wilhelm never forgot or forgave either, and he was just as disturbed by the aloof or neutral attitudes of supposed friends as Jacob. Jacob, however, became hypersensitive in his relations with people, quick to take offense, and suspicious of others' motives. After Göttingen he was less trusting and less open, and he tended more and more to conceal his warmth and friendliness under a mask of cool, impersonal distance. He never became really unapproachable, but the dismissal from the University of Göttingen marked a profound change in his whole inner life as well as his professional career.

✣ XIII ✣

Exile in Cassel

WHEN WILHELM, DORTCHEN, and the children returned to Cassel in October 1838, the family was united again, but in a troubled condition and with an atmosphere of uncertainty and depression prevailing. The brothers had never been truly happy in Göttingen. Even the usually good-natured Wilhelm, always ready to find the bright side of things, wrote disparagingly of the interlude in Hannoverian territory, asserting that he had gone there without enthusiasm and left without regret. But because of the circumstances the brothers' relations with their best friends became strained and difficult. Much of the trouble was imagined by the hypersensitive Jacob, who thought he saw disparagement in every letter that was not rhapsodic in praise of his action. The fancied slights were quite real to him in this period of morose depression, anxiety, and lack of purpose. Wilhelm's troubles were ever present, for Dortchen contracted pneumonia again late in 1838, and for a time she was seriously ill. Not until February 1839 was she able to help in the household again. The children fortunately enjoyed good health, and were a great joy to Uncle Apapa as well as to Wilhelm.

Some cheer came into their lives with a visit from Bettina von Arnim, who arrived in October just after Wilhelm's return from

Göttingen. The fiery lady was not one to be idle in time of trouble. She immediately made the brothers' professional careers her first concern and displayed enormous energy if not consummate tact in promoting their cause with anyone who would listen and many who did not wish to. Jacob, obviously overwhelmed, wrote Dahlmann that she was "an overflowing fountain," but he praised her loyalty and friendship. Wilhelm responded by renewing his dedication of the *Fairy Tales* to her, and the fourth edition (1840) contains sincere words of appreciation. Jacob was impressed by her tirelessness and restless energy. Bettina's greatest wish was to establish the brothers in Berlin. To this end, she addressed letters and appeals to people high and low in the city, government officials, and important university staff. Jacob and Wilhelm had to calm her down and persuade her to proceed more tactfully. They began to take a more realistic view of the political situation, and realized that nothing could be forced. Moreover Jacob felt more reluctant with every passing day to accept a call to Berlin, preferring not to enter Prussian territory, whether invited or not. In August 1838, he wrote to Dahlmann: "The call should have come immediately; now that Prussia has been so pusillanimous and has suppressed our cause, I feel too proud and defiant to devote my services to it." But Bettina had no scruples or inhibitions, and she soon embarrassed the brothers with her eager and reckless activity. Her zeal knew no bounds, and unfortunately did not stop short of intrigue. She had heard of Lachmann's hesitancy in summoning the brothers to Berlin, interpreted this as double-dealing, and started a cabal against him. She even denounced him to Jacob and Wilhelm in such strong terms that they rose to his defense.

Lachmann accused Bettina of being a troublemaker, and all the while he was blaming her he begged the brother's understanding and tolerance in touching terms. He had written immediately and wholeheartedly supported their protest, but apparently never understood the true cause of their displeasure. For a time during 1838 neither brother would write to Lachmann, so that he corresponded with Dortchen. As was nearly always the case Wilhelm was less rigid and strict, being less volatile than Jacob anyway. But his anger was finally aroused, and he came slowly and reluctantly to the reconciliation. The breach was healed in the spring of 1840, when Lachmann wrote a warm and touching letter asking most sincerely and humbly for their understanding. Such an entreaty they could not resist; Jacob answered immediately in May, and the reconciliation was complete. Lachmann, a gentleman of fine character, also defended Savigny's position, explaining the stand of those in Berlin since they knew the situation and the political impossibility of calling the brothers in 1838. Both sides were relieved when the quarrel was over. In spite of all their differences, the Grimms liked Lachmann and appreciated him as a man and as a scholar, for there were many traits held in common.

Only scholars as totally dedicated to work as the Grimm brothers could have continued research during these trying years in Cassel. But neither exile, several trips by Jacob in search of a new home (in June and July of 1838, Jacob visited Kissingen, Würzburg, Bamberg, Erlangen, Nuremberg, Leipsic, Jena, Weimar, and Dresden), worry about the future, Dortchen's illness, nor any other hindrance prevented them from carrying out their normal routine. Jacob edited and published in 1838, together with Johann Andreas Schmeller, *Latin Poems of the Tenth and Eleventh Centuries*. The poems were all written in Germany by German authors, and one of them at least, the *Lay of Waltharius*, was quite well known. Jacob's interest in the poems stemmed from his concern for filling out the gaps in the history of German literature before the flowering of German-language literature in the late twelfth century. Wilhelm, who had been devoting himself more and more exclusively to medieval studies, edited the *Song of Roland* in Middle High German recension; only fragments of it had ever appeared before. Needless to say it was edited critically, with variants and annotations quite in the spirit of Lachmann. Meanwhile Jacob continued work on his *German Grammar* during 1839, and the volume appeared early in 1840. He reworked the entire book, making really significant changes in his presentation of phonology. At the same time he worked on his *Weistümer* (judicial sentences serving as precedents in old German law), continuing in the same channels as his *German Legal Antiquities* (1828). The *Weistümer,* with its many descriptions of old legal practices and common-law judgments, became an important source book for German legal history. By the end of 1839 two volumes were ready to be printed; the second volume was published first, but by early 1840 both were available, although Jacob worried about the sales because of the inverted sequence. In 1839 Wilhelm published a critical text of *Wernher vom Niederrhein,* and in 1840 Konrad of Würzburg's *Goldene Schmiede.*

❧ XIV ❧

The German Dictionary

GERMANY OWES its world-famous dictionary to the dismissal from Göttingen of the two greatest Germanists of the early nineteenth century. The *German Dictionary* is one of the great lexicographical undertakings of all time. Its influence beyond the borders of Germany has been very significant; the format and principles of the great *Oxford English Dictionary,* for example, owe much to the Grimms' pioneering work. The idea could never have been entertained by the brothers except for the enforced period of unemployment following their dismissal. In view of the many publications they completed during the period of intense work in Cassel, it was scarcely a time of leisure, but rather one of uncertainty and financial problems. During the early spring of 1838 Jacob began to form the notion of a complete dictionary of the German language as a project that would support them financially as well as give their work a focus. At first neither brother suspected that with this monumental enterprise they were entering upon what was to become their major life work. At the beginning, while the idea was still a tentative inspiration whose scope they had not yet imagined, they were confident that they could find financial support "for a few years" and a satisfying field of work along with their numerous other interests.

In March 1838, Jacob sounded out Lachmann, suggesting a

"detailed and comprehensive dictionary of the German language," but adding that he felt little urge to start the project while still involved in other plans. By August Jacob's complaints about not having finished the *Grammar* grew silent. He announced to Lachmann that he and Wilhelm had made a firm decision and were going ahead with the dictionary. "The broadly conceived plan of the German dictionary can grant us independence and support, and once the work is started and has some success, I shall renounce any appointment, be it ever so honorable, in order to devote all my strength to the work. . . ." Late in the same month the brothers made a public announcement of their project in the *Leipsiger Allgemeine Zeitung:*

> It is one of the gifts of human nature to be able to extract sweetness from bitterness and gain new fruit from privation. Jacob and Wilhelm Grimm, afflicted at the same time by the same fate, after long and fruitless waiting for a German state to appoint them to some service, have found the courage to insure and fortify their own future. They are undertaking a great German dictionary, which the Weidmann bookshop will publish, as a difficult, far-ranging work which they could not have begun if they had the burdens of ordinary business duties. The dictionary is supposed to contain the infinite wealth of our fatherland's language from Luther to Goethe, a wealth which no one has yet surveyed or measured. All significant writers will be entered completely, the rest will be excerpted; the result will be astonishing. All words with their meanings, all idioms and proverbs are to be verified by their sources; alphabetical arrangement is the most suitable and easiest here. The dictionary of Adelung, the only one worth mentioning among all the predecessors, has fallen far behind the great amount of material and also rests on an insufficient grammatical basis, which, as is obvious, can only be an historical basis. It is only now that the laws of all older German languages have been discovered and presented in their various epochs, now that an Old High German dictionary is nearing completion and a Middle High German one will soon follow,

that our living language can be grasped with full certainty and set down in all its forms of appearance.

Six or seven closely printed volumes, they thought, would suffice. The real magnitude of the task had not dawned on them, and several years were to pass before they realized that it would never be finished during their lifetimes. From the first they counted on collaborators who would read and make excerpts for them. To Gervinus, who gently but firmly refused to help, Jacob wrote: "The work is intended to give an account of all that our written language has achieved in four hundred years. We would never have had the courage for such a difficult work while in Göttingen; naturally we count on collaborators in providing material. . . . Publication cannot begin before 1840. But the deeper I look into the undertaking, the more it attracts me, there will be some surprising and many fruitful, lasting results from the work, even if the working over of the material is not completely successful." Gervinus congratulated Jacob on the new enterprise: "Future times will honor you doubly for having answered a wrong done to you by your fatherland with a new favor, with a work that everywhere else is the result of princely or academic efforts."

The optimism that the brothers felt in the early days of planning the dictionary contrasts vividly with their later complaints. Wilhelm, even more than Jacob, seemed revived in spirit and renewed in strength as he began collecting material. Early in 1839 he wrote Lachmann: "I am not oppressed by the fact that I devote a part of every day to the dictionary. It is going better than I thought; with a little practice one makes fairly rapid progress; of course I know very well that the real work is still to come and demands better powers than are needed for this splitting of wood." To Dahlmann he wrote in much the same vein, again using the figure of "chopping wood for a few hours a day," as if it were a boring chore, but the enthusiasm and pleasure in his work revealed in these letters are refreshing after the months of illness and depression. By the end of the year his remarks grew more cautious, as the realization that it would take several years of sustained and tedious labor made his predictions more sober. Even as collaborators were found—by the fall of 1839 Jacob could count on over fifty—and the work began to take shape, Jacob joined Wilhelm in feeling that it was a task "which will lie heavy on our shoulders for many years."

Disappointments with the contributions from collaborators became a feature of the undertaking. Jacob soon was complaining that he spent more time in corresponding with contributors than in his own research. Some of the task force engaged in the project were lazy and unreliable; others were apparently unable to follow instructions and indulged their own whimsies. In December 1839, Jacob wrote Dahlmann that the contributions were coming in so slowly that no progress in working up the material could be made. Both Jacob and Wilhelm spent enormous effort in trying to manage the process of collecting and collating material. Wilhelm went into great detail, even prescribing the size of the cards on which the notations and excerpts were to be made. "The word must be underlined every time," he wrote to his contributors, but often he had to search whole letters to find what he wanted. Late in 1839 Wilhelm wrote the poet Uhland, gently pleading for his help and pointing out that in a year the number of collaborators had doubled. He spoke of the project as one "which is in its basic idea a general concern of the whole nation." The brothers' persuasive cajoling finally attracted ninety contributors. Too often, however, the helpers turned to the same sources, over and over again, whereas the brothers wished to record the varying literary uses from Luther to Goethe. They often preferred secondary authors, noting that some famous writers like Schiller were "word-poor" and did not have a rich or creative vocabulary. Style and message were of no importance in themselves, since what counted was significant and revealing usage of individual words—a notion that did not immediately become clear to many of their assistants. From 1840 on querulous tones and gloomy predictions dominate all references to the dictionary. But they still had no idea that almost sixteen years would elapse from the signing of the contract (October 1838) to the publication of the first volume in March 1854.

The notion of compiling a German dictionary was not an original thought of the brothers. The first suggestion came from the Leipsic publishers Reimer and Haupt, their chief purpose being to provide income for the exiles in the early months after their dismissal. Both Jacob and Wilhelm reacted with skepticism, and neither showed much enthusiasm or even interest at first. They finally took the offer in the spirit of the publishers, viewing it as a financial problem and not intending to let it interfere with other projects. (Later they came to believe that dictionary-making was a matter of honor.) For several months a move to Leipsic was weighed and tossed back and forth in their discussions. By August 1838, Jacob had decided against Leipsic, having become quite disillusioned with Saxony's treatment of Dahlmann. And by this time also a few months' thought about the plan had awakened his genuine interest. Both he and Wilhelm began to consider it with growing involvement and by mid-summer were eager to start. In August, Jacob wrote to Bettina: "If we live to see the end of the difficult work (after six, eight, ten years), then it will bring us more fame and advantage than if we had to learn anew and strain at some Prussian university." Jacob's resentment of Prussia was not easily mollified; in April 1839, he refused an offer of financial aid for the dictionary from the Prussian Academy of Sciences, maintaining that he wished to be independent and not accept aid from a hostile source. He knew, of course, that the offer came about because of the kind offices of Savigny, but he remained firm, preferring pride to a concession to Prussia.

As work and plans progressed, the original thoughts on the subject began to change. The idea of including the vocabulary of German from Luther to Goethe was soon modified as Jacob proceeded with his etymologies. Jacob's love for philology could not be suppressed for the sake of dry lexical listing. "Etymology is the salt or spice of the dictionary without which its food would remain tasteless," he later wrote in the preface. Thus he gradually moved back in time to include Middle High German, and then even further to Old High German. Luther and Goethe remained the prominent figures for New High German, but they soon ceased to set the limits of research. The upper boundary was abandoned as early as 1839, when Jacob shifted from "up to Goethe" to "up to today." Jacob was the dominant figure in all the work on the dictionary, setting the pace and prescribing the principles. Wilhelm concurred and cooperated, but it is Jacob's voice that one hears most often and most clearly.

Since their procedure marked a new departure in lexicography, they were at pains to explain and justify their methods. "Words demand examples, and examples source references, without which their best power would be lost," they wrote in the preface. Successive examples would produce, Wilhelm believed, a "natural history" of the individual words in their context. Although they carefully avoided anything that could be termed normative or prescriptive, they did have a strong educational urge to record and thereby preserve "beautiful old words" that otherwise might die out: "All words of beauty and power since Luther's time may be brought out again at the right time and used anew; the success and effectiveness of the dictionary is to be seen in the fact writers use it." Jacob used strong invective in discussing the miserable orthography of his time, expressing the fond wish that German spelling would soon be reformed. He noted with regret that the Germans were stubborn in clinging to clumsy and cluttered ways of writing their language. Most deplorable of all was the custom of capitalizing nouns, an aberration against which he inveighed for years. He himself wrote without capitals except for place names and personal names, just as in English. Wilhelm followed his example for several years, but he was as usual less rigid and kept backsliding. Very early during the planning period, Jacob was warned that arbitrary reforms in spelling would make the book impossible to sell. His publishers were aghast at the mere suggestion of reformed spelling. They insisted on the current orthographic standard, regardless of its faults. Scholars too, among them friends like Gervinus, wrote to warn him against introducing his own notions of spelling in a book which readers after all would have to use according to alphabetical listing. Jacob finally yielded reluctantly, but he never missed an opportunity to plead for reform or to point out absurdities in current practices.

The Grimms' first notions of who their audience might be turned out to be wishful thinking. They originally had in mind not a narrow circle of scholars, but, as in the days of the *Fairy Tales,* the whole nation. They hoped that it would become a household book, one which people would browse in and read for pleasure. They intended it not only for writers, and scholars of course, but also for the widest possible reading public—the whole range of users in Germany and abroad wherever German was a living language. For this reason they also included some regionalisms. But the public did not respond. Only 4,000 copies of Volume I were sold in the first year. Soon the sales dipped to 2,000 a year, and after World War II to 1,300. The very virtues which Jacob and Wilhelm saw in their endeavor were what limited the sales; they did not say what was correct usage. Only from careful and extensive reading of long columns could the proper usage be inferred, and this is one of the presumed causes for the dictionary's failure to sell. The price was very high, and the slow pace of production was discouraging: one hundred and six years is a long time to wait for the completion of a reference work, for the dictionary, in thirty-two volumes, was not finally finished until 1960.

They planned generously and broadly in all respects, both brothers being consciously liberal in the material they included. Thoughts of the public to be reached entered into their first ideas of how to proceed. Thus they planned from the beginning to include words from the specialized or technical vocabularies of hunters, artisans, and tradesmen that were not too limited by dialect or province. They even made concessions that belied their usual prudery, for they planned to include obscene words "that a writer might use in stress or a comedian could not get along without. . . . There is no word in the language that is not somewhere the best one and in its proper place. . . . All words are in themselves pure and innocent. . . . The dictionary is not a book of morals, but a scientific book." Thus they wrote in the preface.

Jacob's tics, prejudices, and predilections, from his dislike of Gothic script to his taste for etymologies, were forcefully and emphatically stated on every page of the preface. His likes, dislikes, and idiosyncrasies made up an entertaining, even disproportionate part of the book. But of course there was also much solid history and many fine insights into the nature and growth of the language. And there were good suggestions for improving the language.

The standard literary language in Germany is constantly being enriched by words from the many dialects. The brothers took this into account, operating on the principle that dialect words were to be included if the words had ever been used by a reputable writer, since *any* word once used by a good author, even if provincial, had entered the language and therefore was to be recorded. Regarding words of foreign origin, the brothers, who were neither purists nor reformers, were cautious and sparing in listing them wherever there was the slightest doubt. They were also, unfortunately, quite inconsistent—the word *Cultur,* for example, is missing. But their methods, although clear enough in principle and generally adhered to consistently, were quite flexible in application. Jacob wrote to Savigny, a year after the contract, that they intentionally had formed no fixed plan, and that the rules of procedure should emerge from the practical work itself: "We do not want to tie our hands in advance. Natural tact must be used here, and we must console ourselves with the hope that we shall succeed in infusing the enormous mass of material with an intellectual element." In practice this noble ideal had its disadvantages, however, since the dictionary differs in its approach from word to word. There is a total lack of guidelines. Nearly every word has a slightly different format and treatment— sometimes grammatical interest prevails, sometimes the historical development of differing meanings, and often the idiomatic uses or the special usages and vocabulary that derive from law or other fields. This is delightful and entertaining to someone who is browsing, but an added difficulty for those who wish to use the dictionary as a ready reference book. The definitions and the development of a word's "meaning" occur frequently quite by chance, although of course implicit in the rich material presented, so that the reader must be his own historian and proceed without anything to guide him in semantic nuances. But the rewards are great for whoever wishes to make the effort. And the brothers did succeed in enlivening the "enormous mass of material with an intellectual element."

❧ XV ❧

The Call to Berlin

FOR WHAT SEEMED to them a long time, from 1838 until 1840, the brothers entertained hopes of being called to the University of Berlin as professors. Jacob protested too much—he wanted the honor as a vindication of the path he had chosen in Göttingen. Wilhelm said much less about the whole problem, neither damning Prussia so severely nor stressing his desire to go to Berlin. In the arrangements that were to come, it was always Jacob who took the initiative, made the key plans and decisions, and carried on the correspondence. During the two years of exile in Cassel, they often heard rumors; they waited and worked and wrote letters which expressed their disappointment, but there was no call. Savigny, Lachmann, and the indefatigable Bettina von Arnim all worked long and hard behind the scenes, trying to influence people at court and at the university. Bettina wrote to Alexander von Humboldt, the older brother of Wilhelm von Humboldt, urging him to use his influence. He in turn approached the Minister of Education, Eichhorn, who had known and liked Jacob in Paris. Immediately after the death of the King of Prussia, Wilhelm III, in June 1840, Eichhorn took steps to bring about an invitation to Berlin. The new King of Prussia, Friedrich Wilhelm IV, who had already expressed kindly opinions of the brothers, was receptive to suggestions.

Friedrich Wilhelm IV, often called "the Romanticist on the throne," raised the hopes of all the liberals at his accession in 1840. As crown prince he had been known as a patron of the arts and letters, a reputation he strove to maintain. He started his reign by decreeing an amnesty for many political prisoners, reinstating in Bonn the famous poet and democrat Ernst Moritz Arndt, freeing many members of the persecuted students' associations, and letting Dahlmann accept a call to Bonn. Friedrich Wilhelm's first actions as ruler won him acclaim and support from many groups. But he also possessed many of the faults of a Romantic epigone, and his vague and mystical notions of sovereignty were founded on a sincere faith in patriarchal monarchy. He felt that a constitution was superfluous, if not actually harmful, since "a mere piece of paper" could prevent true communal contact between the sovereign and his people. The favorable auguries of his beginnings were soon forgotten; he not only failed to live up to his early promise, but ended his reign mentally disturbed and remote from a reality he could not master. On the positive side his early reign did attract many scholars and artists to Berlin, and it is to his credit that the Grimms' invitation to the University of Berlin came from him.

Immediately after the new king had assumed the throne, Savigny wrote to Jacob, suggesting that he take advantage of his rights as a member of the Academy of Sciences and come to Berlin to lecture at the university, a privilege which full members enjoyed. Wilhelm too was soon made a full member so that he could lecture. But Jacob was still sensitive and proud; he had waited too long to "smuggle himself into Berlin" or "enter by the back door," as he expressed it. He was determined to wait for an official invitation, since he felt that only such a move would exonerate him from any suspicions with regard to the affair of 1837. Prussia's attitude in those trying days rankled yet in his mind and, still hypersensitive, he wanted full satisfaction. Many years before, in 1818, Jacob had written Savigny that he had a "secret dislike of Berlin, which may be blind and unjust." In 1837 he wrote Wilhelm that he would ten times rather go to Zurich than

Berlin. But Savigny was acting in good faith, confident that if Jacob were once in Berlin all else would solve itself. In August 1840, he sent his wife to Cassel to sound out the brothers. Part of their reluctance to go along with Savigny's suggestion may have stemmed from their dislike of Frau Savigny, whom they considered a bit eccentric and whose aristocratic pose offended them. In addition both brothers were annoyed at the slow progress of affairs in Berlin and were irritated by rumors and newspaper reports that were ambiguous and misleading; of course they could not know the true state of affairs. Inwardly they were torn between their desire to settle their problems with a firm appointment and an instinctive dread of Berlin. Jacob had once said that Würzburg was a city of the proper size; Berlin and Vienna were too big. "An oversized city brings a lot of vices with it and acquires arrogance like the Imperial guards." Going to Berlin also meant lecturing, and this too was something which neither brother really avidly desired. Jacob had written Savigny in 1838 that he wished to be neither a librarian nor a professor, but just a scholar: "For over thirty years I have led a sour enough life in all sorts of service, and now I feel it much more congenial to use my remaining powers in something that will be somewhat more useful to the world than my accomplishments in a professorship."

Jacob's pride and independence asserted themselves to an unusual degree in the years of his exile. To Lachmann he wrote in May 1840: "My nature is such that I have always learned less through association and teaching than by myself." This is a very correct self-assessment; as usual, Jacob saw himself most clearly. It was, however, not the time for such a remark and must be counted as a lapse in Jacob's sense of tact. The argument that Wilhelm had children who might need financial security had no validity for Jacob, who continued in the same letter: "As for Wilhelm's children, heaven will not abandon them, just as it has not abandoned us, and they will have to help themselves as we helped ourselves, every future opens up immeasurable prospects, and the anxious worry for one's heirs is futile in all its calculations. Poverty and deprivation are a spur, whereas in the fat of wealth noble seeds often die."

The resolution of all their difficulties came in November 1840. On the second of the month, Eichhorn wrote Jacob announcing that it was the king's pleasure that they should come to Berlin. The document ended with the words: "His Majesty the King has esteemed your meritorious achievements in the field of linguistic research, belles lettres, and history for years, and His Highness has thus expressed the desire that you be put in the position of completing the great and very difficult task which you have set yourself in the preparation of a complete critical dictionary of the German language here in the capital with leisure, freedom from care, and with the use of all the aid and support available." Jacob received the king's very gracious and generous letter on November 8, and immediately wrote to Eichhorn to accept: "We accept the summons of the King, to whom the longing hope of all Germans far beyond the borders of Prussia is directed, with gratitude and joyous hope. Our lives are on the decline. We strive for nothing but the opportunity to devote our remaining days to the achievement of the work which relates to the language and history of our beloved fatherland. The magnanimity of the King will provide us with the necessary leisure." On the same day he also wrote Bettina to thank her, and the letters of the next few days breathe the spirit of relief and gratitude he deeply felt. Bettina wrote triumphantly: "For my friends I have forged a sword in fire, and I have not been afraid to wield it with my own hands."

In the end, when things were finally resolved, previous resentments and doubts were forgotten, for they were going at last to a situation unlike any they had experienced before. They were offered a well-paid sinecure in the city that was rapidly becoming an intellectual and artistic center where many of their friends were already resident. Since no professorship in German language and literature was open, they were invited to give lectures at the university by reason of their membership in the Academy of Sciences. Thus they were free scholars, who could lecture if they so desired

—quite literally required to do nothing but pursue their own studies while being paid by the Prussian state. The combination of complete freedom and financial well-being was too much to resist. But even victory did not immediately soften Jacob. In 1841 he was still complaining, writing to Savigny to protest the form that the announcement had taken in the press, and that he had sought nothing from Prussia. Not easily assuaged, Jacob could be as tenacious over a presumed wrong as he was firm and constant in research. His last words to Savigny on the subject were that he would have been much happier if he had been called to Berlin because of his actions in Göttingen and not for the sake of his presumed "scientific value."

Early in December Jacob set out in cold weather to look for lodgings in the Prussian capital. His arrival in Berlin was accompanied by ill omens that might have deterred a superstitious person. He reported to Wilhelm:

> Here in Berlin a little adventure awaited me. At the exchange I immediately took a carriage to the house of the Meusebachs, the street was easy to find, but the number difficult, because in the moonlight the shadows were all the deeper and no numbers could be made out. After much stumbling about and inquiring of night watchmen the house was found, my baggage unloaded, and I began to ring boldly. But not a soul appeared and no light was visible. I carried on this way for about half an hour, until someone downstairs finally woke up, opened, and at my questioning answered that the Meusebachs did live here. I therefore went up two flights of stairs, where things were locked up again, and rang again; everyone seemed however to be hard asleep or deaf. So I sat on the steps until six o'clock, until there was finally a flicker of light on the second floor, which I then approached; an unknown man opened up and merely said that the President's wife [Frau Meusebach] seemed to be home, but that she was alone without servants, and that a cleaning lady would not come until the morning. Meanwhile he invited me in friendly fashion

to enter his room, where he served me coffee, brought me a newspaper, and kept me until eight o'clock. When Frau Meusebach
awoke, everything was resolved at once, for she had heard no
ringing, and she received me most cordially, took me into my
room that was all prepared for me, and where I have been asleep
until now when I report this all to you. . . . Bettina is going to
come at noon to eat with us. . . .

After this awkward start, Jacob proceeded to a long series of
receptions and visits with friends as well as important people
eager to meet him. His fame had preceded him; at times he felt it
was a mixed blessing, since he had hoped to return to Cassel
within a few days, but receptions and social engagements occupied much time and energy. Before he left, he was received by
the king in a gracious interview. Finding an apartment that would
offer workrooms for himself and Wilhelm and be close enough to
school for Wilhelm's children took him well into the Christmas
holidays. The weather was cold and windy, and Jacob walked
about Berlin's icy streets for days, trying to find a suitable place for
the family. With the help of Bettina, he located a large house,
Lennéstrasse No. 8, with ten rooms and a balcony, that was only
twenty minutes' walk from a school, and in a quiet section.

Jacob and Wilhelm, about to become pensioners of the Prussian government, had lived most of their lives with inadequate
salaries and had just spent two years without positions of any
kind. The amount of their pension had not been finally settled at
the time of Jacob's trip to Berlin. At the suggestion of Hassenpflug, who had previously been dismissed from Hessian service and was now a member of the High Court in Berlin, the king's
original offer had been two thousand thalers. Jacob made discreet
inquiries of Eichhorn about a possible increase, and the fiery Bettina entered the lists with her persuasive rhetoric. The Prussian
government was more generous than their brother-in-law, and the
Grimms, by special order of January 11, 1841, received three
thousand thalers jointly and the sum of five hundred thalers for

their moving expenses. Hannover protested Jacob's appointment, but the protest was rejected, although the King of Prussia was the nephew of the King of Hannover.

Even while the negotiations were going on, the brothers were able to complete considerable work in Cassel before moving to Berlin. Jacob was busy reworking parts of his *Grammar* and the first volume of *Legal Precedents (Weistümer)*, while Wilhelm completed the fourth edition of the *Fairy Tales*. Some work was done for the projected *Dictionary*, but Jacob was already writing that its success was very doubtful and that it was becoming an ever greater burden. Collaborators continued to send in excerpts and the correspondence with them became an increasing chore, most of which Jacob bore. Nevertheless they were able to leave Hesse with some sense of accomplishment.

In March 1841, Jacob and Wilhelm, with Dortchen and the children, left Cassel again, eleven years after their move to Göttingen. Months later Wilhelm wrote Dahlmann, describing the last days in Cassel and their start to Berlin:

> On the twenty-fifth of February the final break-up in our home began. . . . It was a hard task to order our affairs, to choose what was to be taken along and pack everything. In addition Jacob began to complain of pressure in his chest again, and could not leave his room for three weeks. Dortchen's illness began to become serious again, and she had to stay in bed for almost a week and leave the packing of her things to other people who kindly took pity on us. Not until a few days before our departure were both tolerably well restored, and these days were full of outer disturbances and inner emotion, for it was after all hard for us to leave Hesse, and we received many a proof of love and sympathy. . . . We have been received in friendly fashion everywhere. Minister Eichhorn gives the impression of an honest, sensible, even intellectually alert man, and he spoke without restraint. . . . Humboldt is among those who speak out openly and with calm firmness about the Hannoverian affair, and has, it seems to me, a firm character.

Reminders of Göttingen pursued them even in Berlin. Both Jacob and Wilhelm would have liked to have gone to Marburg and thus remain in Hesse, but despite an effort all the university's plans were frustrated by the Prince-Regent of Hesse, who was loyal in his way to his close relative, the King of Hannover. Leaving Hesse was difficult, and regrets and doubts beset them again when they actually left the corner of the earth they always considered home. Their native land had never requited their loyalty and love, for in Hesse they had been shabbily treated for twenty-five years and then grudgingly received as exiles from Göttingen. But their hearts were Hessian, and they were very conscious of having to leave behind the graves of their mother and sister, as well as living friends and countless memories.

In Berlin they were not entering a small university town as total strangers, but were coming to the capital city of a powerful kingdom as honored citizens invited by the king. They were eagerly received by old friends, prominent people of the capital, and were feted by the king himself. There were, however, also petty discomforts in the move itself. When they finally arrived in Berlin with all their baggage, they found the house not ready for them; they camped out among their belongings for weeks before Dortchen was strong enough to organize the household.

Minister of Education Eichhorn and Alexander von Humboldt were the first to greet them officially and assure them of the abundant good will that awaited them in Berlin. Since they were free scholars unattached to any specific ministry, Wilhelm wrote directly to the king to request an audience and an opportunity to express their thanks in person. After a short wait they were given a brief and cordial audience in the king's private quarters. He greeted the famous brothers with sincere warmth and friendliness, saying that he was glad they had come and repeating that they were welcome in Prussia. Their impression of him was very favorable, and they came away convinced of his benevolence. To Gervinus, Wilhelm wrote that he was able to enjoy the quiet of their new quarters, which were in an area inhabited mostly by scholars and members of the government and therefore called in jest "le quartier latin." But the new freedom was what he stressed most of all: "Our personal position here is as happy as we could wish, full freedom and yet also the opportunity to be active at the university. We are grateful for that. We want to live as withdrawn as possible and hope to be able to. The impression which life here makes on me is just as I imagined it. The people are nice, friendly, and engaging, but I can't say that I've found many to whom I would open my heart."

Even before leaving Cassel, Jacob had announced lectures at the university, and his desire to deliver them on time was a factor in their mid-March departure for the Prussian capital. On April 30, 1841, Jacob gave his first lecture in Berlin on one of his favorite topics—German legal antiquities. His introductory remarks made it clear that he had a different method and approach from that which the students were used to, and he emphasized that he wished to deal with the surviving documents and evidence for their own sake. After the methodological exordium, he continued: "My purpose is in equal measure a practical one, for what could be more practical than awakening a feeling for the fatherland, in so far as I succeed in capturing your attention and putting into your hands old or misplaced keys (but even I do not have them all) which can disclose the bases of German law. In doing so, much material must be adduced which concerns the language, poetry, and religion of former times, and I am setting high goals, for I presuppose much prior information. . . ."

Several hundred students greeted Jacob with an ovation when he entered the auditorium. Their enthusiasm visibly touched him, and for a while he was unable to speak. Although short of stature, Jacob was an impressive and dignified figure. His carriage was erect and his gait firm. Flowing gray hair crowned a high forehead above an expressive face that was always ready to break into a smile. And above all he had a presence that commanded respect. Georg Curtius reported the scene in his biography: "It was a great day for the Berlin students, when Jacob Grimm opened his series of lectures. He was not accustomed to speaking before such a large audience. His emotions hindered the flow of his thoughts.

After a few sentences there came a rather long pause, but completely calm and thoughtful the speaker gazed out at the chestnut trees before the window, and an absolute silence reigned among the hundreds of listeners until he had found words again."

The press in Berlin completely ignored the event. Only a newspaper in Augsburg reported an occasion in the cultural history of the capital of Prussia. The Grimms had no desire for publicity and no regrets about the poor press coverage. Although they themselves did not yet realize it fully, they had changed their lives for good, arrived at a final destination, and found a new home. Their inner lives remained unaffected by their change in fortune, but their public appearances now took on representational importance, and they appeared in the press, in Berlin and elsewhere, more than they liked.

Bettina, who could cast a roseate glow of romance over even trivial things, wrote her brother Clemens of the Grimms' first weeks in Berlin: "In front of their house stand beautiful oaks. . . . Jacob, the simplest and at the same time most peaceful person, who administers the opposition [of the Seven of Göttingen] like a sacred office, suppressing all dissent but not neglecting any right cause or duty, has come forth from this conflict of public opinions and secret calumny and political intrigues with a halo, and this is not to be understood figuratively. The great tranquility which he has acquired from the important questions which he risked his life to answer have lent his features the strength of a wrestler and at the same time the radiance of a martyr, and few people can look at him without feeling put to shame."

Wilhelm did not lecture until May, but his appearance at the university was again the occasion for an enthusiastic student demonstration. He was touched by the students' reception, but he controlled his emotion, and after expressing his gratitude carried on with poise and confidence. He chose as his topic the medieval epic *Gudrun,* opening with the promise that he would lead the students along the paths of German antiquity to discover new vistas and prospects. He then proceeded with a commentary on the poem, relating it and its narrative base to the better-known

Song of the Nibelungs. In the judgment of students and colleagues, Wilhelm with his more relaxed presence was the better
lecturer of the brothers. Treitschke, the historian, said of them:
"Jacob was the greater scholar, but the poorer teacher. He was
really no teacher at all, he was so restless that one could not follow
his lecture, while Wilhelm was a splendid teacher." Jacob was
quite aware of his limitations. In the fall of 1841, he wrote Gervinus: "In preparing for my lectures I noticed how much more
congenial to my nature the quiet working out of problems is than
the public communication of results skimmed off the top. I believe
that by nature, or through long pampering, I am made for diligence in private and that I lack the ways of the world, although I
esteem what is vigorous and capable and would gladly attain it."
To his old friend Paul Wigand, Jacob wrote toward the end of the
year: "This winter I must lecture on grammar and work up a new
notebook for it. Other local obstacles and interruptions are still
not overcome; it is demanding a longer time than I thought for us
to accustom ourselves to the manners and conditions here. It
would be unjust to fail to recognize their positive side; yet I often
long for the greater solitude of my old Hessian study."

Jacob did not lecture after 1848. Wilhelm continued until
1852, although participation in university life became rarer as the
demands of the dictionary grew greater. Jacob lectured on legal
antiquities, mythology, German grammar, and the *Germania*
of Tacitus. Wilhelm limited himself to medieval German epics,
for since Göttingen he had been confining himself more and
more to a single field in order not to scatter his energies.

Jacob's complaints about the time and energy that went into
lecturing soon came to be a constant feature of his letters. To
Dahlmann he wrote:

> The days pass quickly and yet they have not become regular,
> and much seems to me unaccustomed and burdensome. One
> hour of lecturing demands twice the time because of going back
> and forth; the sympathetic and curious crowd has naturally dis-
> appeared, and only thirty paying listeners remain, although that

is honorable enough for a lecture that is not required; this winter, when I want to lecture on grammar, I shall have to be content with an even smaller number.

It was obvious that he was really more interested in quality than quantity in regard to students. While at Göttingen, he had written Savigny: "I feel that universities should bring the best to the top and not be concerned with the great mass." In the realm of the spirit, Jacob was an aristocrat and elitist.

The students appreciated Jacob and Wilhelm as scholars and personalities. The brothers took part in student festivals, meeting with them informally and enjoying friendly relations outside the university. The students took every opportunity to express their devotion, as Wilhelm's description of a birthday celebration in February 1843 shows:

My birthday has been solemnly celebrated, we had invited nobody, but many of our friends and acquaintances came and filled our rooms. The people wanted to see the students and hear the singing, for it had become known that they were going to honor us. Our porter had cleaned the street in front of our house on his own initiative. At eight-thirty the students stood with torches in a half circle about the house, and the circle under the trees looked very pretty, better than would have been possible in the city. They then began to sing, and we went out with our guests to the balcony. Since they had practised for a few weeks, the singing was pure and good and resounded through the street (the students did not let carriages through), and the neighbors came to their windows or stood on balconies. After a few songs had been sung, a deputation came up and presented the festival song, on parchment with delicate gold inscription, that had been especially written and set to music, and another one in Danish composed by a Norwegian who is studying here. The deputation consisted of a Swiss, a student from Offenbach, and one from Brunswick, all three handsome lively faces. One delivered a regular address to us, we shook hands with them, thanked them, and said we wished to answer them all publicly, and invited them to come again and spend the evening with us. Then they went down again, the festival song was sung again, and then a cheer for us. We both spoke to them. . . . After one more song, they put out their torches and sang, as they slowly withdrew, the beautiful old student song *Gaudeamus igitur,* which sounded especially good.

Wilhelm replied to the students:

When I spoke to you here the first time, I expressed the desire that we might find your confidence, just as we came to you in trust. My wish has been most splendidly fulfilled. A year ago I lay ill and could not hope ever again to stand before you and be active on your behalf. I could only ask that heaven maintain my life; but I have received much more and today I can freely enjoy this proof of your friendly attitude toward us. We do not arrogate this proof to ourselves, but accept it as an expression of your love for the studies we have carried on. These studies embrace the whole fatherland; they have the special charm which native material has for everyone and which nothing foreign can replace, be it ever so excellent.

But the investigation of German antiquity demands, like everything which is supposed to vivify, a striving which is serious and dedicated. Part of this striving is the enthusiasm which you still have and with which you approach everything, the finest gift of your age, the gift on which the future rests. May you ever possess it, long live our academic youth!

Unfortunately there were less romantic and idyllic aspects to the university in Berlin. The faculty was composed of heterogeneous types representing all possible attitudes and parties: there were careerists and opportunists taking advantage of the king's generosity, conservatives who wished to prolong the customs of Frederick the Great, liberals who sought reform, and malcontents whose main sustenance in life was professional jealousy. Wilhelm remarked on the academic scene:

As for those who hold office here, the following seems to be the case . . . a third is indifferent to all public affairs, a third is selfish and cares only for further advancement, good salary, the title of privy councillor, medals, and is angry at any who think otherwise, and a third consists of people who have some character. Among them are honest, respectable men, but only the numerically small but influential party of the Ultras, allied with the Pietists, knows what it wants and goes straight for its goal; those who oppose it have no cohesion among themselves, that is, each one has a special opinion about what is good and desirable. The result of such a situation is easy to calculate.

❧ XVI ❧

The First Years in Berlin

ONLY A FEW WEEKS after arriving in Berlin, Jacob and Wilhelm began to accept their new situation and to feel established in the city. At first they were uncomfortable with all the noise and bustle, but their letters soon emphasized the positive side of their position and the many opportunities the capital afforded. Wilhelm gradually learned to love the city. Jacob was overawed by Berlin's size and needed more time to become acclimated. Searching for a house in December 1840, he had felt "afraid" of the city and its breathless pace. But a little over a month after their arrival, Jacob wrote to Dahlmann: "We are living in Lennéstrasse outside the city on the edge of the Tiergarten, which is carefully tended, and with its flowers and fish makes a cheerful impression, especially now that the foliage is coming out. There is a pleasant rustic silence here, at least on most days, whereas in the city the continuous rattling of the cabs is disturbing, and the sight of the straight streets, whose end one cannot see, makes me tired from the start." The Tiergarten was not only a quiet place for walks, but also a refuge where they gathered their inner strength, and thus it became the center and focus of their lives. They arranged their routine in much the same way they had in Cassel, so that every day they could enjoy the rural quiet of the park. Without it, they would not have adjusted so readily to life in Berlin. Wilhelm insisted that he was not a good hiker, but in fact he cherished walking quite as much as Jacob, although of course at his own modest pace. The walks in solitude and silence were recalled years later by Jacob in his memorial address after Wilhelm's death: "How happy I was to meet my brother by chance when he suddenly came along from the other direction, and we then continued next to one another in silence. That can now never happen again!"

According to Berthold Auerbach, who accompanied Jacob on some of his strolls through the park, Jacob knew the quietest and most remote corners where one heard no sounds of traffic and where other people rarely came. Jacob would walk with erect carriage, only his head bent slightly forward as if he were carefully listening for something. He never carried a walking stick and always kept his left hand behind his back as he vigorously strolled along. He was alert to all that was around him, knew the flora of the park thoroughly, and found recreation and pleasure in it at all times of the year. Escape to the Tiergarten meant just as much in Wilhelm's life as in Jacob's, and he treasured the flowers he could identify and the opportunity to refresh body and soul.

By the beginning of 1846, the house in Lennéstrasse had become too small for the family, and they moved to Dorotheenstrasse 47, not far from the Brandenburg Gate. They lived there for only a little over a year, since Wilhelm forgot to pay the rent while away at a conference of Germanists. Their final move in Berlin was to the second story of a house in Linkstrasse near Potsdam Square. Here they were no longer in a quiet, half-rural section of the city, for behind the house lay the Potsdam railroad station. They were now in the busier and noisier part of Berlin, but they had already adjusted to urban living, still finding their special refuge in the Tiergarten. They thus became residents of the city inwardly as well as formally.

The Berlin into which the Grimms moved was a city that had steadily grown and expanded since becoming the capital of Prussia. In 1709 Berlin had 56,000 inhabitants; in 1784, 145,000; and by 1840 about 328,000. During the brothers' years of residence it continued to grow rapidly, and shortly after their deaths (1859; 1863) reached the figure of 825,000 inhabitants. Slums and sections soon to become slums stretched out to the north and east, while the more elegant parts of Berlin were expanding toward the west. The contrasts among the various parts of the city lent the capital its characteristic feeling of tension, which many observers in the mid-century noticed. Wilhelm wrote to Gervinus in 1843: "Since I could not lecture this summer, I have not gone into the city for a long time. It is becoming more and more vast and rambling. When I first went out again after my illness, a new square and two new streets had appeared, so steadily does it grow. I have not been in many parts of the city; once I went out to the Silesian Gate, there one still sees among the walls gardens and tilled fields. Unter den Linden always has a crowd. The square around the palace and beyond must be called splendid and regal, and half an hour from there peace and quiet reign as if in a small town: I don't believe that any other capital city has combined so much that is disparate."

The physical development of the city had fortunately been accompanied by a steady growth in cultural facilities. In 1659 the Great Elector had laid the basis for what later became the Prussian State Library. The Prussian Academy of Sciences, to which Jacob belonged from 1832 on, was founded in 1700, and in 1703 the Academy of Art was established. Frederick the Great had the Opera House built on Unter den Linden in 1743, and opposite it the University of Berlin was established in 1810. From 1840 on, the city attracted more and more artists and scholars. The Grimms found their old friends Savigny and Lachmann already there, but many other distinguished men of learning graced the capital, among them Alexander von Humboldt, Ernst Moritz Arndt, Schelling, Franz Bopp, the legal historian von Richthofen, the Egyptologist Lepsius, and the historian Leopold Ranke. Already known to many of these scholars, the brothers soon found themselves in an exciting but rather tiring round of visits and receptions in the learned world of Berlin.

The Grimms lectured at the university by right of their membership in the Academy of Sciences, where the luminaries of Berlin's intellectual scene gathered. But Jacob noted that these sessions had little attraction for him. There was supposed to be a lecture every week, but the lecturers did not keep to the schedule, and a wealth of committees proliferated to take care of worthy causes, some pious, some trivial. Jacob was elected a member of a committee to edit the works of Frederick the Great; far from being flattered, he was much annoyed that Wilhelm Schlegel was brought all the way from Bonn just to write a preface.

The membership of the Academy represented a colorful miscellany. There were people like the Grimms and Savigny, who had earned some recognition for what they had accomplished. But there were also many others whose names have rightly been forgotten. Friedrich Wilhelm IV called to Berlin the favorites of his childhood and youth. When they arrived in Berlin in the 1840's, many were past their prime, if not in their dotage. Ludwig Tieck, whose creative period was long past, is one good example. Most representatives of the arts and letters were heroes of a bygone age. In the sciences the situation was much better, owing to the guidance of Alexander von Humboldt—and it was he who was largely responsible for bringing the Grimms to Berlin.

Both Jacob and Wilhelm took the sessions of the Academy very seriously, in spite of all complaints. They were rarely absent from formal meetings, and they contributed regularly. From 1842 until his death in 1859, Wilhelm gave seventeen lectures. Jacob also gave a great many, and both had their lectures printed for publication. Even where they found grounds for criticism, they entered into the activity and spirit of both the university and the Academy—they would have been untrue to their natures not to have participated.

The court of the King of Prussia followed his example in cultivating the company of artists and scholars, so that the general atmosphere of the capital was congenial to the muses and contrasted favorably with the earlier experiences of the brothers. For the first time in their lives, they were residing in a state where they were honored and esteemed by the ruling family and the government. They could not help but enjoy the atmosphere, which was so different from previous unhappy histories in Hesse and Hannover. Reminders of their former troubles occasionally interrupted their new life in Berlin. In 1842 King Ernst August of Hannover visited Berlin, wearing the uniform of a Prussian hussar the entire time. His manners were as bad as ever and his jibes as caustic; he took the trouble to insult several prominent people in Berlin, apparently just for fun, in his boorish style. To one of the dinners he gave in Berlin, he invited Alexander von Humboldt, a man of great dignity and a splendid old cavalier and scholar. At the table the king called across to Humboldt: "Well, Mr. Humboldt, what are my runaway Göttingen professors doing? But you know that one can always get professors, dancing girls, and whores for money anywhere." Humboldt replied: "Your Majesty, with the last two classes I have never had any connections, and as for the professors, I too am half a professor." After dinner Humboldt announced loudly and deliberately in the presence of some officials from Hannover that he had heard of people in high places insulting others gratuitously, but that it was new to him that one was especially invited to dinner to receive the insult.

Ernst August's visit was an embarrassment for his younger relative Friedrich Wilhelm IV of Prussia, who chose a sly form of revenge for his boorish guest from Hannover. The password issued by the king for the morning of Ernst August's departure was "Oxford." Given the English background of the guest, this might have been appropriate enough, except that Oxford, pronounced in the German fashion, sounds like *Ochs fort*, that is, "the ox has gone."

Echoes of Göttingen persisted even when the "ox" of Hannover was not in Berlin. The French ambassador conveyed to Jacob in the spring of 1841 the Cross of the Legion of Honor with a diploma that referred to Jacob as a professor at the University of Göttingen. It is quite understandable that the French were ignorant of the niceties of the crazy-quilt political divisions of Germany, but there was another aspect to the honor: Wilhelm reported it to his friend Moritz Haupt with the ironic comment that Jacob was amazed to find himself now a colleague of Prince Metternich, who received his diploma at the same time. Jacob and Wilhelm were more amused than offended at being placed in the same category with a politician whom they despised. They had been the recipients of enough honors to be able to take them calmly and humorously.

More meaningful was the presentation in 1842 of the order of *Pour le mérite*. In May 1842, King Friedrich Wilhelm IV of Prussia established the order of *"Pour le mérite* for arts and science." In 1740, upon his accession to the throne, Frederick the Great had founded the order of *Pour le mérite* as a military award, and in 1810 it was made the highest in the land for military achievement. Alexander von Humboldt, the first chancellor in the new reign, helped to design and promote the order as an award for highest distinction in civilian service. Both he and the new king were concerned with changing Prussia's image in the world and redressing its reputation as a *Soldatenstaat,* or purely military state on the Spartan model. By an odd coincidence Jacob was involved in the wording of the statutes of the new order. Humboldt turned to him with the question of how to spell "deutsch" (German), reporting a debate among the ministers of state as to the proper spelling and calling upon Jacob as a final authority. The king regularly wrote "teutsch," a fashionable misspelling of the time, and ordered Humboldt to find out the correct spelling from Jacob.

Since Jacob was among the first to receive the new order, his pleasure was genuine, and Wilhelm, sharing as always, wrote of the occasion to a friend in Göttingen: "Jacob was invited Sunday to dinner on Tuesday in Sanssouci . . . learned of his award, however, only on Tuesday. . . . General satisfaction with the selection of people to receive the medal could not be expected, but only few would be content with any other choice. . . . Several who failed to get it are said to be very bitter. . . . It is not only something new but very fine that it is called a German order and that the right to vote [co-opt] is given to recipients of the order in other German states. When the remark is made that mainly Prussians have received it, then one should also note that among them most are not born, but adopted Prussians."

In point of fact, twenty-two of the thirty German members of the order were Prussian subjects. There were distinguished names among them: Schelling, Savigny, Ranke, Jacob Grimm, Minister Eichhorn, among others. Many who seemed important at the time of election are now happily forgotten. The statutes prescribed that new members should be co-opted by the existing members, and so it has remained to this day. The king wished to see the members of the first chapter immortalized, and therefore had them all sit for their portraits. Jacob was painted by Karl Begas; Jacob liked Begas's portraits, but was suspicious of him as a person: "I did not like him so well, and it seems that he himself believes that everything he says is the voice of the oracle. These Berlin artists all speak like printed reviews; they all believe that they alone have hit the nail on the head and they know everything better because they consider themselves unsurpassable." Jacob's portrait turned out very well, although oddly and inappropriately for one who disliked ostentation, it portrayed him draped in a long, rather pretentious fur coat.

Since the brothers, whether they liked it or not, were prominent, they were much sought after by portrait painters. One sure test of their "social importance" in the status-conscious city is the large number of portraits made of them during their first few years in Berlin. Neither Jacob nor Wilhelm strove for status; neither was a social climber, but they could not avoid behavior in accordance with their position. Prior to their move to Berlin, no one besides their brother Louis had seriously studied them as subjects for portraiture. The new art of photography was just being developed during their early years in the capital. As early as 1843, Jacob, Wilhelm, and Lachmann had themselves daguerreotyped, and were rather pleased with the results. Neither brother was at all vain, but both enjoyed seeing their likenesses fixed in pictures. They prized portraits above daguerreotypes, and they kept pictures of the family in their rooms as pious reminders of its continuity.

Membership in exclusive and distinguished groups such as *Pour le mérite* brought with it contacts with many interesting people as well as new social obligations. It was an age that still required formal visits, which obligated one to equally formal return visits. Wilhelm seems to have enjoyed this social life more than Jacob, although both complained equally. Wilhelm was basically an optimist who was eager to see the best in everything and everybody. Yet his critical faculties never slept, and his comments on characters and personalities in Berlin are witty and rather sharp at times. He enjoyed gossip and wrote long and chatty letters to friends. Without being malicious himself, Wilhelm relished the infighting of the city as a keen observer. During the first years at Göttingen, Jacob had often complained of Wilhelm's melancholy, knowing of course that it was due to his constantly recurring bouts of illness. In Berlin Wilhelm recovered his normal good humor and even temper, although he could not boast of perfect health, for he was sick for many months in 1842. Jacob first noted his ill health early in February, and from then on for the rest of the year Wilhelm never fully recovered. In the fall he wrote to Dahlmann:

I have not been able to gather my strength all summer. For about a month now I feel stronger and the wilted leaves are beginning to freshen again. I believe that only a spiritual power has preserved me in this illness which gnawed at my noblest organ, my heart. When I was conscious—for I was busy with all sorts of notions while unconscious, so I was told afterward—I could not form a single thought without violent pain in my forehead, and I could not remember the most familiar things, there was nothing else to do but give myself up to my imagination which sped across the sea like a bird which can no longer alight anywhere. At other times I was calm, and then past events, mostly from my youth, appeared without my making any effort but quite in context and so lively and vivid, that they were like carefully painted Dutch pictures. I even built a beautiful, fancy house, when a ship from Malaya, loaded with treasures, put into port, and I can still describe the clever plan of the house. . . . It was lucky that we do not live in the city but as if half in the country, for I could stroll slowly back and forth in the open air during the cool morning and evening hours. . . .

Jacob and the whole family were worried by the continued palpitations of the heart and the intervals when Wilhelm seemed quite remote from reality and hard to communicate with. Jacob's turn for illness came in 1843, when he was unwell for a long period. In the spring he wrote to Gervinus thanking God that the doctors had not sent him to a spa to drink the waters—he considered that very boring—but had let him stay in the Tiergarten. He added, without comment but probably with relief, that he was taking a vacation from lecturing on account of his illness. Jacob never let anything interfere with his scholarship, but he could be persuaded not to lecture. He had a tendency for hypochondria that did not improve with age. Even before the dismissal from Göttingen, his premonitions of an early death led him to make out his last will and testament:

I want after my death all my possessions to go to my brother Wilhelm or his children Herman, Rudolf, and Augusta, and belong to them without claim or conflict. Since I have owned everything from youth on together with Wilhelm and shared continuous, uninterrupted management, increase or decrease of property, no separation is possible anyway. In my other brothers and sisters, all of whom I love, I have the firm faith that they will keep this my cordial and well-considered will just as sacred as if it were expressed in the most formal way. I also will that all my literary gleanings shall be burned. An exception should be made for the collection of legal precedents as well as everything written down in bound books that can perhaps be used by future persons. Göttingen, February 7, 1837.

In February 1841 and again in August 1843, Jacob confirmed

the document as his valid will. Thoughts of death did not terrify Jacob, but they came to him regularly at times of illness or inner reflection on his condition. He worried more about Wilhelm's health than his own, and only in letters to confidential friends did he ever mention his health or lack of it. But periods of introspection and melancholy were not unknown to him, and at such times his sense of obligation to survivors was very strong. The late summer and early fall of 1841 was a bad time for Jacob, who felt just well enough not to take to his bed. He confessed to Gervinus that he felt inwardly restless and dissatisfied, blaming it on his poor health but also, it must be assumed, weighed down by the obligations he had incurred and the uncertainties he faced. In September he wrote the following memorandum for Wilhelm and Dortchen:

> If work on the dictionary should falter because of my death, then I will that the good people Hirzel and Reimer [the publishers] be recompensed for the expenses they have incurred; if you agree, we shall give the finished excerpts to Haupt [professor of philology], who will perhaps have the courage to finish the task; I have carried it around in my head more than I have written it down. Other people can do nothing with the collections I have made. About six [actually four] years ago in Göttingen I made provisions for my estate, and that must still be valid, it lies in a briefcase and has not been read over again. My thoughts and feelings are calm and clear at this time, but in the last few days such heaviness and weariness have come over my body that I long for resolution in God, who is an only God, and who will take me as He has created me, and who knows why He wishes that our eyes grow dim, our hands rest, and our hearts stop. Compose yourselves in my regard, love of relatives is still the most sacred thing in the world, and think of me, as I think of our dear mother.

The last months of 1843 were a time of renewed ill health for Jacob, who assured Dahlmann that he was not melancholy, but just "thoughtful," surely a euphemism. He remarked slyly that the doctor had forbidden him to go out in the evening, "and that, you may believe, suited me just right." Dortchen, herself frail and often suffering from respiratory trouble, still was able to run the household and keep the two scholars fed, clothed, and reasonably contented. The early years in Berlin saw the family of Wilhelm and Dortchen rapidly growing up. By 1844 Herman, now sixteen, was steadily improving in health after years of chronic illness. Rudolf continued to follow his parents in being sickly, but he too gradually improved and became a lively boy with a sense of fun and playfulness. Auguste, as the only daughter, received special attention in accordance with the family tradition. Jacob took great delight in the development of his niece and nephews, reporting their doings and successes with glowing avuncular pride. On his sixty-first birthday in 1846, he noted that his hair was graying, but that his senses were still fresh and lively. But he also remarked with sorrow that many of his classmates had died, that his younger brother Ferdinand had died the year before, and that his only wish was to preserve his health long enough to accomplish the tasks before him. By then, however, he realized that the dictionary would never be finished in his lifetime, and this thought always saddened him. He remarked with some surprise that he had lived longer than his father, although for years he had not hoped or expected to achieve this.

Complaints about the hectic social life in Berlin were so frequent and insistent during the early years that it is hard to believe that the brothers accomplished any serious scholarly work. Besides the lectures, which taxed their energies, they had the constant meticulous work on the dictionary. Evenings were their sacred time for work, but the evening social calls were demanding and exhausting. They really preferred to keep up their contacts by letter or by travel, but their hospitality and courtesy made them a part of the social whirl. If one brother was ill, the other took over the duty of representation. Dortchen attended most of the visits in their own home, and her yawns were often the signal for the departure of the guests. Wilhelm's letters of the period reveal some pleasure in the parties and festivities as well as his ability to find amusing aspects in what was otherwise a disturbance of his routine.

In June 1843, brother Louis came to Berlin with his little daughter to visit Jacob and Wilhelm. The activity that developed in the next few weeks was astounding and must be considered exceptional, but it indicates some of the things which made life in Berlin so distracting. Bettina von Arnim came to call, as she did so often, on the very first night that Louis was at the Grimms' home. A few days later Bettina came again, and brother-in-law Hassenpflug (not a favorite of Jacob and Wilhelm) paid a call in the evening. Three days later Louis went out calling with Wilhelm, and the following night the brothers had a house full of guests, among them, of course, Bettina. The next day, the twenty-third of June, there were guests for lunch. On the following day there were noon guests again, among them Savigny, now a government minister. In the evening they all went to a large party where Louis had an opportunity to see celebrities. On the twenty-fifth they dined at Savigny's home, returning in time to receive evening guests. The next evening the Grimms had house-guests, and on the following day they all went to dine with Eichhorn, again meeting several celebrities. During the next few days, guests continued to visit the Grimms, Bettina coming twice, and finally on the fifth of July there was a wedding party at the home of Minister Eichhorn. Louis enjoyed the pace and de-lighted in meeting so many famous people, but one cannot help wondering how his older brothers, who had so loved their quiet routine in Cassel, stood up under the pressure. When not enter-taining guests or dining out, Wilhelm took Louis to the university for lectures or around the city to see the sights, showing him entertainment spots as well as cultural monuments. They even visited a session of the Academy of Sciences, whose dignity and grandeur much impressed Louis.

Bettina von Arnim visited so often and so regularly that Her-man Grimm grew up thinking of her as an aunt and a special member of the family. The Grimms owed her much, and they were grateful to her and as tolerant of her fiery temperament as they could be. Very revealing is a letter of Jacob from this period: "Almost every evening, just at the time when I like best to devote myself to quiet contemplation, Bettina comes and disturbs us with her endless, exuberant, and yet charming conversation. Night or day, her nature is to be tireless, and if she does not see that Dortchen's eyes are closing, she doesn't think of leaving; at the same time she brings into our house people from her entourage with whom we would otherwise never think of making acquaintance. I hope, to be sure, that this style of living will gradually come to a halt and that everything will go back to its natural limits." Her brother-in-law Savigny, now a dignified and slightly stuffy minister in the Prussian government, was sometimes shocked at the excitement and exuberance generated by Bettina, but he never did more than shake his head, since he had learned long ago that it was impossible to curb or convert a Brentano.

Many of the guests who enjoyed the Grimms' hospitality during those years have left accounts of their visits. Almost all were impressed with the warmth and cordiality of the family and the intimate bonds of love and trust that united it. A traveler from Hesse, Julius Rodenberg, wrote of his visit with the Grimms:

I spent a cordial, happy evening with the Grimms. Immediately upon entering their house I felt warm and comfortable as I hardly had for all my time here. Wilhelm's wife is a dear woman, full of Hessian good-heartedness and without any pretensions, the most charming mistress of the house that one can imagine. Auguste, her daughter, awoke old Marburg memories in me. . . . Wilhelm came in first, a man with a calmly content visage, with blue eyes and long, gray hair. He looks more affable than intellectually significant. His gentleness is attractive without making one feel overwhelmed by his intellectual superiority. Jacob, who came in after him, is different. One feels immediately a certain shyness in his presence; the vivacity of his eyes captivates and holds one, but when his hearty smile softens his features and the whole haste of his carriage turns to good-natured mobility, then one's sense of constraint is changed into a quite unaccustomed fondness and a feeling of attraction, one feels related to him and loves him, just as once as a child one loved his household tales. The title "Councillor" I could hardly pronounce, for I kept feeling as if I should call him simply Jacob, as his brother did, or uncle, as the flattering Auguste called him. He is a little man, but in his old-fashioned dress-coat he looks like the good old times, and has nothing of the ivory tower scholar and even less of the aristocratic Berlin professor about him. A full head of gray hair surrounds his high forehead, and his eyes sparkle. The whole company that evening was just as unaffected as the people of the house.

The Grimms preferred quiet, intimate conversation with friends as a form of entertainment and relaxation to the more ceremonial affairs to which they were often invited. An evening with friends and family at home in the style described above was a welcome and rewarding form of interruption in their work. There were, however, invitations which they could not well refuse. In January 1843, Wilhelm described to Dahlmann a court reception in Charlottenburg: "The King addressed me by remarking: 'You are thinner after your illness, but I envy you.' And in fact he seemed to me to have put on weight. He was cheerful at table and jested in his accustomed manner. Afterwards he talked with both of us for a rather long time, and I again had an opportunity to observe his intelligent and ingratiating manner and his well-meaning nature. I was then presented to the Queen. She asked me if I missed the region of Göttingen, which she knew and liked very much. Even more the region of Cassel, I answered, the city of Berlin can really not compete here, but the Tiergarten, where I live, is nevertheless very beautiful. She then began to speak of Hesse, praised the deceased Electress and her good intentions, and said: 'Things are no longer good there.' She speaks simply and naturally and has something kindly and generous in her eyes and whole expression."

Not all the entertainment at court was interesting and pleasant, since some occasions were formal command performances. Even in the most informal gatherings, there was a certain amount of stiffness and an atmosphere of ceremony or constraint. The court was under obvious obligation to follow the king's lead in all matters. Just as he chose the literary luminaries from the favorites of his youth, so he insisted on lending social gatherings a veneer of culture by having some distinguished person perform. Bismarck recounts with some irony an average, deadly boring tea at court where Alexander von Humboldt, now approaching dotage, held forth:

> At the house of our illustrious lord I was the sacrificial victim when Humboldt entertained the company in his special manner in the evening. He usually read aloud, often for hours at a time. While reading he stood and held the page close to the lamp. At times he let the page drop, and when he did, covered up with a learned remark. Nobody listened to him; but he had the floor. The Queen sewed steadily away on some tapestry and surely understood nothing of his lecture. The King looked at pictures—engravings and woodcuts—and turned the pages noisily, obviously with the intent of not having to hear anything. The young people on the side and in the background conversed quite without constraint, giggled and drowned out his lecture completely. The talk, however, went on murmuring without surcease like a brook. Gerlach, who usually was present, sat on his small round chair and slept so hard that he snored. . . . I was Humboldt's only patient listener; that is, I kept silent, pretended to listen to the talk, and thought my own thoughts.

Relations between students and faculty at the University of Berlin existed in forms that may seem strange today. The students took proud pleasure in honoring professors whom they admired and respected. On festive occasions they often feted chosen members of the faculty. In 1843 Wilhelm wrote to his brother Louis in Cassel, describing a party hosted by the students for the faculty:

The day before yesterday the students arranged a party for the professors. Only students sang and played in the concert, and a few among them had good voices, and nothing that they presented was poor. Since the organizers had arrived in carriages and had invited people personally, no one could refuse to come. And since such a party was being put on for the first time this way, everyone gladly took part. Only a selection of professors, with their wives of course, was invited, and the whole group amounted to about four hundred persons. The main hall was new and brilliantly arranged and contained the whole company. At the table rhymed toasts were given, and the students alternately sang on the gallery or the orchestra played on the other gallery. The whole festival was fine and decent, and I went home about twelve o'clock, when the meal was over, but the ball naturally lasted until late at night.

Not every party organized by the students was successful. Through no fault of the well-meaning students, one affair caused the Grimms considerable grief. On the occasion of Wilhelm's fifty-eighth birthday (February 24, 1844), the students marched to the house to do homage to their revered teacher. They came in a torchlight parade to serenade Wilhelm and to cheer as they had before. A writer named Hoffmann von Fallersleben, who had recently been evicted from Breslau for writing political poems, was a guest of the Grimms that evening and appeared on the balcony when the students presented their ovation. When the students saw Hoffmann, they burst into cheers and put on a lively and noisy demonstration. Hoffmann went down, addressed them for a few minutes, and expressed his gratitude for their cheering support. The police, who had been keeping Hoffmann under surveillance, observed the whole incident and interpreted it as a provocative antigovernment demonstration. Hoffmann was evicted from Berlin and steps were taken against the student leaders. The liberal press seized upon the affair as an example of political repression, criticizing the Grimm brothers, who had been at pains to dissociate themselves from Hoffmann. The Grimms were amazed and upset by the commotion, sincerely believing that Hoffmann had played a trick on them. Both were loyal to the king as well as grateful to him, and they wanted no misunderstanding on that score. Embarrassed by the whole occasion, derided in the press, and bitterly angry at Hoffmann for "betraying" them, they finally felt moved to publish a declaration stating their case. This statement merely incensed the liberal press, whose short memory had completely forgotten the heroes of 1837, and Jacob and Wilhelm were subjected to renewed vilification.

Bettina von Arnim, in typical fashion, took Hoffmann's side, defending and justifying his actions with her usual eloquence. This embittered the brothers even more, since they felt that their trust had been betrayed by a person to whom they had always looked for sympathy and understanding. Wilhelm could not get over the injury for a long time, refused to see Bettina when she visited, and nurtured distrust and hostility toward her for months.

It was a topsy-turvy situation. Bettina had no intention of offending the Grimms, since she had instinctively taken sides with someone who seemed unjustly oppressed, just as she had been bold in her defense of the wronged brothers in 1837. Seven years later, the relationship was turned upside down, and it now seemed that the brothers were wrong and that Bettina, always impulsive, had once again championed the cause of an underdog. Jacob and Wilhelm were firm in their belief that Hoffmann was guilty of abusing their hospitality and exceeding the bounds of taste and judgment. They considered his conduct inexcusable, being convinced that he knew of the torch parade in advance and had arranged the whole scene with the students. Bettina's position they could not understand, and for a while forty years of friendship seemed about to be annulled by something quite fortuitous. However, Herman, Wilhelm's oldest child, soon became engaged to Gisela von Arnim, and this proved to be a restorative reconciliation. Finally, in 1852, Jacob and Hoffmann met again and were reconciled. But Wilhelm never forgave him. He was slower to anger than Jacob, but all the more unyielding once his wrath was aroused.

Jacob's ill health in 1843 finally persuaded his doctor that he should travel to the warmer, friendlier climate of Italy. Jacob gladly took the opportunity to see the classical "land of longing" for all Germans of his generation, and enjoyed both the country and the people he met. He loved its natural beauties and praised its landscapes. In December 1844, he gave a lecture to the Academy of Sciences describing his experiences. He opened his talk with the characteristic remark that he would "rather learn without traveling than travel without learning." He naturally included many linguistic and historical remarks of a kind that he alone could make. Three things, he said in summary, made up the riches of which Italy could rightfully boast: the grandeur and splendor of its natural beauty, the richness of its history as former ruler of the known world, and the greatness of its many art monuments scattered throughout the land. Italian was the Romance language he liked most—French was the Romance tongue he knew best, but he disliked the French. He was charmed by the people of Italy and found them "in harmony with their native landscape." The lecture, later published in his *Minor Works,* is a poetic and appealing document of his travels to the south.

A year later he visited Scandinavia, the land of his own special longing, since it stood in close relationship to Germany and represented a parallel Germanic development: "For a German scholar Scandinavia is a classical land, just as Italy is for everyone who follows the paths of the old Romans." His lecture on Scandinavia contrasted his impressions of the Germanic north with his experiences in Italy. Sweden and Denmark he found attractive in a different, "sterner" way than the lands of the Mediterranean. His preference for the sturdy Norsemen found expression in a comparison of the Icelanders and their rich contribution to European culture with the inhabitants of Sardinia, "who have lived since the beginning of our time reckoning in useless sloth." Jacob, the lifelong bachelor, was not blind to the charms of women and he was an alert observer of the fair sex. He noted that the red-cheeked Danish women looked "fresher, pale Swedish women more delicate." But basically he remained a philologist wherever he went, so that his observations on language are perhaps more important than his remarks on Scandinavian ladies. He preferred the full vowels of the Swedish language to Danish, but he gave Danish literature and scholarship its due, for after all he and Wilhelm owed the start of their careers to the Danes—the advantage they held over many other scholars of their time was due in large part to their knowledge of Scandinavia's language and literature.

The spirit of nationalism was strong in the German lands during the 1840's. Conferences of professional people, who came from the many states and principalities with a common mission and common professional bonds, usually had political overtones. The dream of a unified Germany, frustrated after the Napoleonic Wars and the unsatisfactory settlement of the postwar political map, was a common topic of discussion. During this period a conference of lawyers and legal historians called for a unified law for all the German states, and various conferences of Germanists also sought to create the impression of unity at their business sessions. When the Germanists met in 1846, they convened in the *Römersaal* (or Hall of the Romans) in Frankfurt am Main, a setting that recalled imperial splendor and was an appropriate symbol of a Germany that one day might be united in a single state. More than two hundred scholars were gathered, and it may be assumed that most of them were united in their hopes for a unified Germany. The poet Ludwig Uhland came forward during the deliberations over the choice of a president and proposed Jacob Grimm, whose representational value at such a moment was inestimable. Jacob was unanimously elected by acclaim and given an ovation. The minutes of the proceedings reported the event as follows:

On the twenty-fourth of September, 1846, the pictures of our Kaisers in the old Hall of the Romans looked down on two hundred of the most distinguished German men, and breathless silence reigned when Ludwig Uhland took the floor: "It seems to me," he said, "that the first election of a president can proceed without delay. In addition a wish has been expressed with which I heartily agree: that by this election a man be summoned, in whose hands for many years all the threads of German historical studies are intertwined, and from whose hands many of these threads have first come forth: to wit the golden thread of poetry which he himself has spun in German law, a study which one is otherwise accustomed to consider a dry study. People have expressed to me their wish that this man be chosen president of this conference by acclamation. I hardly need to utter the name of Jacob Grimm."

Storms of applause followed these words, and Jacob, with warm words of thanks, took over the presiding office of the conference. He opened the proceedings with a profound lecture on the interrelations of the three branches of study represented at the conference: law, history, and philology. At the same session Wilhelm Grimm presented a broad survey of the preliminary work on the German dictionary. The next day Jacob gave a second lecture, in which he emphasized the great value of studies concerned with the fatherland. For the foreign scholars present, he gave his lecture in French as well.

The next year, when the conference was held in Lübeck, Jacob was again unanimously elected president. At the final farewell dinner, he gave a speech in which he dealt with the long and interesting history of the Hanseatic city of Lübeck. In reply a member of the Supreme Court stood up and proposed a toast to the "ruler in the three realms of language, history, and law." The minutes of the meeting reported Jacob's response to the toast: "Grass will soon grow over my head. If I am still remembered, then I wish that people will say of me what I may say of myself, namely that in all my life I have never loved anything more than my fatherland." Then, overcome with emotion, Jacob sank into the arms of his old friend Dahlmann. It was the high point of the whole conference and a moving experience for all who attended. For Jacob it was also a gratifying form of recognition and a kind of restitution after the distressing publicity surrounding the Hoffmann affair.

Jacob and Wilhelm did not spend all their time attending parties and conventions. Jacob was able to prepare and publish a second edition of the *German Mythology* in 1844. In the preface he again undertook to defend the ancient Germans from the slander of barbarism:

> One may say that to deny the genuine existence of this mythology is tantamount to rejecting the great age and life span of our language: every nation needs belief in gods just as much as language. . . . I find repugnant the arrogant view, that the life of whole centuries was absorbed in gloomy, joyless barbarism; that would be contrary to the loving kindness of God, who causes the sun to shine upon all times and who gave man the consciousness of a higher divine guidance just as He bestowed upon him the gifts of body and soul: In all ages of the world, even the most infamous, the blessings of happiness and salvation have been granted. . . . In our heathen mythology there appear in purity and vigor those ideas which the human heart needs most and by means of which it maintains itself. . . . Because I discovered that our fatherland's language, law, and antiquity were held in much too low esteem, I wished to exalt the fatherland. One task led to another, and what furnished proof in one place gave support in another, and what laid the foundation here served to confirm there. Perhaps my books will mean more in a calm, happy time, and such a time will also come again; they are to belong to the present, however, since I cannot imagine our present day without our past reflecting radiance on it, and the future will avenge any belittling of our past.

During research on the dictionary, it became evident to Jacob that a history of the German language was more urgently needed by students and teachers alike than a lexical reference work. Jacob had clear in his own mind the basic outlines and much of the detail. In just a few weeks in 1847, he wrote out most of the whole long, complicated book; the *History of the German Language* appeared in Leipsic in 1848 in two volumes. The dedication to Gervinus recalled in cordial terms their cooperation in Göttingen in teaching and in suffering the same fate. Jacob mentioned with sincere appreciation the fact that Gervinus had followed Jacob's research with sympathy and understanding. The book was finished during the March 1848 revolution, and these political events reminded Jacob anew of the difficulties he and Gervinus had experienced eleven years before.

The political turbulence of the time left its mark on the book, since Jacob's patriotism took a rather aggressive form. The preface, written at the convention in Frankfurt am Main, urged the necessity of studying Germany's history and cherishing it so that Germans might maintain their identity and not become submerged "in a bottomless sea of generality that is supposed to inundate all individual countries." At times the *History* is distressing in its glorification of the German people: "The book teaches that our nation, after the Roman yoke had been thrown off, brought its name and its fresh freedom to the Romance people in Gaul, Italy, Spain, and England, and decided through its great power alone the victory of Christianity and set itself up as an impenetrable dam against the violently pressing Slavs in the middle of Europe. The fate of the whole Middle Ages was directed by this race. . . ." Jacob postulated two basic types of people: the great and ruling races and the submissive and conquered types. He foresaw a day when only three European nations would exist—Romance people, Germans, and Slavs. In the last sentence of the dedication, he expressed the belief that as soon as Germany had been properly unified, Denmark could not possibly continue to exist as previously.

Jacob's *History of the German Language* may be viewed not only as an upsurge of patriotic fervor but also as a Romantic revolt against the demanding and confining work on the dictionary, or even as a "poetic" work that represented in many respects a relapse into the Romanticism of his youth. Jacob was intent on recapturing the entire Germanic past, but he channeled his data into a strictly German path, projecting German tribal history into the remote past without proper evidence or documentation. Certain flights of fancy and a lack of strict method recall his style and approach of the period before the *Grammar*. Jacob's systematic treatment of Gothic inflections was an important and scholarly achievement, but his fixation that "Getae" and "Goths" were identical was a damaging aberration and systematic error that led to odd results. The Getae, an ancient people of Thrace akin to the Daci, are first mentioned by Herodotus in the fifth century B.C. By about the third century B.C., the Getae disappear from history. They can have no possible relation to the later Goths, whose origins may be traced to Scandinavia. It was an exciting notion to think that as early as Herodotus a Germanic tribe was known to history and had existed on the periphery of classical Greek civilization. Unfortunately the assumption of the identity of Getae and Goths was central to Jacob's arguments on the course of German history, so that an error, even if an imaginative one, was built into the core of the book.

Jacob's erudition and lively style are redeeming features of a book that in spite of its faults is still a magnificent document and a storehouse of information on the early history of the Germans. Data from nonphilological fields were brought in much more frequently than in the *Grammar,* so that the *History* is by no means a variation or abridgement of the early work. Folklore, legal and religious history, and archaeology all play an important role, although Jacob emphasized the certainties of philology in contrast to the hypotheses of archaeology. As he promised in the preface, he used the history of the language to reveal the history of the nation. Poetry, legends, and ancient customs supported the findings in the field of philology. The book has had great influence on later scholars, especially in the use of etymologies to establish relationships, the close attention to toponymy, and the concern for social structure. Jacob was a proponent of the tripartite division of ancient Germanic society: warrior, shepherd, and farmer. Observations in these related fields buttressed his arguments in a way that set the fashion for later generations of scholars. But he still had his own special idiosyncrasies, believing even at this date in his system of three basic vowels. And there is evidence of provincial pride too, for the Hessians head the section on the High German tribes.

Wilhelm was not idle either during these years. In 1841 he published a manuscript of the medieval legend *Silvester* by Konrad of Würzburg and reedited *Count Rudolf* in 1844. With Jacob he oversaw the publication of the fifth edition of the *Fairy Tales* in 1843. In spite of periods of ill health, he continued both his lectures at the university and his work on the dictionary. He shared with Jacob the burden of correspondence with dictionary contributors, yet, as he emphasized in his many letters, lived a rich and full life.

❧ XVII ❧

1848:
The Year of Revolution

In 1847 Friedrich Wilhelm IV summoned the representatives of the Prussian estates to attend the "United Diet of the Monarchy" in order to get them to grant a government loan to build a railway from Berlin to Königsberg. What started as a matter of finance soon developed political consequences of a far-reaching nature. The Diet refused to grant the loan until a constitution had been formulated. The king, obsessed by the doctrine of the divine right of kings, resented the proposal of a constitution as something that would destroy the family community which he imagined he headed. He repeated his request for a loan as a matter of obedience to his (divine) will, meanwhile rejecting all proposals for a change in the structure of government. The liberals in the assembly refused to comply with his wishes. Thus a serious conflict developed between the representatives of the estates and the crown, setting a pattern for resistance and hostility.

In February 1848, France experienced revolution again; a republic was proclaimed amid a burst of enthusiasm, and the waves of popular uprising poured over the border into Germany. Popular assemblies began to meet in many regions, and new demands for long-overdue reforms were presented to alarmed governments: freedom of the press, arming of citizens, trial by jury, governmental status for popular assemblies, and above all, a German parliament. In Austria events moved even faster than in Germany. Metternich was driven from Vienna and sought refuge in England. A constitution was promised, and revolts broke out in Bohemia, Hungary, and Italy, some of which had to be quelled by foreign troops. In Prussia the king at first seemed conciliatory —in fact, he kept vacillating—and conceded freedom of the press and a constitution on March 18, 1848. But on that same day troops in Berlin fired on demonstrators in the square in front of the palace. The citizens arose in wrath against the army and government, erected barricades, and fought in the streets until the next day, with great loss of life. The king issued an appeal to stop the fighting, and on March 21 paraded through the streets of Berlin, promising that Prussia would seek a unified Germany.

In the midst of the general turmoil, Schleswig-Holstein revolted against its overlord, Denmark, since the German population of the area feared incorporation of Schleswig into the Danish state. Danish troops marched to meet the uprising and soon encountered Prussian troops dispatched by the king. A foreign war only added to the confusion, arousing nationalistic demands at a time when most liberals were chiefly concerned with internal reforms.

The revolution had two main goals: the unification of Germany and the establishment of constitutional government. In Frankfurt am Main fifty leaders of the movement for national unity from all the German-speaking territories met to arrange for a constituent national assembly. After their resolution had been approved by the individual governments, the "Frankfurt Parliament" was elected and assembled in the Paulskirche in March 1848. From the first the assembly, whose main aims coincided with the revolutionary ones, was beset with many vexing problems that gradually eroded both its purpose and its effectiveness. The assembly elected Archduke John of Austria as "imperial vicar" to preside until a final form of executive power had been selected. But all the deliberations and proposals were dependent on the reactions of the individual states, since these states would have to surrender their sovereignty in favor of a united Germany.

The parliament had no army or other power to enforce its will and could invoke sanctions only with the approval of the individual governments. In spite of this feeling of operating in a political vacuum, the assembly proceeded to formulate a constitution. Some problems were quickly settled—for example, the question of rights for the citizens of the new state to be formed. But other problems were more difficult to solve, and the parliament eventually foundered on the questions of the territorial extent of the new state, its relationship to the existing states, and the general division of powers. Austria refused to yield its sovereignty, so that the members resolved by a very close vote to exclude Austria and unite Germany under Prussian leadership, with the King of Prussia as hereditary emperor. The powers of any future emperor were to be limited by the constitution and by a freely elected parliament. Friedrich Wilhelm rejected the offer and refused to lead the proposed state, so the assembly was unable to implement its proposals, persuade its opponents, or achieve even its minor goals. As the resolutions it did pass were binding on no one, the whole affair ended in futility and frustration.

Jacob and Wilhelm watched the gathering storm with alarm and anxiety. When the king had first rejected the proposal of a constitution in 1847, Jacob wrote to Dahlmann: "The King's speech is discouraging and lies heavy on my mind; it will leave the most unfavorable impression far and wide. To be sure, I am touched by several remarks, and I find everything very honestly stated, even if very unpolitical. Up to now I had always kept hoping, but now I am convinced that he is not capable of understanding the spirit of the times and his position. . . . On such occasions one really feels the great value of a constitution with which one can live proudly and calmly. All other projects and plans appear shallow without it."

When the street-fighting broke out in Berlin, students escorted Wilhelm home after his afternoon lecture, guiding him through the fire of musketry and cannon. On the twentieth of March, Wilhelm wrote Louis in Cassel:

I have never yet spent a day in such fear and emotion as the eighteenth of March. At two o'clock the jubilation at the King's promise, and already at three the beginning of the deplorable fighting. For a good fourteen hours, from two to three thousand people battled the troops violently in the streets. The rattling volleys of rifle fire, the roar of the cannon and the shells were frightful, especially in the night. At the same time there were fires in several places and when the guns were silent for a few minutes, then one heard the dreadful alarm bells. Our street was protected to a degree by its situation on the canal, which closes it off at one end, so that the fighting did not touch it, but not far from us at the Anhalt Gate, it was all the more violent. We naturally stayed up the whole night.

The eighteenth of March also saw the delegates in Frankfurt opening the constituent assembly. The Grimms, busy as always with their work, were not immediately involved in the events of the exciting times. But they were not forgotten by a public that now recalled their courageous stand in 1837. The twenty-ninth electoral district, which included the city of Essen and several neighboring towns and cities in the Rhineland, elected Ernst Moritz Arndt, the well-known writer and political figure, to represent them in Frankfurt. But Arndt, who had also been chosen by the city of Solingen, chose to represent that city instead. His deputy should properly have succeeded him, but the city of Essen was determined to seek a famous candidate as its representative. The press in the Rhineland had recently published an article regretting the omission from the list of candidates of a "star of first magnitude," namely Jacob Grimm, "of whom one may rightly say that he is every inch a German." The press reported "with great enthusiasm" that on the nineteenth of May Jacob had been elected as their representative. Within a week it was able to publish Jacob's letter of acceptance. Jacob expressed his gratitude at having been elected and assured the election committee that he "thought like Arndt in all important matters."

He continued: "I am for a free, united fatherland under the rule of a powerful king and against all republican longings."

The election of a philologist as a delegate to Frankfurt is no more puzzling than his acceptance. In fact it was delayed recognition of Jacob's role in the Göttingen affair of 1837. In reporting Jacob's acceptance, the press emphasized that he was "one of the seven men of stern character who left their positions at the university in Hannover in 1837 because they refused to recognize the abrogation of the free constitution which had been given the land. They sacrificed their livelihood for noble principles. The brothers Grimm deserve the respect of all Germans because of their firmness of character as well as their research in the field of German language, German customs, and German life. The election of Jacob Grimm redounds to the honor of the electors." Jacob accepted the honor in the spirit in which it was offered. Eleven years after his dismissal from Göttingen, a significant national vindication of his position finally came, and with it the comforting and inspiring knowledge that the nation had understood him. Four of the famous "Seven of Göttingen" sat in the assembly in Frankfurt's Paulskirche, all of them in the section of the Right Center, the so-called Casino: Jacob Grimm, Dahlmann, Albrecht, and Gervinus.

When Jacob presented his credentials and was seated at the sixth session of the assembly on the twenty-fifth of May, 1848, he immediately turned his attention to the problems at hand. He entered into debate, participated at every opportunity, and was an active member in every sense. But his speeches, and indeed his whole contribution to the constituent assembly, were political only in a general way. Contemporary reports agree that his effectiveness as a member owed more to his character, reputation, and impressive presence than to the substance of his speeches. He was considered too much of an idealist to be effective in the infighting of the parliament and, as his biographer Scherer asserts, he trusted the natural power of truth to conquer. Jacob tended to stray in his addresses into the paths of history and philology, speaking elegantly and with learned assurance, but pressing only general points and not swaying opinions even while commanding respect. Jacob was primarily interested in spiritual forces, and believed in them and their ability to conquer unaided by political jockeying and intrigue. With his natural faith in the good will of men and the force of abstract ideas, it is a wonder that he was able to hold the attention of his listeners at all. The problem that did involve Jacob in heated debate was the question of incorporating Denmark into a united Germany. He entered the discussion with passion and conviction, writing articles for the press as well as addressing the assembly with unwonted fervor. He claimed that Schleswig was originally German territory which the Danes had entered as intruders. He distinguished the "Germanic Jutes" from the other Scandinavian tribes, remaining true to his concept that what was "Germanic" was also German. His philological good sense deserted him in the ardor of his polemics, so that he could claim that the Jutes had "gradually become Danish," although the larger part of the inhabitants of Schleswig "remained faithful to German language and customs." Both his historical claims and his philological reconstructions are totally untenable.

True to his normal working habits, Jacob did not devote himself single-mindedly to the political problems before him to the exclusion of his scholarly work. He finished the *History of the German Language,* writing the preface during heated debates on the future of Germany. Gervinus, who left the assembly in disillusionment before Jacob, wrote to his old friend and ally from Göttingen to express his amazement at Jacob's ability "to lucubrate over such a book in the midst of this confusion in Frankfurt." Jacob's powers of concentration on scholarship were not impaired by his passion for a German Schleswig. He spoke to the assembly eloquently, if irrelevantly, on the subject of old German freedom and law, attended most of the sessions, but was also able to write letters as usual and carry on his research.

Jacob reproached Gervinus for leaving the assembly and for not attending regularly while still resident in Frankfurt. But soon he too became restless. In the course of the meetings it became more and more evident that nothing was going to be accomplished by debate in Frankfurt. Jacob's discouragement was complete when the parliament approved a settlement of the Danish dispute that left affairs as they had been before. During the last week of September he left for home, giving as an excuse his concern for his family's health. He also had doubts about his own health, which he felt was not capable of enduring meetings in Frankfurt during the winter months. In his official letter he made no mention of his real reason for renouncing the mandate he had so optimistically accepted four months before. His letters home, however, reveal a deep disillusionment with practical politics and continued resentment of the peaceful settlement of the Danish problem. Prussia, he felt, had failed again and had yielded when it might have settled the matter by force of arms. Jacob's idealism and his patriotic fervor are curiously inconsistent during this whole period of political unrest. On the one hand he had a noble view of a united Germany, but on the other his desire to include all that was "Germanic" led him to chauvinistic claims on foreign territory in a pan-Germanic spirit that casually included Denmark, the Netherlands, and the Baltic provinces as part of a "German union that could defy the Slavs and Latin nations."

Wilhelm spent the summer of 1848 in Berlin, watching developments with concern and worrying about his brother in Frankfurt. On the sixth of December he wrote to Louis: "Since the state of siege we have lived in peace and quiet, and the people here have become cheerful and happy again. I saw the beginning of it, as the first Guard Regiment arrived on the great square of the Potsdam railroad, formed ranks, and then marched behind its banners to the Brandenburg Gate. I felt as if I could breathe freely again. No decent citizen was molested or bothered in the slightest. We fed six men, who were quartered in our neighborhood for a week, giving them lunch a few times and lending them our silver spoons; after a few hours they brought back the silverware and everything we had lent them and thanked us most heartily. Now the new constitution has been issued. The King has not reneged on anything that he promised.

Everything proceeded from his initiative. Only those who do not know him can doubt his noble and humanitarian heart. Now the cries of the reactionaries will grow silent, but the miserable political agitators will try something else."

The brothers naturally welcomed the new Prussian constitution and the popular elections that it introduced, since they had advocated such notions for years, and they did not hesitate to participate in the new political activities. They took part in caucuses, without real enthusiasm, but sustained by their strong sense of duty and a desire to contribute what they could to a cause they had long espoused. In March 1849, Wilhelm wrote to his brother-in-law's sister, Amalie Hassenpflug: "In the caucus, which I did not refrain from attending although an eight-hour stay in the tobacco smoke and noise was painful for me, I heard an ordinary citizen speak with such thorough sincerity and cogency that I still take pleasure in it." The novelist Theodor Fontane reported on Jacob's appearance at an electoral assembly in the Royal Theater: "And then the old Jacob Grimm strode up to the podium, the wonderful face full of expression—impressing itself on the memory like the face of Mommsen—surrounded by radiant snow-white hair, and he spoke about Germany, something quite general in nature that would have earned him, in any regular political gathering, the cry 'to the point!' The cry was not uttered, however, since everyone was touched by the sight and felt that however far from the subject his speech might be, one must still follow him, whether wanting to or not."

Jacob's sincerity and patriotic enthusiasm were so obviously genuine that he commanded respect. But he was not really a politician, nor was he capable of speaking effectively to sway opinions and win votes. He did not enjoy his role as a public orator on a political platform, and his appearances at political assemblies were a nervous strain for him. He came gradually to look back on his four months in Frankfurt as an aberration. The return to his quiet scholarly work in the privacy and silence of his study was a great relief. In retrospect, he realized that he had stepped out of his proper role in life, although he never regretted having tried to make a contribution. Like Wilhelm and many other intellectuals, he had been carried along by the upsurge of optimism as the events of 1848 unfolded, but in the end he felt disappointed and disillusioned. In a letter to a friend, he summed up his feelings and retrospective wisdom: "The older I get, the more democratic I become. If I were to sit once again in the Paulskirche, I would vote along with Uhland and Schröder more, for forcing the constitution into the paths of existing conditions can lead to no good. We cling to our many achievements and are afraid of the outbreak of crude violence. Yet how petty is our pride when there is no greatness of a fatherland standing in the background." The failure to unify Germany made all other accomplishments seem insignificant. And the failure to support the German inhabitants of Schleswig in their struggle rankled in his mind for years. In 1850 he wrote a newspaper article, which closed with the bitter words: "Why learn history, if it does not prevent us from making such a cruel mistake?"

❧ XVIII ❧

The Last Years in Berlin

THE DICTIONARY DOMINATED the lives of both Jacob and Wilhelm from the year of revolution until their deaths. They found time to write letters, receive visits from friends, and even take short trips. Their work routine, long since established, continued to rule their lives. But more and more the work on the dictionary absorbed their creative efforts, so that the story of their final years has as its leitmotif the trials and tribulations connected with their Frankenstein project. They lectured less frequently at the university, attended sessions of the Academy only rarely, and utilized any time and energy they could find in reediting earlier works. All the while the demands of the dictionary weighed on their collective conscience and cast a shadow over everything they undertook. Both were now aware that they would never live to see its completion, and this thought saddened them.

Although complaints about their burdensome task crept into their most optimistic reports, they nevertheless were able to maintain a cheerful attitude toward life. By the early 1850's they were so at home in Berlin and such confirmed Berliners that the tones of regret at having to live outside their beloved Hesse were rarely heard and then only in letters to friends still residing in that region. Jacob especially began to show signs of aging in his growing tendency to look back over his life and career as something

finished. In 1851 he wrote: "My own work proceeds uninter-
ruptedly, but with advancing age things are more troublesome
and difficult in the situation of the fatherland and this weighs on
us all. The greatest part of my life was filled with lively hopes
and it is painful to have to renounce them at the end; but I retain
my courage and confidence, even though one prospect after the
other disappears."

The loss of unlimited opportunity and new horizons was difficult for someone who had always been an adventurer of the spirit.
Jacob began to feel life's end coming with an intensity and sadness which were new even for one accustomed to the thought of
death. In the routine of daily life Jacob was as cheerful and industrious as ever, a kind brother and loving uncle, but in letters
to friends he frequently expressed a growing irritation with petty
annoyances, reaffirming his habitual dislike of social events which
disturbed his work. Jacob's complaints about the infirmities and
disadvantages of old age were offset by positive considerations,
however, and the tone of many letters remained one of guarded
cheerfulness. In January 1852, he wrote his friend and col-
laborator Professor Weigand: "On the fourth of this month I
became sixty-seven years old and still have three years to go in
order to reach the allotted number; if I do reach it with a modi-
cum of health, then much must be done and worked on, and
after that I only desire more free time and rest, if I should be
granted the ability to undertake some of my favorite projects."

With the passing years both Jacob and Wilhelm tended more
and more to turn to the past to recall events of earlier days.
Reminiscence is a major theme in their letters to old friends as
shared experiences became more precious with every year. To
Gervinus, Wilhelm wrote in 1855: "We wander on, step by step,
on our path, and the days disappear and the years, and the past
moves into the background like high mountains over which a delicate haze moves but which glow splendidly at twilight." Many
letters seek to recapture the glow by recalling even trivial incidents once shared with good friends; Göttingen is a recurrent

theme in much of their correspondence, for their experiences there left indelible impressions.

The political scene continued to occupy their attention, but without their former keen interest. Their sense of involvement became less with the passage of time, although they never ceased to observe the political arena and still felt quite free to comment and criticize. Jacob especially was annoyed by the raucous voices of the Left, and his innate conservatism grew stronger every year. He was as always quite inconsistent in his feelings toward popular government, welcoming "an awakened popular element that has established itself and the undeniable reconstruction of the father-land," yet hoping that the democrats would not win. Wilhelm too remained an intellectual aristocrat at heart and complained of the "general, unlimited suffrage." Neither brother ever developed a coherent political philosophy; their responses were intuitive and guided by no system or ideology. Both strove to be good citizens by contributing to the nation and serving it as scholars and guardians of its heritage. But their service was to an ideal community and their contribution was to the spiritual wealth of the nation, not to the practical forms of governance.

Reflections on the past and preoccupation with the dictionary did not prevent the brothers from pursuing favorite lines of research. They found time to reedit works which they had first published years before, and they also published some of the lectures which they gave at the Academy of Sciences. Many of these were issued in pamphlet form by the Dümmler publishing house in Berlin. Jacob intended to collect his minor works and lectures in a single edition to be put out by Dümmler, but he kept postponing the project and it was not completed in his lifetime.

One of Jacob's most famous lectures, delivered to the Academy in 1851, was published in 1852. Entitled *On Old Age,* it is a delightful blend of philological speculation and bits of homely wisdom. Erudite comments on ancient Greek and Latin authors alternate with insights gained from Jacob's own experience. Personal observations are informally interwoven with the text to a greater degree than in his usual scholarly essays. His praise of the virtues and advantages of old age is clearly confessional, and it is elegantly combined with supporting quotations from classical authors. Walking, he asserts, is wonderful for old men, and it was while walking, he added, that he had his best ideas and solved his most vexing problems. Meeting a friend or encountering his brother Wilhelm were also rewards to be found when out walking. Love of Nature increases with age, he believed, and he maintained that in old age one has both greater freedom as well as freedom of judgment. General thoughts about life lead, as they so often do with Jacob, to observations on language. Language is usually the key to a people's thinking, he asserts, and the importance of language in culture is a central if unobtrusive theme in the essay. The warm personal notes and the lightly worn scholarship make this one of his most charming writings.

The year 1851 also saw the publication of a more professional work, *On the Origin of Language*. Originally also a lecture, this work shows him at the height of his powers. The essay opens with the programmatic statement: "Our language is also our history." Language, he maintained, is older than any written document and was in its very beginnings more than just a means of communication. He believed that speech began with assigning names to people and things. Speech is coeval with thought—with cognition in any form, the awakening to consciousness of an individual produces language. After the names of things and persons (and the personal pronouns), verbs arose to define relations and activities. Speech developed as a means of expressing the essential characteristics of man and was a necessary concomitant of the process of becoming human. Jacob rejected all theories of language as an innate capacity of man, preferring to link the development of speech with that of thought and emphasizing that both were acquired. With equal incisiveness, he refuted the theory that language had been "revealed" to man by some higher power, thus putting to rest a widely held theological interpretation.

Uncle Apapa developed his theory of the origin of language in part through his observations of children. He noted how small children awaken to language and consciousness of their environment at the same time. His instinctive tendency to view all creation as the product of growth and development led him to see the acquisition of speech in harmony with the general history of mankind. His view was by no means irreligious, however, since he emphasized the fact that the Creator endowed man with the fundamental creative power of generating speech: "The Creator gave us as precious gifts a soul, that is, the power to think, and the organs of speech, that is, the power to speak, but we do not think until we use that ability and we only speak by learning language. Thought and speech are our property on which the developing freedom of our nature rests. . . ." Language he conceived of as social in nature, not given just to individuals but bestowed on mankind for the formation of community and as a bond that unites people over time and space. Jacob's essay is filled with awe and wonder at the miracle of language, and he rejoiced in it as a "natural" miracle of the Nature which God had created.

Jacob's idiosyncrasies find a place in this essay together with his less controversial views. Greek and Sanskrit he considered more "poetic" than later, less well-inflected languages. Epic poetry he held to be the noblest and finest achievement of the human mind. Among modern languages, he gave first place to English, regretfully setting it above German, praising its concision and power of expression, and prophesying a great future for it. His national pride and love for his native tongue did not prevent him from suggesting that German would have to be improved and polished in order to compete with the perfection of English. His own style waxed poetic in many passages which are noble and lofty without being sententious. Language was for him a "spirit whose guardian eye watches over all and which heals all wounds overnight and causes the scars to heal. . . ." In all his studies, Jacob tended to find organic growth guided by the power of the spirit, and he habitually expressed this feeling in metaphors of personification as naturally as he explained forms and inflections in expository prose.

Jacob found the time and energy to publish a second edition of the *History of the German Language* in 1853, and in 1854 he brought out a second edition of *Legal Antiquities*. Wilhelm, although distracted both by his own chronic illness and Dortchen's ill health, published in 1851 a *History of Rhyme,* which had originally been delivered as a lecture at the Academy of Sciences. Wilhelm praised Goethe's "free" rhymes, censured the hypercorrect and artificial rhymes of Platen, and was generous with value judgments throughout the work. Like Jacob, he complained that many other favorite projects had to be abandoned in order to concentrate on the dictionary, but he continued to devote himself to the main task. In 1852 he ceased lecturing at the university, where Jacob had also given up teaching a few years before. Both brothers quietly withdrew from the university without dramatizing the end of their teaching careers.

Poor health and the need for diversion occasioned several trips during the early 1850's. Wilhelm usually traveled with Dortchen to quiet resorts in Thüringen or the Harz Mountains. In 1853 he undertook a longer journey, going back to see the Rhein, the most romantic of rivers, and passing through Steinau and Hanau on the way. In the same year Jacob traveled to southern France, returning by way of Venice, Austria, and Bohemia. The journey was prompted by a desire to escape from his duties, but immediately upon his return he could write to Wilhelm, who was still sojourning on the Rhein: "It is a comfortable feeling to be home and at rest again."

The first fascicles of the great *Dictionary* were in print by 1852, and in 1854 the first volume finally appeared with the heading *A–Biermolke* ("A" to "beer posset"), an unintentionally comic note for an epoch-making work of lexicography. The labor involved had been immense; as the time drew near for publication, Dortchen related that she often had to coax Jacob from his desk late at night with many pretexts and exhortations. The first volume represents work done by Jacob alone; Wilhelm's contribution is only the volume beginning with the letter D. At the inception Jacob had offered to start by taking A and suggested that

Wilhelm begin with B, but Wilhelm objected that B and C "came too soon" and devoted all his efforts to D.

Although the profound significance of the vast undertaking was understood and appreciated by most scholars, the publication of this first volume occasioned adverse criticism. There were objections to the use of Latin letters instead of Gothic ones, omissions were noted, and unnecessary words enumerated. Jacob immediately started to complain of unjust criticism from many sides; several critics found petty fault and completely missed the revolutionary sense of the principles and methods employed by the Grimms. Jacob wrote in despair to his publisher Hirzel: "I know of no other example of the persecution and defamation of a patriotic work—and right at its inception—that insults no one, attacks no one, and at the very first glance offers so much that is new as well as a wealth of words that no one knew about." Even before the first fascicle went to the printer, Jacob realized that only a second, revised edition would be satisfactory, and he was doubly saddened by the thought that he would never live to see even a first edition completed. His old friends from Göttingen, Dahlmann and Gervinus, were among the first to acclaim the volume, and other voices were soon heard in appreciation of the undertaking.

Jacob's good humor was somewhat dimmed by the tone of the carping critics, but he was mollified by the positive appreciation that soon greeted the work. In his letters he continued to speak of the dictionary's inordinate demands and emphasized that the work "forced him under a yoke." He worried too about Wilhelm's methods, writing to Dahlmann's wife: "I am secretly afraid of the time when Wilhelm's work starts, it will necessarily make an uneven work, since in such things two cannot work in unison. In addition he is constantly melancholy, and I am doing everything possible to encourage him and cheer him up." A year or two later, he wrote to Dahlmann:

The fact that we are both working on the dictionary at the

same time has much to be said against it. The great amount of books which have to be used have to be carried now here, now there. Since we do not sit in one room, a constant running and fetching would be necessary. Almost all the books are piled up along the walls of my room, and Wilhelm has the tendency to take them into his room where he lays them on tables, so that they are hard to find again. If however he carries them back to their original spot, then there is a ceaseless closing and opening of doors that is annoying to both of us. This is only an external difficulty that arises from working together—the inner difficulties are much more severe. You know that we both have lived together in brotherly fashion since childhood and have kept up an undisturbed community of work. Everything that Wilhelm works on is done with industrious care and fidelity, but he does work slowly and does not force himself. In my heart I have often reproached myself for having driven him into matters of grammar which are contrary to his inclination—he would have proved his talent and everything in which he is superior to me better in other fields. This dictionary work does to be sure afford him some pleasure, but really more pain and distress, and in it he feels quite independent and is slow to agree where opinions differ. And thus it comes about that the uniformity of the plan and the execution suffer. Do not think that the dictionary brings no reward and no pleasure. It forces me to discover and observe countless details which I otherwise would not have thought of, and the gain is welcome. But I also realize how much I am losing all the while.

The centennial of Schiller's birth was widely celebrated in Germany in 1859. Jacob was requested to give a speech before the Academy of Sciences, and in November he delivered one of his finest addresses to that distinguished audience. He took the opportunity to appeal again for the unification of the German states, quoting from Schiller to strengthen his plea. The speech was published almost immediately. Weigand, professor of German literature at Giessen, wrote in January 1860: "Your Schiller address has won great applause here, and my copy of it has gone from hand to hand. You have spoken profoundly and cogently for all of us; it was the voice of the people, and thus your words reach their hearts in edifying fashion. I have often wished that I could have heard the speech from your lips."

In the fall of 1859, Wilhelm traveled with Dortchen to Pillnitz on the Elbe. The vacation seemed to restore both his health and his spirits. He found time to write several cheerful letters to friends describing his stay and expressing confidence about his work. But early in December he suddenly fell sick. At first it seemed like a minor infection from which he apparently recovered rapidly. He began to check the manuscript of *Freidank* and also arranged the distribution of complimentary copies of a new edition of the *Fairy Tales*. On the fifteenth of December, he was supposed to give a lecture on a medieval poem and was busy preparing it when the infection suddenly spread throughout his body. During the night of the fifteenth, his fever rose, he began to hallucinate, and he then dropped off into a deep slumber from which he recovered only fitfully. During the morning of the sixteenth, he died, with the faithful Jacob at his bedside watching over his labored breathing, still hoping for recovery.

The funeral took place on the twentieth of December. Many notable and famous people gathered for the interment. Of the "Seven of Göttingen," only Gervinus, who chanced to be in Berlin at the time, was present. Jacob walked to the grave steadily and vigorously, flanked by Wilhelm's sons, Herman and Rudolf. At the grave in the Schöneberg cemetery, Jacob threw a piece of earth onto the coffin as a last farewell to his brother. Jacob's outward composure and firm carriage gave no hint of how deeply the loss touched him. The thought that his brother might predecease him had always been terrible for him. In letters to his friends, the depth of his sorrow and bereavement was expressed in loving recall of the years together. In the preface to the second volume of the *Dictionary*, published in 1860, Jacob also paid tribute to his beloved brother: "In his gentle and pleasing manner of presentation, he was always superior to me in all that we undertook together."

After the funeral Gervinus wrote to Dahlmann: "I did not leave Berlin until we had buried Wilhelm Grimm. . . . It was a sad pleasure for me to have once again seen the good, peaceful man, and the family in their naturally very profound sorrow I was able to console, as far as that was possible. His wife lays more and more claim to our respect and love; his brother was very touching, even when in the bitterest feelings of sorrow one could not help smiling at the odd and childlike simplicity of the man. The bad turn that the illness took seemed to affect him at first like a completely unexpected, unforeseeable occurrence; it seemed to force upon him a warning to think of his own goal in life and work. . . . For although he was deeply and emotionally affected and was touching for others too in his sorrow, I do not doubt that he will soon pull himself together and that his rugged nature will soon be restored and give him new courage and strength in his occupations. He is an indestructible person."

In July 1860, Jacob gave a memorial address before the Academy of Sciences that was a moving testimony to the brothers' years of loyalty and cooperation. He contrasted Wilhelm's habits with his own, noting how much more music meant to Wilhelm than to himself, how Wilhelm was able to take pleasure in gay parties, "while I spent many an evening until late at night in blissful solitude over my books." He felt justified in speaking of himself in commemorating his brother, "for one must consider whether we belong together and whether I, in speaking of him, can avoid mentioning myself." He closed his speech with a reference to the *Fairy Tales*: "As often as I now take up the book of fairy tales I am moved and touched, for on all the pages his picture stands before me and I recognize his distinctive path."

Now began the lonely years for Jacob. He kept his brother's memory in his heart and saw to it that nothing was changed in Wilhelm's workroom, which was dominated by a large desk with a chair before it as if ready for use. The pictures and plants that

Wilhelm had loved so well remained where he had left them. Jacob immersed himself in his work, but even his strolls in the park would not let him forget that he could no longer meet Wilhelm by chance. Dortchen cared for him as best she could, coddling him as before and catering to the little whims she knew so well, but she could not replace Jacob's real life partner. His niece Auguste was able to cheer him up better than anyone else. She devoted much time and thought to making his days brighter and was a great comfort to him. Dortchen tried to protect Jacob from importunate visits, but the stream of visitors was more than she could turn away. Some callers came from as far away as Japan, and there were also distinguished guests, old friends, and former students who could not be refused. Jacob kept up his correspondence with friends, answering their letters of condolence and always mentioning the great loss that had come into his life.

Often during his last years he lay awake during the night and could not get back to sleep. But this did not depress him; rather he took the opportunity to study the stars and reflect on his life. In June 1862, he wrote a note, found only after his death, in which he commented on his insomnia: "How beautiful are the long summer days to which men and birds look forward with pleasure! They remind us of our youth when the hours drink in the light and pass slowly; what is left is quickly devoured by the dark of winter and age. Now I shall soon be seventy-eight years old, and when I lie sleepless in bed I am comforted by the dear light which gives me thoughts and memories."

In the fall of the same year Jacob went on what was to be his last trip to a convention of the historical commission of the Bavarian Academy of Sciences in Munich. He took this occasion to present the manuscript of the fourth volume of his *Deutsche Weistümer*, which was published in 1863. He was now quite hard-of-hearing and unable to travel alone; Auguste accompanied him on the journey, from which he returned quite well and content. In April of 1863 his youngest brother, the painter Louis, died in Cassel. Jacob now felt more alone than ever, but had no presentiment of his own end. But in the fall, upon returning from a vacation in the Harz Mountains, he fell ill. In mid-September he was acutely ill for a time, but seemed to recover and immediately took up his work and his plans. A stroke then suddenly paralyzed his right side. One of his last conscious acts was to take up a photograph of Wilhelm near his sick bed, hold it close to his failing eyes, and then lay it gently on the covers. On the evening of September 20, 1863, he died peacefully under the careful watch of Dortchen and Auguste.

Scholars and friends from all over Germany sent letters of condolence or came to the funeral. Jacob was buried beside his brother in what Professor Weigand, who had hurried to Berlin from Giessen, called the most beautiful part of the cemetery. Jacob's death came at a time when the Germanists were convening in Meissen. The news of his passing was the occasion for a solemn memorial service at which the main address was given by Professor Zarncke, the president of the assembly. At the end of his speech, tears choked his voice so that he could not continue, but his audience waited in silence, moved by his genuine emotion. Hoffmann von Fallersleben proposed to the assembled Germanists that an appeal be issued to collect funds for a monument honoring the brothers, but the project was never carried out.

After Jacob's death Dortchen and Auguste moved to Schellingstrasse in Berlin. In 1867 Dortchen's chronic lung condition became worse and she undertook a cure in Eisenach, where toward the end of her stay she contracted pneumonia. She died after a short illness on the twenty-fourth of August. Her son Rudolf remained unmarried; Herman, who had married Gisela von Arnim in October 1859, had no children. Auguste, who also did not marry, lived until February 1919, dying at the age of eighty-seven. Her death meant the end to the direct line of descent from the family of Jacob and Wilhelm Grimm.

Epilogue

EVEN DURING THEIR LIFETIMES the brothers had become legendary figures, known and honored throughout the world. Jacob's death was the occasion for tributes from many lands besides Germany. But more significant and more in the true spirit of the Grimms was the memorial erected in their honor in Hanau, not built in response to an appeal of Germanists and other scholars, but contributed by rich and poor, learned and humble alike. Like figures from one of their own tales they had become folk heroes.

After their death, work on the dictionary continued under the guidance of Rudolf Hildebrand, aided by many of the collaborators whom the Grimms had attracted to the project. Professor Weigand continued, as did Matthias Lexer, a specialist in medieval German. All the successors naturally differed in their personal styles and preferences, so that the work gradually came to represent an interesting cross section of German scholarship. Progress was slow, funds were frequently nonexistent, and interest often flagged. The task required not only enormous industry and zeal, but also organizational skill, and at times both were lacking. In 1908 the German Commission of the Berlin Academy, under the leadership of Gustav Roethe, assumed responsibility for the dictionary and a collection point for contributions was set up in Göttingen. After World War I, which brought work to a halt for over a dozen years, the first significant reorganization was undertaken by Arthur Hübner in 1930, and a committee was established at the Academy in Berlin, and later in Göttingen. World War II interrupted the work again, but under the leadership of Theodor Frings the task was finally completed in 1962 in thirty-two volumes.

The historical principles established by the Grimms were maintained throughout the work by many hands. Various personalities left their stamp on the project: Gustav Roethe, Edward Schröder, Rudolf Meissner, to mention only a few. The dictionary has a history all its own; Jacob died while writing up the word *Frucht* (fruit), and this has always been considered symbolic for the whole enterprise. The scholarly work of the Grimms has been updated, their discoveries have become history, and their great dictionary has been completed by others. They were giants in an age of greatness, leaders and pioneers in an age of discovery. Yet their greatest gift was not to scholars, but to the youth of the world and all who are still young in heart and open to the bright world of the imagination.

Chronological Table

1785   January 4. Jacob born.

1786   February 24. Wilhelm born.

1791   Family moves to Steinau.

1796   Death of the father, Philipp Grimm.

1798   In school in Cassel.

1802   Jacob to the university in Marburg.

1803   Wilhelm to the university in Marburg.

1805   Jacob in Paris; their mother moves to Cassel.

1806   Jacob at the War College.

1807   Jacob unemployed.

1808   Death of the mother, Dorothea Grimm. Jacob a librarian for King Jérôme. Both brothers publish in Arnim's *Zeitung für Einsiedler.*

1811   Jacob publishes first essay: *On the Old German Meistergesang.* Wilhelm publishes first book: *Old Danish Heroic Songs.*

1812   Brothers publish *Hildebrandslied* and *Wessobrunner Gebet.* First volume of the *Fairy Tales.*

1813   Jacob secretary to the Hessian legation. Brothers start their own periodical, *Altdeutsche Wälder* (until 1816).

1814   Wilhelm assistant librarian; Jacob in Paris and Vienna.

1815   Volume 2 of the *Fairy Tales; Der Arme Heinrich; Songs of the Elder Edda.* Jacob publishes *Irmenstrasse und Irmen-*

säule and *Silva de Romances Viejos*. Concerning Poetry in Law.

1816   Jacob librarian in Cassel. *Folk Tales*, volume 1.

1818   *Folk Tales*, volume 2.

1819   Jacob and Wilhelm receive honorary doctorates from the University of Marburg. Second edition of the *Fairy Tales*. Jacob publishes first volume of the *German Grammar*.

1821   Wilhelm's *Über deutsche Runen*.

1822   Lotte marries Hans Ludwig Hassenpflug. Third volume of the *Fairy Tales*. Second edition of first volume of the *German Grammar*.

1825   Wilhelm marries Dortchen Wild. "Minor" edition of the *Fairy Tales*. [Further editions: 1833, 1836, 1839, 1841, 1843, 1847, 1850, 1853, 1858.]

1826   *Irish Tales of Elves*. Volume 2 of the *German Grammar*.

1828   *German Legal Antiquities*. Wilhelm edits *Graf Rudolf*.

1829   *German Heroic Tales*.

1830   The brothers move to Göttingen.

1831   *German Grammar*, volume 3.

1834   Jacob: *Reinhart Fuchs*. Wilhelm: *Freidank*.

1835   *German Mythology*.

1837   Protest of the "Seven of Göttingen." *German Grammar*, volume 4. Third edition of the complete *Fairy Tales*. [Further editions: 1840, 1843, 1850, 1857.] Jacob returns to Cassel.

1838   Wilhelm returns to Cassel. Start of work on the *German Dictionary*. Jacob publishes *Concerning My Dismissal*, edits *Latin Poems of the Tenth and Eleventh Centuries*. Wilhelm edits the *Rolandslied*.

1840   *German Grammar*, third edition of first volume. *Weistümer*, volumes 1 and 2. Wilhelm edits Konrad von Würzburg's *Goldene Schmiede*.

1841   The brothers move to Berlin.

1843   Jacob visits Italy, publishes third volume of *Weistümer*.

1844   Jacob travels to Scandinavia.

1846   Conference of Germanists in Frankfurt am Main.

1847 Conference of Germanists in Lübeck.

1848 Jacob at the Paulskirche in Frankfurt am Main. *History of the German Language.*

1851 Jacob: *On the Origin of Language.* Wilhelm: *On the History of Rhyme.*

1852 First fascicle of *German Dictionary* published in Leipsic.

1853 *History of the German Language,* second edition.

1854 *German Dictionary,* volume 1. *German Legal Antiquities,* second edition.

1856 Second edition of third volume of the *Fairy Tales.*

1859 Jacob's address on Schiller. Wilhelm dies on December 16.

1860 *German Dictionary,* volume 2. *On Old Age. In Memoriam Wilhelm Grimm.*

1862 *German Dictionary,* volume 3.

1863 *Weistümer,* volume 4. [Further volumes: 1866, 1869, 1878.] Jacob dies on September 20.

Selected Bibliography

Andresen, Karl Gustaf, *Über die Sprache Jacob Grimms,* Wiesbaden, 1968.

Arens, Hans, ed., *Sprachwissenschaft,* Freiburg/München, 1955.

Bausinger, Hermann, *Formen der "Volkspoesie,"* Berlin, 1968.

Benz, Richard, *Die deutsche Romantik,* Leipsic, 1937.

Berendsohn, Walter A., *Grundformen volkstümlicher Erzählerkunst in den Kinder- und Hausmärchen der Brüder Grimm,* 2nd ed., Wiesbaden, 1968.

Bolte, Johannes, and Polivka, Georg, *Anmerkungen zu den Kinder- und Hausmärchen der Brüder Grimm,* 5 vols., Leipsic, 1913–32.

Bramsted, Ernest K., *Aristocracy and the Middle Classes in Germany,* Chicago, 1964.

Denecke, Ludwig, and Greverus, Ina-Maria, eds., *Brüder Grimm Gedenken,* Marburg, 1963.

De Vries, Jan, *Altgermanische Religionsgeschichte,* 2 vols., Berlin, 1956.

Dundes, Alan, ed., *The Study of Folklore,* Englewood Cliffs, 1965.

Fraenger, Wilhelm, and Steinitz, Wolfgang, eds., *Jacob Grimm zur 100. Wiederkehr seines Todestages,* [East–] Berlin, 1963.

Gerstl, Quirin, *Die Brüder Grimm als Erzieher,* München, 1964.

Gerstner, Hermann, *Die Brüder Grimm. Ihr Leben und Werk in*

Selbstzeugnissen, Briefen und Aufzeichnungen, Ebenhausen bei München, 1952.

Ginschel, Gunhild, *Der junge Jacob Grimm,* [East-] Berlin, 1967.

Grimm, Herman, *Essays on Literature,* Boston, 1888. (Contains his essay on his father and uncle.)

Grimm, Herman, and Hinrichs, Gustav, eds., *Briefwechsel zwischen Jacob und Wilhelm Grimm aus der Jugendzeit,* 2nd ed., ed. by Wilhelm Schoof, Weimar, 1963.

Grimm, Jacob, *Deutsche Grammatik,* 4 vols., Göttingen, 1822–37.

———, *Deutsche Mythologie,* 3 vols., 4th ed., ed. by E. H. Meyer, Berlin, 1875–78.

———, *Deutsche Rechtsaltertümer,* 2 vols. (reprint of 4th ed.), Darmstadt, 1955.

———, *Deutsches Wörterbuch,* 32 vols., Leipsic, 1854–1960.

———, *Geschichte der deutschen Sprache,* 2nd ed., Leipsic, 1853.

———, *Reden und Aufsätze,* ed. by Wilhelm Schoof, München, 1966.

———, *Sprache, Wissenschaft, Leben,* ed. by Hermann Gerstner, Stuttgart, 1965.

———, *Von der Poesie im Recht,* Darmstadt, 1957.

———, *Vorreden zur Deutschen Grammatik von 1819 und 1822,* Darmstadt, 1961.

———, *Weisthümer . . . ,* 7 vols., Darmstadt, 1957.

Grimm, Jacob, and Grimm, Wilhelm, *Kinder- und Hausmärchen,* München, 1966.

———, *Deutsche Sagen,* München, 1956.

Grimm, Wilhelm, *Die deutsche Heldensage,* 3rd ed., ed. by R. Steig, Gütersloh, 1889.

Hammond, Muriel E., *Jacob and Wilhelm Grimm—The Fairy-Tale Brothers,* London, 1968.

Hansen, Wilhelm, ed., *Grimms' Other Tales,* New York, 1966.

Jackson, Kenneth Hurlstone, *The International Popular Tale and Early Welsh Tradition,* Cardiff, 1961.

Jolles, André, *Einfache Formen,* 4th ed., Tübingen, 1968.

Kuhn, Hugo, and Schier, Kurt, *Märchen, Mythos, Dichtung* [Festschrift für Friedrich von der Leyen], München, 1963.

Leitzmann, Albert, ed., *Briefwechsel der Brüder Jacob und Wilhelm Grimm mit Karl Lachmann*, 2 vols., Jena, 1927.

von der Leyen, Friedrich, *Das deutsche Märchen*, Düsseldorf, 1964.

———, *Das Märchen*, Heidelberg, 1958.

———, *Die Welt der Märchen*, 2 vols., Düsseldorf, 1953.

Lüthi, Max, *Das europäische Volksmärchen*, 2nd ed., Bern, 1960.

———, *Es war einmal . . . Vom Wesen des Volksmärchens*, 2nd ed., Göttingen, 1964.

———, *Märchen*, 3rd ed., Stuttgart, 1968.

———, *Volksmärchen und Volkssage*, 2nd ed., München, 1966.

Lüthi, Max, and Fohrer, G., *Sagen und ihre Deutung*, Göttingen, 1965.

Mann, Golo, *Deutsche Geschichte des 19. und 20. Jahrhunderts*, Frankfurt am Main, 1967.

Neumann, Friedrich, *Geschichte der altdeutschen Literatur*, Berlin, 1966.

Ottendorf-Simrock, Walther, ed., *Die Grimms und die Simrocks in Briefen*, Bonn, 1966.

Pedersen, Holger, *Linguistic Science in the Nineteenth Century*, Cambridge, 1931.

Röhrich, Lutz, *Gebärde, Metapher, Parodie*, Düsseldorf, 1967.

———, *Sage*, Stuttgart, 1966.

Schneider, Hermann, and Wisniewski, Roswitha, *Deutsche Heldensage*, Berlin, 1964.

Schoof, Wilhelm, ed., *Briefe der Brüder Grimm an Savigny*, Berlin, 1953.

———, *Die Brüder Grimm in Berlin*, Berlin, 1964.

———, *Jacob Grimm, Aus seinem Leben*, Bonn, 1961.

———, ed., *Unbekannte Briefe der Brüder Grimm*, Bonn, 1960.

———, *Wilhelm Grimm, Aus seinem Leben*, Bonn, 1960.

———, *Zur Entstehungsgeschichte der Grimmschen Märchen*, Hamburg, 1959.

Schulte-Kemminghausen, Karl, and Denecke, Ludwig, *Die Brüder Grimm in Bildern ihrer Zeit*, Cassel, 1963.

Steffen, Hans, ed., *Die deutsche Romantik*, Göttingen, 1967.

Steig, Reinhold, *Achim von Arnim und Jacob und Wilhelm Grimm*, Stuttgart, 1904.

———, *Clemens Brentano und die Brüder Grimm*, Stuttgart, 1914.

Thompson, Stith, *Motif-Index of Folk-Literature*, 6 vols., 2nd ed., Bloomington, 1955–58.

Vossler, Otto, *Die Revolution von 1848 in Deutschland*, Frankfurt am Main, 1967.

———, *Heldenlied und Heldensage*, Bern, 1961.

Waterman, John T., *A History of the German Language*, Seattle, 1966.

———, *Perspectives in Linguistics*, Chicago, 1963.

Welchert, Hans-Heinrich, *Aus der deutschen Idylle 1805 bis 1871*, Stuttgart, 1949.

Zuckmayer, Carl, *Die Brüder Grimm*, Frankfurt am Main, 1948.

INDEX

Index